A NEEDLE, A BOBBIN, A STRIKE:

Women Needleworkers in America

Women in the Political Economy,
a series edited by Ronnie J. Steinberg

A NEEDLE, A BOBBIN, A STRIKE:

Women Needleworkers in America

Edited by
Joan M. Jensen and
Sue Davidson

Temple University Press
Philadelphia

Temple University Press, Philadelphia 19122
© 1984 by Joan M. Jensen and Sue Davidson. All rights reserved
Published 1984
Printed in the United States of America

Library of Congress Cataloging in Publication Data
Main entry under title:

A Needle, a bobbin, a strike.

(Women in the political economy)
Includes index.
1. Women clothing workers—United States—History—
Addresses, essays, lectures. 2. Strikes and lockouts—
Clothing trade—United States—Addresses, essays,
lectures. 3. Trade-unions—Clothing workers—United
States—Addresses, essays, lectures. I. Jensen, Joan M.
II. Davidson, Sue, 1925–   . III. Series.
HD6073.C62U56   1984   331.4'887'0973   83-24338
ISBN 0-87722-340-8

"the endless, endless stitches"

Gertrude Whiting,
Old-Time Tools and Toys of Needlework

The Seamstress

Hark, that rustle of a dress,
Stiff with lavish costliness;
Here comes one whose cheeks would flush
But to have her garments brush
'Gainst the girl whose fingers thin
Wove the weary broidery in;
And in the midnights, chill and murk,
Stitched her life into the work;
Bending backward from her toil,
Lest her tears the silk might spoil;
Shaping from her bitter thought
Heart's-ease and forget-me-not;
Satirizing her despair
With the emblems woven there!

Scientific American, 4 (Feb. 17, 1849), 1

Time was when half the human race were occupied chiefly in making clothes. When the machines took that avocation away from them they turned to other employments. The invasion of all occupations by women and the sweeping changes which have taken place in their relations to the law, society, and business can be ascribed in large measure to the sewing machine.

Speaker before the patent centennial celebration of 1891 celebrating one hundred years of patent laws

I remember the first time of the walkout we were all in break, eating, have some coffee. And then suddenly there was a whole bunch in the cutting room—the girls and everything. They went over to my table and said, "Alma, you've got to come out with us." And I just looked at them. I was so scared I didn't even know what to do. What if I go and lose my thirteen years? So long, having seniority and everything. I just looked at them and said, "Yeah, yeah, I'll go." That's all I said. And I had a whole bunch of people sitting there with me and I said, "Let's go."

Women at Farah: An Unfinished Story (1979)

CONTRIBUTORS

JOAN M. JENSEN is professor of history at New Mexico State University. She has published *With These Hands: Women Working on the Land* (1981), and *Decades of Discontent: The Women's Movement, 1920–1940* (1983) with Lois Scharf.

SUE DAVIDSON is information director of the National Female Advocacy Project. Formerly an editor for The Feminist Press, she served as a co-director of its Women's Lives/Women's Work series. She is editor of *Justice for Young Women: Close-up on Critical Issues* (1982) and co-editor of *The Maimie Papers* (1977).

NINA ASHER has taught labor and women's history at the University of Vermont, and is currently teaching history in New York City. Her specialty is female leadership within unions.

AVA BARON teaches sociology at Rider College in Lawrenceville, New Jersey. Her primary research interest is the relationship between women's work and changes in the labor process.

LAURIE COYLE is a student of film production in San Francisco.

DEBORAH S. GARDNER, a member of The Institute for Research in History in New York, is an archivist-historian. She is co-author of a forthcoming documentary text on the history of low-income housing reform.

HARDY GREEN is a labor writer based in New York. He has taught history at the State University of New York at Stony Brook.

GAIL HERSHATTER teaches history at Williams College in Williamstown, Massachusetts.

EMILY HONIG teaches history at Lafayette College in Easton, Pennsylvania.

SUSAN E. KLEPP teaches history at Rider College. Her specialty is the demographic history of Philadelphia.

LOIS SCHARF is director of National History Day in Cleveland. She has published *To Work and to Wed: Female Employment, Feminism and the Great Depression* (1980).

ANN SCHOFIELD teaches American studies at the University of Kansas at Lawrence. Her primary research interest is American labor press attitudes toward women.

N. SUE WEILER has taught at the University of Illinois at Chicago Circle. She is interested in the problem of aging in an industrial society.

ELIZABETH WEINER is managing editor of a New York City weekly newspaper and writes frequently about labor and urban affairs.

CONTENTS

INTRODUCTION

Sue Davidson

OFTEN by necessity, sometimes by choice, sewing has long been women's work. As with other work done by women, little attention has been given to its significance in the lives of those who have performed it and in the social and economic systems of their times. Yet the story of women needleworkers in North America raises issues that not only are central to the lives of women, but apply to labor history generally. The selections in this volume encompass themes that include changes in the conditions and rewards of work, the effects of new technologies, tensions among and within social classes, the impact of political ideas, the interactions of urbanization, immigration, and international trade. Most enduringly for women workers, the selections reflect the unsolved conflicts between responsibilities in the home and the need to earn a livelihood.

In colonial America, when all but a very few articles of use were produced by household members, women performed sewing tasks along with other domestic and farm labor. Industrialization and the rise of a market economy reduced the kinds and quantity of household manufactures, including cloth and men's clothing, but it was not until the mass production of the sewing machine in the latter half of the nineteenth century that most garment making shifted from the home to the factory. Young, unmarried women followed, moving into the apparel industry as, earlier, their counterparts had moved into the textile mills. By this time, the household labor of both farm and urban daughters was less needed than the contribution they could make to family income.

In the large cities of the Northeast, in Baltimore, and in Chicago, women had been concentrated in the men's clothing industry since its inception. Unmarried women and widows mainly, they sewed by hand, taking the work home and delivering shirts or piecework to the factories. Later, they also worked at machines within factory walls and in small shops run by contractors. The better-paying occupations—

such as cutting and custom tailoring—were dominated by men. With thousands of poor women competing for sewing work, employers could pay wages so minimal as to keep the masses of them on the edges of starvation, as they toiled long hours under unspeakable conditions. The development of the sewing machine and the increasingly detailed division of labor in garment making led to the gradual deskilling and downgrading of the needlework done by most women. The young women who poured into the factories to become "operatives" at the close of the nineteenth century were carrying on a female tradition of hard work, but not one of an exacting personal craft.

Although single women were leaving the home to become wage workers, married women, except in the most impoverished families, attempted to remain at home. Once the workplace of all family members, the home had now become "woman's place," where she organized living space, processed food, and cared for the personal needs of husband and children. The hard work performed by women at home was only vaguely reflected in the ideology of domesticity, an ideal that developed after 1830 to rationalize the changing situation of women who belonged to the rapidly growing urban middle and working classes. Although thousands of urban married women took in boarders, sewed, and engaged in other market activities to enable their families to survive periodic hard times, the idea that women were primarily consumers and nurturers grew after mid-century. Employers, especially, viewed women as transitory workers who could be depended upon not to clamor in large numbers for job advancement, improved working conditions, and better pay. Their stay in employment was supposed to be a temporary one, until they became wives and mothers who did not need to "work."

The domestic arts became a means to achieve a better standard of living at home. Domesticity was not just an ideal for the white American middle class and the average "working girl." The ideal touched the lives of nonwhite ethnic groups, as well. Ex-slave and abolitionist Ellen Craft, for example, set out in 1874 to teach freed black women who had been field hands not only how to read and write, but also how to be proper housewives. Sewing was an art that even poor women could practice for the enhancement of domestic life, and Craft—herself an accomplished dressmaker—taught the freed women to sew clothing for themselves and their children, as well as how to cook and clean.[1] Earlier in the century, in Hawaii, white women of missionary families brought "civilized" domestic culture to native women through needlework, persuading them to cover their nakedness from neck to foot with a loose-flowing garment called a "muumuu," and to engage in making American-style patchwork quilts of imported cloth, which gradually displaced the native tapa (bark cloth) bedcovers.[2]

In the crowded cities, middle-class reformers turned their attention to urban immigrants—domestic and foreign—as potential carriers of the ideal of domesticity. Native white working-class mothers who had migrated from farms could inculcate in their children habits of thrift, punctuality, industriousness, and obedience to authority. Poor immigrant women in highly industrialized areas were a special concern of female reformers, who organized innumerable domestically oriented projects aimed at teaching American values and at improving the living standard of the new arrivals.

The values of domesticity coincided with employers' interests in a dependable and docile work force, but factory women proved to be anything but docile in the early twentieth century. In a pattern that was to repeat itself up to the present day, immigrant women flocked to the garment industry. Jewish and Italian women were the most numerous of the new recruits, and the most militant. They were moving spirits in the great period of unionization which began almost simultaneously with the century. Other industries were organized in this period, but union strength in the garment industry, with its large concentrations of urban working poor, was particularly significant in labor-capitalist struggles. Industrialists' fears of labor agitation and of radical ideas among immigrant workers turned out to be well justified. Industrialists seem not to have anticipated that women workers would be central to the unrest, however.

Male workers had not expected the women in their ranks to be crucial to their own collective power. Most male workers did not regard women workers as important or trustworthy allies; attitudes toward them were at best ambivalent, at worst hostile. On the one hand, women were competitors for the lowest paying jobs, in which their ready availability further reduced wages; on the other hand, poor families could not survive without the earnings of female members. Early union organizers in the needle trades focused on skilled workers, ignoring women as a matter of course. But as mechanization increased the proportion of unskilled jobs in the apparel industry, so too did the proportion of women workers increase. They could not be overlooked by the new unions that sought to attract the rank and file, organizing by industry rather than exclusively by craft. From the beginning, women's participation was an important element in the growth of the International Ladies Garment Workers Union (ILGWU) and the Amalgamated Clothing Workers of America (ACWA). Women were indispensable to organizing and to the use of strikes, which established the unions as bargaining agents able to negotiate demands for improved wages, hours, and working conditions, and even to bring the sweatshop system under control for a long period of time.

In the clothing strikes, women emerged as expert practitioners of techniques that have been perceived in a labor context almost solely as "confrontational," but in which the shape of many conscious campaigns of nonviolent resistance can be discerned. Although journalists and historians have stressed the violent aspects of these strikes, what is more apparent today is the disciplined willingness of workers to risk the violence of superior force with relatively little recourse to mass retaliation.[3] It was not the workers' muscle power or fire power that brought employers to the bargaining table, but the determination of workers to withhold their labor and their ability to bring favorable opinion to their side. In strike after strike, workers endured far more punishment than they delivered or were capable of delivering, neither police forces nor jails being at their disposal. The official violence visited upon unarmed women strikers was particularly effective in eliciting public sympathy and in rallying the support of progressive leaders.

As clothing workers organized, women who were predominantly middle class were also taking to the streets and to the jails. Militants in all sectors of the feminist movement, from the cause of suffrage to that of birth control, were engaging in public protest and acts of resistance. The organization of women into trade unions was a matter of prime importance to some feminists. A group of these women, including settlement house leader Helena Stuart Dudley and Wellesley economics professor Emily Greene Balch, joined with labor representatives in 1903 to found the National Women's Trade Union League (WTUL). Middle-class WTUL members, along with other middle-class women who were socialists or urban reformers, forged multiple alliances with working-class women and provided support to union struggles in ways that ranged from walking picket lines to pressuring employers and public policy makers.

The interaction of the feminist movement and the labor movement was limited by factions among feminists and by class divisions. The great number of feminists who centered all their hopes on suffrage were, on the whole, much less responsive to labor issues than feminists who were concerned with the broad questions of woman's sexual and economic exploitation. On their part, working-class women could more readily perceive their common lot with workers of both sexes than with middle-class women; they looked to union successes for the amelioration of their condition, rather than to feminist victories. With few exceptions, a worker solidarity that excluded feminist issues endured until the 1970s, in spite of continuing bias against women in union activities. It was in large part the unionization of women and their militant action that established the new needle trades unions on the American scene by the 1920s. Yet the ILGWU and the ACWA remained firmly male dominated, little affected by efforts of union women to gain a voice in decision making.

Runaway shops tested the new union strength. With its legions of small entrepreneurs, the clothing industry has always been fiercely competitive, and the risk of business failure high. Confronted with unionized shops, many firms packed up and moved westward in search of cheaper labor and better profits. The unions followed, attempting to organize the new labor force as one means of protecting the interests of workers in the Northeast. These efforts met with mixed success. Meanwhile, in spite of the Red scares of the post–World War I period, which weakened support for organized labor among some progressives, and in spite of business devastation during the Great Depression, the clothing unions made gains. Consolidating their position over the years, they managed to raise wages and to secure such benefits as pension plans, disability pay, unemployment insurance, health and housing programs.

In the process of this forward march, however, the stance of the clothing unions became increasingly conservative. The price that was paid for recognition of the unions as legitimate institutions was their growing spirit of compromise, as they adopted an ideology of "partnership" between capital and labor for the good of both. In order to maintain their influence and also to stem the tide of runaways, the unions undertook cooperation with management to hold down wages, relax environmental standards, and head off strikes. It was true enough that jobs depended upon persuading footloose companies to stay fixed; yet to the rank and file, now effectively excluded from participation in union strategy, the concessions made by the union leadership often smacked of "sellout." In its opposition to strikes and in its discouragement of union democracy, the entrenched male leadership of both the ILGWU and the ACWA grew more and more distant from the mass of low-paid women workers.

Furthermore, the unions' strategy of pacifying employers failed in its objectives; for with every passing decade, the geographic dispersal of the clothing industry widened. The most dramatic shifts took place in the post–World War II period, with the flight of more and more companies not only westward and into the American South, but to Mexico, the Dominican Republic, South Korea, Hong Kong, and other Third World areas. The needle trades have remained sex segregated, employing more women than any other United States industry; but the ethnic composition of the work force has changed. Whether at home or abroad, the women laboring at sewing are now overwhelmingly Latinas, Asians, and blacks.[4] And the conditions and rewards of their work represent a return to those against which women needleworkers rose less than a hundred years ago.

In common with many other business enterprises, the clothing industry has sought out locations in which low-skilled workers have few alternative employment opportunities, and in which the official climate—whether in the Philippines or Alabama—is hostile to union organizing. But even in locations in which labor has long been organized, such as New York and Chicago, conditions for thousands of needleworkers have deteriorated. Sweatshops have reappeared and multiplied in the jungle of an industry characterized by small establishments. The various tasks required for producing a single garment are not usually performed under one roof. More typically, manufacturers supply precut material to small contract shops, in which women do the sewing. Because very little capital is needed to set up a few sewing machines in small, substandard quarters, contractors are numerous, and manufacturers may choose from among those offering the lowest bid. The contractors, in an effort to underbid their competitors and still turn a profit, must find workers who will accept the lowest possible wages—wages that compare unfavorably with welfare, and even with the pay that a working-class white high-school age male would consider worth his labor. Ultimately, in fact, the apparel industry in the United States must compete against manufactures abroad, based on pay scales to women needleworkers that are as low as 25 cents an hour. Where can these willing United States workers be found—including those who, taking work home, provide the highest profits, as they supply their own sewing machines and pay all overhead costs? By and large, they are relatively recent immigrants, some of them "illegals," living in their own ethnic communities. They are women who are the sole or partial supporters of their families, often mothers of young children. They are also elderly women unable to survive on tiny pensions. They are unfamiliar with the ways of the city and the country in which they reside, and many have only the most rudimentary command of its language.

The case of Chinese apparel workers offers one illustration.[5] The most recent heavy immigration of Chinese began in the mid-1960s with the liberalization of United States immigration laws. The major portion of immigrants settled in the existing Chinese ghettos of New York, San Francisco, and Los Angeles. Non-English speaking and with few transferable skills, the new immigrants found their way into the most available jobs in their communities—restaurant work and labor in the apparel industry. Those able to get together a little capital have become contractors, often working alongside their employees in the pattern of earlier immigrants in the garment trades.

For Chinese women with family responsibilities, the proximity of sewing work to home is important, as are informal arrangements with Chinese employers. Poor women with no access to day care may bring small children to the sweatshop, or sew at home. Flexible hours permit women to shop for groceries and do other family errands, pick up children at school, tend to the ill. Such "advantages" are illusory, however, masking gross labor abuses. Paid by the piece rate rather than at an hourly wage, most women must work ten to twelve hours daily, six or seven days a week, during the peak season, in order to earn even the minimum wage. Earnings of Chinatown sewing women in San Francisco average $3000 to $6000 annually.[6] Violations of minimum wage and overtime regulations go unchallenged even when investigated by state agents, since women are fearful that complaints will cause them to lose their jobs. Many are bullied by employers with threats of deportation, and frequent shop raids by the Immigration and Naturalization Service (INS) add credence to the threat. Employment during the slack season is scarce and erratic. In California, seasonal employees are entitled to "partial unemployment" insurance, but a recent case brought against garment companies and employees for unemployment fraud may help to discourage sewing workers from applying for this relief.[7]

The clothing unions have been slow in responding to the plight of immigrant Chinese and Latin American workers, whose cheap labor keeps the garment industry going in New York City and on the West Coast. Often, the unions have been part of the problem, as in the ILGWU's opposition to minimum wage laws in the 1960s, and its cooperation with INS raids on garment shops. Similarly, neither the ILGWU nor the ACWA has risen adequately to the challenge of labor conditions in the American South. With declining memberships, however, both unions have begun to give more attention to "organizing the unorganized" in recent years. The women needleworkers of the present day have shown themselves no less willing to engage in collective action than those of the past. The ACWA-supported strike during 1972–1974 of hundreds of Chicana workers at the Farah plant in El Paso, Texas, provides one example; the 1975–1976 strike of 125 Chinese women at the Jung Sai garment shop in San Francisco, ending with an ILGWU contract, provides another.[8] Yet while sewing women of today are capable of militant action, there is no assurance that the established clothing unions can make a successful adaptation to the contemporary female work force.

Unions determined to "organize the unorganized" must learn to speak the language of contemporary needleworkers. This may be taken quite literally to mean Spanish, Chinese, Tagalog, and other new immigrants' languages. Language differences have made it difficult for workers not only to know their rights under law, but also to understand the terms of contracts negotiated by the unions. Women workers are kept out of participation in decisions on contracts and other union affairs both by language barriers and by the clothing unions' continuing adherence to centralized, top-down control exercised by white males who have not risen from the ranks. Although the ILGWU and the ACWA employ some female organizers, as they have done from time to time in the past, their executive boards remain male clubs penetrated by less than a dozen females added together.

Grotesquely unrepresentative of union membership, the male union leadership has shown little concern for specifically female issues: sex-biased practices in hiring, promotion, and wages; sexual harassment, particularly of immigrant women; the lack of child-care programs; and the urgent need for internal training and education that can equip women needleworkers to assume union responsibilities and thereby exercise some control over their working lives.

Outside the unions, women needleworkers have found new allies who are sensitive to their unique needs. These allies come from both within the ethnic/racial communities of needleworkers and mainstream society. In the San Francisco Bay area, the Asian Law Caucus is a watchdog of Asian women needleworkers' interests, through legal action on behalf of women often not organized into unions, and through educating women to understand and demand their rights as union members. A much older organization, the Quaker-based American Friends Service Committee (AFSC), in cooperation with the Mexican Friends Service Committee, has established projects for women needleworkers on both sides of the Mexico-United States border—one among women employed in the *maquiladores* (U. S.-owned partial assembly plants in Mexican border cities), the other among El Paso women needleworkers. Staffed by Mexicanas, these projects have begun in the setting of small, all-female groups, in which women may feel comfortable in speaking up about problems ranging from sexual harassment on the job to violence in families hard pressed by poverty. Once they have begun to express themselves among their peers, the women move on to analyzing their working conditions and finding strategies for bringing about change. For example, women in groups on the Mexican side, who began with no understanding of their rights vis-à-vis management or union, decided to study labor law. They then began to take their own cases to court, challenging unfair firings and suspensions, and sometimes winning. The groups have now formed themselves into a council of workers to pursue the employment problems they view as most immediately relevant to their welfare.[9]

The project just described required more than three years of patient building before its effects were evident in action. It is not an isolated effort, but part of a coherent AFSC drive to expose and challenge the exploitation of women working for United States companies in many other countries.[10] With considerably richer coffers than such human rights organizations as the AFSC, and a good deal more political clout, neither the ACWA nor the ILGWU has made a forthright attack on the multinationals now linking the fate of U. S. needleworkers and their sisters abroad. The "buy American" campaign of the ILGWU is a particularly sterile and unrealistic response, even apart from its offensive jingoism. As for the patient work of cultivating self-confidence and independent organizing skills through all-female groups, male clothing union leaders apparently do not wish to commit generous resources to such feminist techniques.

The one exception to union neglect of women needleworkers is the work of the Coalition of Labor Union Women (CLUW). Founded in 1974, CLUW has used a variety of feminist-inspired approaches to strengthening women's position within unions, not excluding reliance on small group meetings as a starting point for many women workers. With 15,000 members from many sectors of the labor force, and programs demonstrating much political sophistication, CLUW has begun to enjoy recognition among established unions. In the summer of 1982, CLUW and the Industrial Union Department of the AFL-CIO joined together in a pilot project aimed at unionizing women in the Washington/Baltimore area. The "Women's Organizing Campaign" sought cooperation from regional women's groups and stressed distinctively female workplace issues. It was not long before the campaign ran into difficulties with AFL-CIO officials, evidently much distressed by its strong feminist flavor. Ideological conflicts have continued. The venture, now expected to fold before 1984, does not encourage hopes of a speedy turnabout in old-style union dealings with the needs and aspirations of female members.[11]

No turnabout is taking place in the clothing unions, and although there are occasional progressive stirrings, these have not had an impact on the ugliest issue of them all: the continued flourishing of the sweatshops abroad, and in our own midst. Although the ILGWU has somewhat repaired its reactionary stance toward immigrants by accepting undocumented workers as union members, the mass of sewing women—"illegals," lawful permanent residents, and U. S. citizens alike—remain trapped and unprotected at the bottom of the clothing industry heap. Feminist organizations, although interested in the "feminization of poverty," have not demonstrated special awareness of this group of poor women. Today the story of women needleworkers sometimes appears to be a film running backward, with a fresh cast of characters and some new, foreign settings. Any record of that story, however, would include innumerable scenes of women struggling against the injustices of their condition. That part of the story, also, repeats itself today.

NOTES

1. Dorothy Sterling, *Black Foremothers: Three Lives* (Old Westbury, N.Y.: The Feminist Press, 1979), 54. That married black women needed, almost universally, to be gainfully employed did not impede the steady growth of the domestic ideal among black families in the nineteenth century and beyond. For one discussion, see David M. Katzman, *Seven Days a Week: Women and Domestic Service in Industrializing America* (New York: Oxford University Press, 1978), 83–85.

2. The permanent collections of the Bishop Museum, Honolulu, and the Lihue Museum, Kauai, include artifacts and pictorial records that reflect the uneven transition from native household furnishings and dress to Western linens and clothing. On Christian missionary vs. Hawaiian mores, including differing attitudes toward clothing, see Gavin Daws, *Shoal of Time: A History of the Hawaiian Islands* (Honolulu: The University Press of Hawaii, 1968), 61–105.

3. *The Power of the People: Active Nonviolence in the United States*, ed. Robert Cooney and Helen Michalowski (Culver City, Calif.: The Power of the People/ Peace Press, 1977), 33–36, 62–73. Many socialists and anarchists in the early labor movement opposed violence on practical as well as philosophic grounds, and were interested in the application of nonviolence to class struggle, particularly through the use of the general strike.

4. North American Congress on Latin America, "Capital's Flight: The Apparel Industry Moves South," *NACLA's Latin American Empire Report*, 11 (March 1977), 7.

5. Unless otherwise noted, material in this discussion is drawn from the following sources: Dean Lan, "The Chinatown Sweatshops: Oppression and an Alternative," *Amerasia Journal*, 1 (Nov. 1971), 40–57; Peggy Li, Buck Wong, Fong Kwan, "Garment Industry in Los Angeles Chinatown, 1973–1974" (unpublished paper, n.d.); Abeles, Schwartz, Haekel & Silverblatt, Inc., "The Chinatown Garment Industry Study: An Overview" (paper submitted to Local 23–25 ILGWU and the New York Skirt and Sportswear Association, June 1983).

6. Deborah Morris Farson, "Chinese Garment Workers Resist Fraud Charges," *Union Wage* (Nov.–Dec. 1981), 1.

7. *Asian Law Caucus Reporter* (issues from Apr.–June 1981 through Jan.– June 1982); *San Francisco Examiner*, Oct. 5, 1981; *Oakland Tribune Eastbay*, Mar. 22, 1982.

8. Barbara Ehrenreich and Annette Fuentes, "Life on the Global Assembly Line," *Ms.* (Jan. 1981), 56.

9. *AFSC Quaker Service Bulletin* (Winter 1983), 3.

10. Women and Global Corporations Project report, *AFSC Women's Newsletter* (Fall 1980), 7–14.

11. Richard Moore and Elizabeth Marsis, "Will Unions Work for Women?" *The Progressive* (Aug. 1983), 30.

PART I

NEEDLEWORK AS
ART, CRAFT, AND LIVELIHOOD
BEFORE 1900

NEEDLEWORK AS ART, CRAFT, AND LIVELIHOOD BEFORE 1900

Joan M. Jensen

ART. Meditation. Liberation. Exploitation. Needlework has been all these to women. From the time that early woman fashioned her first bone needle to the contemporary sweatshops of the Third World, women have had the primary responsibility for clothing both mankind and womankind. Men have been tailors and factory workers; sailors at sea have sewn their own clothing. But women have most often held the needle, whether for sewing on buttons or for taking the fine stitches that created the great women's art of quilting. Quilting is now receiving attention long overdue as art, but the everyday craft of sewing and the women who practiced it for a living—their techniques, their tools, their materials, their working conditions, the ways they distributed their work, the changes caused by the nineteenth-century invention of the sewing machine—these have been virtually ignored.

A NEEDLE

In the eighteenth century, to know how to handle a needle well was to possess an important skill. Parents provided in their wills that daughters be taught how to read and sew. And while one wishes the daughters might have been taught to write, as well, so that they could have left better records of their craft, both daughters and their peers apparently held in high esteem the ability to sew well. Afro-American women in the South and Euro-American women in the North counted these skills as valuable avenues to work away from the fields. Elizabeth Ashbridge, one of the few women to leave an account of her sewing in the eighteenth century, recalled her harsh indentureship in New York. Looking for a way to escape from her master, who made her go barefoot in snowy weather and do the meanest drudgery, she began to do extra sewing to buy her freedom. After three years, she bought the

3

remainder of her time "and then fell to my needle, by which I could maintain myself handsomely."[1]

Many articles sewn by eighteenth-century women have survived and are on display in museums. Probably it is the work of the most skillful sewers which has survived, work that can only be described as elegant. With a few simple tools—for her tool kit consisted of needles, scissors, thread, and thimble—the seamstress was able to create clothing both serviceable and ornamental, of such high quality that it was passed on from mother to daughter and, in some cases, from father to son.

Few descriptions of the clothing actually sewn by the ordinary country woman exist. Among them, Ellen Gehret's *Rural Pennsylvania Clothing* is the most detailed account of the way in which clothing was made. Gehret estimates that much of the eighteenth-century male clothing, even in rural areas, was made by traveling tailors who visited farmhouses to measure and fit the men of the farm with leather, wool, or linen tow breeches, linen shirts, waistcoats, coats, and great coats. These were carefully made by men who had apprenticed to tailors when young. Occasionally, a woman might also apprentice to learn to make male clothing. Mary Gravely apprenticed in Philadelphia in 1773 for four years to learn the trade of making leather breeches. Usually, however, men learned to sew custom clothes for men, including learning to make buttonholes and covered buttons of bone or cork.[2]

Buttons and buttonholes seem to have been one of the major differences in the construction of clothing for men and women in the eighteenth century, for women's clothing almost always fastened with draw strings and pins. This simpler construction allowed women to construct their own clothing and children's clothing at a time when the button-clad male had to be clothed by a specialist. It was, of course, possible for women to learn these skills along with other types of plain sewing, but women apparently usually did not learn them. Like the skilled cordwainers who sewed leather shoes, tailors early developed themselves into a highly skilled and mobile work force capable of supplying clothing at a price that allowed even rural farmers to hire their services. Women, meanwhile, concentrated on producing linen bedsheets, tablecloths, bed cases, pillowcases, and quilts, along with the clothing they and their children needed.

Most women's clothing of the eighteenth century was constructed with narrow flat-felled seams. When finished, the seam usually measured only one-quarter inch. With double thread, sewn in small back stitches, these seams were stronger than those later sewn with machine stitch. The strength of these seams accounts for the age of the garments that still exist in collections and for the lists of garments in eighteenth-century wills indicating that clothing did pass from generation to generation until finally it was made over in so many styles and sizes that the fabric could no longer serve for garments requiring large pieces. Whereupon women cut the cloth still smaller, fashioning it into quilts of intricate and subtle designs.[3]

A woman's eighteenth-century wardrobe in rural areas involved considerable time and effort to construct. Although most rural people had only two sets of clothing—one for the work week and one for Sunday—work clothes had to be replaced more frequently than Sunday clothes, the latter most often being those treasured garments passing between generations. In Pennsylvania, women sewed for themselves a shortgown—a top, usually long sleeved, sometimes with a fitted bodice and peplum (an extension below the waist). It had no buttons, buttonholes, snaps, or hooks, but instead it closed with a tie and was fastened with a pin. Women also constructed petticoats with drawstrings to wear over what they called under-petticoats, both typically ending six to eight inches above the ground to allow free movement for chores. To these basic garments, the woman added kerchiefs for over the shoulders, aprons without pockets, caps, and separate pockets tied over or under the petticoat. Women usually braided their own summer hats of straw and often made cloaks for winter. Wealthier women might purchase a cloak—the first garment commonly purchased for women outside a household. A store-bought flat beaver hat with a one-half-inch-high crown and a six-inch brim, and a pair of shoes—usually leather soles with cloth uppers—completed a rural Pennsylvania woman's winter wardrobe. In summer many women went barefoot or wore wooden clogs. The clothing worn by women in other areas was quite similar.[4]

Because shoes were a specialized item requiring the cutting and sewing of leather as well as sewing of cloth uppers on women's shoes, the shoemaking trade developed early in the colonial period. Even in the eighteenth century, farm families seldom made their own shoes.

Traveling cobblers went about the countryside fitting custom shoes
and repairing old ones, while gradually certain towns began to
combine summer farming with winter shoemaking in what came to
be one of the earliest and most important cottage industries. While
shoemakers sold shoes from their farm factories in most colonies, New
England developed an urban trade that gradually moved many farm
families into an industry dependent upon the urban market place.
Though factories were in homes rather than in separate locations,
these enterprises were among the first sewing establishments to com-
mercialize.

By the late eighteenth century, Lynn, Massachusetts, had become
a leading center of the shoemaking industry. As William Mulligan
has shown in his analysis of the women shoemakers of Lynn, the
family became the basic work unit there, with mothers and daughters
sewing the uppers together while fathers and sons attached the sole
and heel to the uppers. Until the mechanization of shoemaking after
1850, these skills were handed down from mothers to daughters, and
practiced whether the women were single or married. By 1880 the
introduction of the sewing machine had drastically changed the life
cycle of Lynn women. Single women were moving out of the home
into the factory; married women were left economically dependent on
husband and wage-earning children, and the home was changed from
a locus of production to a unit providing mainly for the reproduction
of labor. This shift of the cottage industry from home to factory
brought a clear change in the role of married women needleworkers,
moving them into a far more domestic role. The relationship between
women's lives and industrialization was nowhere so clearly illustrated
as in the lives of the women shoemakers of Lynn.[5]

The first technology to affect the sewing of garments was the
introduction of factory-spun yarn and woven textiles. While the
sewing process remained essentially unchanged, the availability of
factory cloth at low prices quickly revolutionized household production in most areas of the country. As inexpensive cotton yardage
became available, farm women phased out their processing of flax and
weaving of linen, purchased cloth, and developed new cottage industries that could bring in the cash income needed to purchase the new
textiles. Often this new cottage industry was butter making. Even
when new cash income was used for purchase of cloth, women had to
provide their families with more clothing. It may have been necessary

to sew more. Cotton clothing was probably less durable than linen; it also may have soiled more easily, thus wearing out more quickly with more laundering. A greater quantity of clothing was also an important indicator of affluence in the new nation.[6]

The transition from linen to cotton, from homespun to storebought, is recorded primarily in the account books women began to keep in the early nineteenth century. One of the most complete accounts of this transition may be found in the detailed records kept by Martha Ogle Forman, who, with her husband, managed a large wheat plantation in northern Maryland, worked by over a hundred black bondsmen and women. In 1814 the Forman plantation women hackled flax and spun both flax and wool. Either a male or female weaver usually came in to weave the yarn into cloth, which was then sent out for fulling, bleaching, and dying. Martha Forman and a skilled black seamstress, Rachel Teger, did most of the cutting and sewing. They produced frocks, petticoats, aprons, coarse linen trousers and shirts for the black workers, and also made overalls, waistcoats, and pantaloons for Martha's husband, General Forman. Long trousers were not yet commonly worn among the upper class gentry: General Forman wore pantaloons, while his workers wore trousers. The women also made up all the children's clothes, the sheets, the tablecloths, and all other household "linen" necessary on the plantation. In 1818 the plantation women produced over one thousand yards of homespun to make into clothing and domestic items.[7]

The Formans had already purchased some clothing, however. Tailors made General Forman's better pantaloons and suits, and Martha purchased a "riding dress" in 1816. Outside purchases soon increased. The Formans purchased fifteen tablecloths in Philadelphia in 1818; by 1819 they were buying sheeting at 47 cents a yard for shirts for the men. In 1820 they purchased 88 yards of linen for the women's and children's clothing; in 1821, 57 yards of sheeting and thirty yards of domestic cotton; in 1822, 276 yards of material for clothes for the black families. By the 1820s the Formans were regularly buying cotton for their own and their worker's clothing. By the 1830s entries in Martha's account books indicate that she was also buying ready-made dresses in Wilmington, Philadelphia, and Baltimore. In 1836 she recorded: "The General and I went to Ceciltown and purchased for Henney a black bambazett frock, a blue domestic frock, two pair of black stockings, three handkerchiefs, a shawl, a straw bonnet, a pair of shoes, three check aprons. We made her three new domestic schemeese with stitched wristbands, five aprons, a flannel petticoat, a pair of corsets, and a workbag, two white aprons." This entry is an excellent indicator of transition in women's clothing. While Henney was an upper-class young woman, probably going away to Baltimore to a private school, and much of her wardrobe was still made at home, at least a portion of it was now being purchased ready-made.[8]

Democratization is a theme emphasized by a number of historians who have studied the history of clothing manufacture in the nineteenth century. Usually historians use the term to mean the spread of fashion from upper-class women to other classes through inexpensive mass-produced clothing and patterns. This spread of fashion then becomes the means whereby the great majority of American women can dress in fashions that no longer distinguish them by class. They share a "democracy" of fashion, almost all having equal access to whatever status dressing fashionably may bring.

These changes in clothing did occur, but they brought a leveling of labor as well. The mass production of clothing depended on large numbers of women engaged in sewing under conditions that were often brutal, exhausting, and sex segregated. There was a continual tension between the democratization of clothing and the conditions under which women workers mass produced this clothing.[9]

The term democratization does reflect the reality that in the nineteenth century "fashion" became the concern of middle-class as well as upper-class Americans. This spread of fashion (or styles that changed, rather than repeating traditional modes) probably was due to the ultimately successful experiment in creating accurate standard patterns for clothing the male and female bodies. During the period between 1812 and 1853 the United States government pioneered in manufacturing military garments of predetermined sizes. Centered in Philadelphia, this military garment manufacturing was usually completed by widows and other "meritorious females" who would stitch up the garments by hand in their homes. Meanwhile, tailors were beginning to create ready-mades during slack season for the urban middle-class males who staffed the new commercial sectors of the cities. Other entrepreneurs in such towns as Baltimore were beginning to produce cheaply made men's clothing for sailors and simple clothes to be sent south for black workers. While black bondswomen such as Rachel Teger had cut and sewn much of the plantation clothing in the early nineteenth century, the spread of textile manufacturing and the increase in cotton prices meant that plantation owners would consider women workers too valuable as field hands to train them as seamstresses. Black women were thus among the first women to be affected by industrialization of sewing. Their sewing skills were no longer valuable; their agricultural work became all-important for the profits of plantation owners. The availability of urban Euro-American northern sewing women desperate for employment made it cheaper to hire them to sew, while sending Afro-American women into the fields.[10]

The development of ready-made clothing for middle-class women lagged behind that being sold to working-class and middle-class males. Early clothing, to fit properly, had to be measured and sewn to fit individual women. Upper-class women could afford to hire dressmakers to create new fashionable clothing in response to some group that set the fashion. Among the eighteenth-century elite in Europe and America, men and women abandoned traditional clothing for fashions introduced by the wealthy. Like the housing of the new merchant class, clothing was designed to catch the eye of the beholder, to impress neighbors with the ability of the consumer of these new fashions to deviate from traditional styles. In the later nineteenth century, Thorstein Veblen would label this phenomenon "conspicuous consumption," and would identify women as the group mainly preoccupied with material culture. The phenomenon, however, began much earlier among the newly rich, and males seemed quite as preoccupied with fashionable display as females, if not more so. Whatever the origins of the phenomenon, people relied increasingly upon material items to help establish themselves in society, and to mark their place visibly in that society's growing stratifications. The results were a greater demand for fashion and for ready-to-wear that could provide quick changes in style. Male ready-made clothing evolved from earlier sturdy working-class clothing to ready-made "fashion" in the 1870s. Women's clothing, still crafted by most women in the home, could not be democratized or subject to fashion until more simple ways of fitting the complicated fashions could be devised.[11]

In the 1880s dressmakers' drafting systems, touted as magical devices, finally allowed dressmakers and home sewers to improve the fit of women's clothes. While techniques for cutting men's suits remained geared to professional tailors, the complicated devices created to assist in the cutting of women's clothes were designed to serve a dual market—amateur and professional sewing women. The tools of these systems provide an important visual record of attempts in paper, cardboard, wood, and metal to make the work of the sewing women easier in the late nineteenth century. [12]

Traditionally, the terms "tailor" and "seamstress" had described a division of labor in garment construction, in which men cut and women did most of the sewing. Until the end of the seventeenth century, laws in France and England enforced this separation. Gradually, seamstresses began to cut as well as sew. In England, they took the name mantua makers from the popular eighteenth-century dress that had back pleats stitched down to the waist. Later mantua makers were called dressmakers. In effect, dressmakers were tailors who measured and cut the material. Seamstresses usually continued to perform the most time-consuming task, that of sewing seams. [13]

The inch tape measure and proportional drafting systems began to be used widely in the early nineteenth century. Smithsonian curator Claudia Kidwell believes these new tools spread as the result of increased literacy and the decline of secrecy that had surrounded the trades of tailor and dressmaker. Previously, the dressmaker made as many as sixteen measurements for each customer, then used the measure as a guide to cut and sew the garment. The process demanded time and patience on the part of the skilled craftswoman as well as her client. By the end of the eighteenth century, however, an increasing number of urban middle-class women were demanding access to information on how fashionable clothing might be produced and procured. Abigail Adams's letters as First Lady are full of comments about ordering fabrics and inquiries about the latest styles in Europe and America, as well as descriptions of these styles for her rural correspondents. [14] By the first decades of the nineteenth century, middle-class American women had at their disposal *Godey's Lady's Book*, with its fashion illustrations. By mid-century, women could also find simple pattern diagrams there.

Godey's was also one of the first magazines to sell full-size patterns. These patterns came in one size only, however, thus necessitating adapting the pattern to the individual woman. The pattern merely provided a shape; the sewer still did all the fitting by traditional methods. At least two factors led to the new drafting systems. The first was the need of an increasing number of women to use sewing as a source of income for themselves and their families. The second was the desire of more women for more tightly fitting clothes. As Elizabeth Gartland, the creater of one new drafting system said in 1884, "The close-skin-fitting busts and sleeves of today require scientific cutting and fitting."[15]

And so professional and amateur dressmakers struggled with ever more complicated systems designed to simplify the process of creating fashionable women's clothing. After the 1870s, however, these drafting systems became the province of professional dressmakers. Equipped with one of the various drafting systems, women could set up their own businesses in their homes. Often combining millinery with garment making, married women or women who chose to remain single could make a comfortable living as respected and valued members of small towns. The integrity and self-sufficiency of these women was portrayed vividly in Mary Wilkins Freeman's story "A Mistaken Charity." Published in 1887, it describes two aging dressmakers who had made a comfortable living in a small New England town, and who refused to accept charity in their old age. Breaking out of the "Old Ladies Home," the two sisters returned to their own home to continue their life of independence.[16]

In cities, women might establish either dressmaking or millinery businesses, cater to the new or old rich, or both, and hire their own assistants. Ellen Louise Curtis was the best known of many dressmaker-milliners who, through dressing their wealthy New York clients, became wealthy themselves. Nearly four hundred dressmakers operated in New York City alone in 1894. Hundreds of other women ran millinery establishments similar to the one described by Edith Wharton in *The House of Mirth*. Wharton's character Lily Bart, reduced from high society to making a living with no training, is described in a workroom with twenty other women sewing spangles on hats. The women were, wrote Wharton, "fairly well-clothed and well-paid, but the youngest among them was as dull and colourless as the middle-aged." Lily, who had imagined herself presiding over "the charming little front shop," while subordinates prepared the shapes and stitched the linings, was unable to adjust to the life of a work woman; thus, her sewing experience became the final step in the disintegration of a woman unable to find her place in society. Other women did succeed, however. Like the dressmaker, the milliner carved out a place in the business world which gave her status and an income much envied by working-class and lower middle-class women who still dreamed of using needlework skills to create an independent way of life.[17]

For the amateur sewer, the mass production of sized paper patterns which began in the 1860s provided a simple and inexpensive alternative to the more complex drafting systems. Ellen Louise Curtis, later married to a merchant and calling herself Madame Demorest, began to publish fashion magazines and then to provide paper patterns to professional dressmakers and to a mass market. Demorest gradually lost out to other pattern makers because she continued to focus on individual *haute couture* clients. The Massachusetts tailor Ebinezer Butterick was thus the first to capitalize on mass distribution of patterns sized for men, women, and children. By 1871, the Butterick company was producing 23,000 patterns daily. That year, it sold more than six million patterns. Handsome profits for marketing the patterns soon made them widely available in the smallest towns throughout the country. By that time, as Margaret Walsh has said, fashion had become democratized. Women across the nation could now make fashionable clothing without specialized training.[18] Moreover, they were expected to keep up with fashions or suffer social ostracism.

Women would keep sewing in their homes for almost another fifty years. Combined with the spread of home economics classes that would teach working- and middle-class daughters how to cut and sew from patterns in the home, patterns indeed democratized fashion. They also helped preoccupy large numbers of females with fashion as a means of showing their ability to assimilate middle-class urban culture. As urban middle-class women turned more to ready-made clothing in the late nineteenth and early twentieth centuries, working-class urban and rural women spent more of their time creating imitation fashions. The Agricultural Extension Service, created in 1914 by the Smith-Lever Act, would develop as part of its federal mission the teaching of farm daughters how to sew fashionable clothing by using standardized patterns. Settlement houses performed the same teaching function for urban immigrants. Democratization also meant "Americanization," the equipping of all females in America—urban, rural, native born, immigrant, black, Hispanic, and Anglo-Saxon—with standardized clothing. All middle-class and an increasing number of working-class women had access to this clothing, but all now also were subject to a new conformity of style. Dress became as ordered as other aspects of society during this era which historians have labeled progressive.[19]

While patterns helped women to conform to national dress norms, new merchandising practices spread both fashion ideology and dress. The department store system, as Deborah Gardner shows in her article on New York, was also an early transitional phase to women's ready-made clothing. Department stores began their invasion of women's consciousness by providing urban space that women could, in many ways, consider their own. Although still sold by males, the consumer items appealed mainly to women shoppers. For the wealthier, there were enough material items to occupy their attention for many hours each week. For the less wealthy, there was the beginning of window shopping and bargain clothing. On the upper floors, sewing women were already doing piece work, as managers split work into various functions. Beginning as emporiums for the upper middle class, department stores increasingly provided for a broader-based consuming public. As purveyors of fashion, the department stores provided desirable urban space for women, and through competition for customers, the department store provided more variety in clothing for more women. Although available in fewer standardized sizes than those of men, women's clothes would soon be available in a large variety of styles. Yet, aside from the shirt waist and walking skirt, the democratization of clothing gave rise to few uniquely American styles in the late nineteenth century. Conformity in dress came with availability of ready-made styles, and European styles still ruled.[20]

Catalogs, meanwhile, spread the image of the well-dressed man and woman into rural areas. The 1897 Sears catalog still carried a greater variety of men's than women's clothing, but enough styles were shown to indicate to rural women what they should be wearing. The sewing machine provided the tool that enabled most farm women to conform to the prevailing fashions of the day.

By late ninteenth century, the sewing machine had spread through most of the country. Women may have delayed the introduction of the sewing machine by fifteen years with their opposition to using an invention that appeared to some at least as capable of putting women out of work. Walter Hunt invented the first practical sewing machine in 1834 and suggested to his daughter Caroline that she manufacture corsets. But, according to one history of Hunt's invention: "After discussing the matter with older women, experienced in the business, Miss Caroline declined to go into the business and use the new invention to perform the difficult heavy stitching required, for the sole reason that the introduction of such a machine would be injurious to the interests of hand sewers, and would be very unpopular." Elias Howe found the same opposition when, ten years later, he took his first sewing machine up to Quincy Hall Clothing Manufacturers in Boston. One woman at a Howe machine could sew five seams faster than five women could sew five seams. Yet he made no sales. Not only was the machine too expensive; the Quincy Hall owner said it would put women out of work.[21]

Within eight years, such concern for women clothing workers had disappeared, as clothing manufacturers began to compete for the newly developing ready-made male clothing trade. Machines gave manufacturers a competitive edge. With the Singer Standard No. 1 in 1852, and the introduction in 1856 of an installment plan, sewing became mechanized. By 1865 half a dozen factories were each producing over 25,000 machines a year. Five years later, in 1870, Singer alone was producing nearly 130,000 a year. Companies exported hundreds of thousands of machines to Germany, Great Britain, Cuba, and Mexico. In what was perhaps the first multinational corporation, Singer built a huge plant in Russia to corner the market there. It was one of the plants nationalized by the Russians after the Communist Revolution in 1917.[22]

Women stitched on, but now they worked both by hand and with the machine. The bobbin—a word once used to describe a small tube or stick upon which thread for lace-making was wound or a circular wooden pin to hold thread for weaving—now became a term, as the *Dictionary of Needlework* explained, "employed to denote the small reel on which thread is wound in some sewing-machines."[23]

A BOBBIN

Sewing machines spread rapidly during the Civil War, as the demand for uniforms launched a number of northern capitalists in large-scale clothing factories. Women who sewed by hand now had to compete with those able to work at a machine, the former working for a few cents an hour; the latter, a few dollars a week. The young women of a family might work in a factory; the married women, especially those with children, usually worked at home. Sometimes the whole family stitched at home—mother, father, and children.

The economics of the machine were relentless. In a patent claim occurring in 1860, the Winchester Shirt Factory of New Haven, Connecticut, explained the figures which brought higher wages and higher unemployment of women. Before adopting the sewing machine, the Winchester Shirt Factory made 800 dozen shirts per week by hiring 2,000 hand sewers at about $3 per week. After the introduction of the sewing machine, it could hire 400 women at $4 a week and pay off 400 machines at $150 each in fourteen weeks. The company could sell the shirt more cheaply, and 1600 women were out of work. The United States Commissioner of Labor later estimated that machines reduced labor time by 77 to 93 percent.[24]

At first, machine sewers in factories seemed assured of better pay and working conditions than those left sewing by hand at home. There was a good deal of public sympathy for the efforts of the hand sewers to gain higher wages, and earliest organizing activities, including those of Susan B. Anthony and other feminists in the 1870s, were directed at these hand sewers. Most organizing efforts were short-lived and unsuccessful, however, as more and more married women turned to home hand sewing to service the expanding factory operations. The availability of thousands of skilled hand sewers and young women desperate for factory jobs eventually lowered the wages of factory machine sewers as well, while an increasingly competitive industry forced owners to push factory workers to produce more, faster, for longer hours.

While working-class urban women struggled to control the new industrialization of their old art, rural middle-class women eagerly sought the new machine to lighten the burdens of their home sewing. During the 1880s, Granges provided buying cooperatives for rural women. In Illinois, for example, the Grange purchased thousands of sewing machines for members. Traveling salesmen of the 1880s bartered sewing machines for poultry or other farm produce, developing the rural market for catalog sales in the 1890s. Farm women not only used the machines for clothing, they sewed sheets, quilts, curtains, and feed sacks. They sometimes also sewed gloves, shirts, and other articles of clothing for country stores. The sewing machine was a versatile tool for the farm woman.[25]

Democratization can be seen in still other aspects of the sewing

machine. Early colonial women divided their sewing into two types—
plain sewing, on which we have focused so far—and fancy sewing,
that elaborate and largely nonfunctional sewing that mainly displayed
a woman's skill with the needle. No discussion of women needleworkers can overlook fancy sewing, for through it women created and
maintained uniquely female artistic forms, now included by art
historians in the special category of fiber arts. In colonial times, these
fancy works took the form of samplers, some of which displayed
complex and beautiful patterns. By the early nineteenth century,
according to Susan Swan, the quality of fancy work had declined and
the golden age of needlework was over. Upper and middle-class
women found other interests. Whereas reading and sewing had been
traditional skills, young women now learned letter writing, music,
dancing, and other polite occupations at the private boarding schools
they attended.[26]

Yet the artistic needlework tradition in fiber arts never died. It
lived on during the nineteenth century in the quilts that American
women pieced by the millions, fashioning both traditional and innovative patterns. The great American art, as art historians now
designate quilting, lived on into the early twentieth century, passed
on by women who refused to concentrate on the newly expanded
machine-made "plain sewing." One Home Extension agent in New
Mexico complained in 1918: "New Mexico farm women need to be
trained to place higher values upon neat, plain sewing and mending,
etc., rather than upon crazy quilts and difficult crochet patterns." The
importance of this sewing is clear from the comments left by early
twentieth-century quilters who resisted the efforts of home econo-
mists to make their work purely functional. Quilting was something
more. Aunt Jane of Kentucky, interviewed about 1900, said:

> I've been a hard worker all my life, but 'most all my work has been the kind
> that "perishes with the usin'," as the Bible says. That's the discouragin'
> thing about a woman's work . . . when I'm dead and gone there ain't
> anybody goin' to think o' the floors I've swept, and the tables I've scrubbed,
> and the old clothes I've patched, and the stockin's I've darned. . . . But
> when one of my grandchildren or great-grandchildren sees one o' these
> quilts, they'll think about Aunt Jane, and, wherever I am then, I'll know I
> ain't forgotten.

Another quilter at about the same time put it this way:

I'd rather piece as eat. . . . Whenst I war a new-married woman with the children round my feet, hit 'peared like I'd git so wearied I couldn't take delight in nothing; and I'd git ill to my man and the children, and what do you reckon I done them times? I just put down the breeches I was patchin' and tuk out my quilt squar'. Hit wuz better than prayin', child, hit wuz reason.[27]

While rural women clung tenaciously to the joys that fancy sewing could bring into their hard lives, middle-class women found other diversions. At the end of the nineteenth century there was one attempt to reverse the trend toward plain machine sewing. Influenced by the Arts and Crafts movement, middle-class women attempted to redefine needlework as art. New Yorker Candace Wheeler organized a Women's Exchange, where women could sell needlework, and helped professionalize home decoration for women. Art schools added needlework to their curriculum and women formed needlework guilds around the country. While these innovations reinforced the sexual division of art and reinforced domesticity, such groups kept alive an interest in women's traditional crafts, created places where women could keep their artistic interests alive, and fostered a sense of sisterhood in the arts. For some women, crafts were an important attempt to found businesses, but these attempts ultimately led back to the home and to a second-class status for the needlework practiced by women on the fringes of the male-dominated art world.[28]

Despite the determination of women to keep alive their traditional arts in the twentieth century, needlework and needleworkers increasingly came to be associated with factory work. The introduction of the sewing machine essentially altered the role of women in the fabrication of clothing. The individual and local markets declined, as a national market based on competitive capitalism demanded low-paid workers to run the new machines. Factories and sweatshops would be the dominant workplaces within which women would work with needle and bobbin.

NOTES

1. "Some Account of the Forepart of the Life of Elizabeth Ashbridge," Friends Historical Library, Swarthmore College.

2. Ellen J. Gehret, *Rural Pennsylvania Clothing: Being a Study of the Wearing Apparel of the German and English* (York, Pa.: Liberty Cap Books, 1976).

3. Ibid., 24.

4. Ibid.

5. William Henry Mulligan, Jr., "The Family and Technological Change: The Shoemakers of Lynn, Massachusetts, during the Transition from Hand to Machine Production, 1850–1880," PhD diss., Clark University, 1982. The drastic increase in the total number of women sewers in shoemaking is also documented in Susan E. Hirsch, *Roots of the American Working Class: The Industrialization of Crafts in Newark, 1800–1860* (Philadelphia: University of Pennsylvania Press, 1978), 28. The percentage of women in shoemaking dropped from 34 percent in 1850 to 14 percent in 1860.

6. Joan M. Jensen, "Cloth, Butter, and Boarders: Women's Household Production for the Market," *Review of Radical Political Economics*, 12 (Summer 1980), 14–24.

7. W. Emerson Wilson, ed., *Plantation Life at Rose Hill: The Diaries of Martha Ogle Forman: 1814–1845* (Wilmington: Historical Society of Delaware, 1976).

8. Ibid., 374.

9. Claudia B. Kidwell and Margaret C. Christman, *Suiting Everyone: The Democratization of Clothing in America* (Washington: Smithsonian Institution, 1974); and Margaret Walsh, "The Democratization of Fashion: The Emergence of the Women's Dress Pattern Industry," *Journal of American History*, 66 (1979), 299–313.

10. Kidwell and Christman, *Suiting Everyone.*

11. Claudia B. Kidwell, *Cutting a Fashionable Fit: Dressmakers' Drafting Systems in the United States* (Washington: Smithsonian Institution, 1979), 3.

12. Ibid. has many illustrations of these devices.

13. Ibid., 11.

14. Ibid., 8.

15. Ibid., 45.

16. Mary Wilkins Freeman, "A Mistaken Charity," in Barbara H. Solomon, *Short Fiction of Sarah Orne Jewett and Mary Wilkins Freeman* (New York: New American Library, 1979), 301–311.

17. Walsh, "Democratization," 302.

18. Ibid., 313.

19. For the urban revival of sewing see Louise J. Kirkwood, *Illustrated Sewing Primer, with Songs and Music: For Schools and Families* (New York: Ivrson, Blakeman, Taylor, 1884).

20. Paul H. Nystrom, *Economics of Fashion* (New York: Ronald, 1928), 370.

21. Frederick L. Lewton, "The Servant in the House: A Brief History of the Sewing Machine," *Annual Report, The Smithsonian Institution, 1929* (Washington: Smithsonian Institution, 1930), 563.

22. William Ewers and H. W. Baylor, *Sincere's History of the Sewing Machine* (Phoenix: Sincere Press, 1970).

23. Quoted in Gertrude Whiting, *Old-Time Tools and Toys of Needlework* (New York: Dover, 1971; repr. of 1928 ed.), 202.

24. Grace Rogers Cooper, *The Invention of the Sewing Machine* (Washington: Smithsonian Insitution, 1968), 58.

25. D. Sven Nordin, *Rich Harvest: A History of the Grange, 1867–1900* (Jackson: University Press of Mississippi, 1974), 135. The Indiana Grange sold $43,000 worth of sewing machines in 1875.

26. Susan Burrows Swan, *Plain & Fancy: American Women and Their Needlework, 1700–1850* (New York: Holt, Rinehart and Winston, 1977), 159.

27. Mirra Bank, *Anonymous Was a Woman* (New York: St. Martin's Press, 1979), 94, 121. See also Second Annual Report for Year ending June 30, 1916, New Mexico College of Agriculture, New Mexico Extension Service, National Archives Microcopy T876, Reel 1.

28. Yet another tradition, sewing for charity, has not been discussed here. The widow of Grover Cleveland and other antisuffragists were active in the Needlework Guild of America, founded in 1885. See Thomas J. Jablonsky, "The Ideology and Identity of American Suffragists, 1894–1920," paper delivered at the 1981 OAH conference, Detroit, Mich. For the crafts movement, see Eileen Boris, "Art and Labor: John Ruskin, William Morris and the Craftsman Ideal in America," PhD diss., Brown University, 1981.

CHAPTER 1

"If I Didn't Have My Sewing Machine...": Women and Sewing Machine Technology

Ava Baron and Susan E. Klepp

The editors of *Godey's Lady's Book and Magazine* wrote in 1855:

> A friend of ours from Chester County, lately visited Philadelphia for the purpose of securing a sewing-machine. . . . She herself calculated to do up her year's sewing in a week, and then have plenty of time for mental culture, for society, and general recreation, privileges from which women are often excluded solely by the neverending labors of the needle.[1]

Four years later, in 1859, Caroline H. Dall wrote in Boston:

> Nor would I have the sewing done with machines, unless those of the highest cost could be procured and ably superintended. The best machine is as yet a poor substitute for the supple, human hand; and many practical inconveniences must result from its use. It requires more skill and intelligence to manage man's simplest machine, than to control with a thought that complicated network of nerve, bone, and fibre which we have been accustomed to use.[2]

IN SUCH terms, middle-class women debated the merits of the introduction of the sewing machine.

In spite of these debates, between 1830 and 1880 sewing machine technology was developed, and the machine came into widespread use. In these decades there was, as one historian put it, "a ferment, a stew, of sewing machine ideas."[3] The growth of this technology, however, needs to be understood in the context of changes in clothing manufacture and the working conditions of the sewing women who had to come to grips with these changes.

This article deals with the development and uses of sewing technology as a social phenomenon and not solely as a technical or scientific one. The specific questions addressed here are: What social factors stimulated the development, production, and distribution of sewing technology at a historically specific time, and, what were the consequences of the implementation of this technology for the garment industry and its workers?

THE SEWING WOMEN: DRESSMAKERS AND SEAMSTRESSES, 1800–1860

Professional dressmakers had supplied the clothing needs of well-to-do Americans from colonial times. Very wealthy women had all their clothing custom made, while middle-class women employed dressmakers on special occasions, especially for making trousseaux and mourning clothes. Such dressmakers were highly skilled and were expected to keep abreast of the very latest fashions. Aside from making quality garments, they had to know the stages of mourning attire, the proper clothing for weddings, balls, and other special events, the accepted fashions in gloves, hats, and other accessories. They were consulted not only on questions of fashion, but on etiquette. Dressmakers seem to have come from middle- or even upper-class families, and to have served frequently as companions. The more exclusive dressmakers were often described as "gentlewomen in reduced circumstances."[4]

There was little or no subdivision of labor in the dressmaking trade. Dressmakers generally designed, measured, cut, basted, sewed, trimmed, finished, and pressed a garment. Only the larger establishments in the major cities employed apprentices and seamstresses for the simpler tasks such as basting garments. Dressmakers received good wages plus room and board. Some of these women were also shopkeepers and importers. Cloth, buttons, trimmings, feathers, beads, ribbons were sold at a central retail shop and the more exclusive of these establishments imported much of their merchandise from Paris, along with dressed dolls that exhibited the latest fashions. The dressmaking itself, however, was done in the homes of the clients.

The great majority of women who made their living by sewing in the nineteenth century were not dressmakers but seamstresses, who did piecework for clothing manufacturers or labor contractors. These women received bundles of precut garments from their employers and did the basic construction of the garment. They basted, lined, seamed, trimmed, made the buttonholes, and sewed on the buttons. In most cases they also washed, ironed, and folded the clothing before returning it to the shop for payment of work done. This work was considered unskilled because it involved only straight sewing, a skill the women had learned as girls. There was no training or apprenticeship for seamstresses. The skilled labor was generally done in the shop, most often by tailors or journeyman tailors. These men designed the garment, made the pattern, selected the fabrics and trimming, cut the cloth. From the early decades of the nineteenth century, seamstresses had no control over the quality of the goods they produced, or over its pricing.[5]

Sewing women were very poorly paid. A shirt could require up to 20,000 stitches.[6] Women in the 1820s could finish no more than six to nine shirts a week, laboring twelve to fourteen hours a day for six days. For this they were paid, on the average, 12 1/2 cents a shirt. Not only were wages low, but sewing women had to absorb the costs of production overhead. Since they worked at home, the expenses of rent, fuel, candles, needles, and in some cases, thread came out of their meager earnings. In addition, seamstresses could not devote full time to sewing. They had to travel the city looking for work, wait to pick up material, wait to deliver the garments, wait to be paid. The clothing industry was seasonal and few women could work the year round. Matthew Carey estimated that if a woman worked full time in 1833 she might earn $58.50 per annum, but if the periods of unemployment were taken into account, her annual income would be $36.40.[7]

The low wages of sewing women did not rise substantially over the next few decades. Even in those branches of the clothing industry where increases in weekly productivity were brought about by the further subdivision of labor or by the simplification of garment construction, wages did not rise. Rather, where productivity increased, piece rates fell. In New York City, in 1853, women might make three shirts a day, but the average paid per shirt was only 5 cents; the weekly wage, taking into account unemployment, was 50 cents.[8] This was at a time when skilled workmen earned $12 a week, and even women working in the factories might make a weekly wage of $3 or $4.[9]

To grind wages down even further, employers engaged in such tactics as claiming shoddy workmanship and then paying less than the price agreed upon, paying in kind rather than in cash, paying in depreciated script, or withholding pay for a month or more until a certain amount of work had been done.[10]

That sewing women's wages were so low—that these women were more exploited than any other wage laborers in America—was in part the result of clothing manufacturers' efforts to lower costs. The other important factor in low wages was labor supply. There were thousands of women in the cities desperate for employment. The women who turned to sewing had peculiar demographic characteristics. While most women in the labor force in the nineteenth century were young single women, seamstresses were more likely to be widows, wives abandoned by their husbands, or women with disabled husbands—many with young children at home. They were the breadwinners of their families. With dependents at home who needed their care, they could not search out work as domestics, teachers, or factory workers. These women needed to work at home; they needed flexible work hours so that they could take out time to prepare meals and nurse the sick. Because these women were poor, they could not become boardinghouse keepers or shopkeepers, since both occupations required capital investment in a house or a shop. With the lack of social services—no day care, no free apprenticeships, little welfare, and no workman's compensation, pension funds, or social security—thousands of women were forced to work at home with their needles. Matthew Carey estimated there were 5,000 or 6,000 seamstresses in Philadelphia in 1830, 3,000 of whom were widows with small children. There were more than 40,000 seamstresses in New York City in 1857.[11]

Labor supply affected full-time sewing women in still other ways. Women who were attempting to earn a living by sewing were also in competition with prison labor, poorhouse labor, farmers' wives and daughters who sewed to contribute to the household income, and—especially by the 1850s—with church women's sewing circles, which used the money earned for charity. None of these groups depended upon sewing income for their entire support, and consequently they could work for very little. Labor contractors used all these groups, sometimes because they needed additional labor in the peak seasons, and sometimes specifically to reduce the wages and stifle the protests of the professional seamstresses.[12]

The final factor affecting labor supply was the value structure of Victorian America. The cult of true womanhood restricted the opportunities available to women who had to work. Sewing was women's work and therefore respectable. Many other occupations would not have been deemed proper. The statement of Caroline Dall in 1859 sums up this attitude: "the command of society to the uneducated class is, 'Marry, stitch, die or do worse.' "[13] Marriage was the ideal state for a woman. If you were unmarried, single, widowed, or abandoned by your husband, then sewing would still be respectable. However, if sewing was impossible, then death was preferable to the only other viable option—prostitution. The constraints on sewing women can be seen not only in the literature of the times but also in the general absence of strikes. At various times after 1830 women seamstresses did organize. In general, however, most organizations of seamstresses seem to have been benevolent societies designed to help women while sick rather than to raise wages or improve working conditions.[14] The large number of seamstresses and their isolation in their homes made organization virtually impossible. Most seamstresses could ill afford to offend their employers for they had no other legitimate options.

The factors of labor supply, aggravated by the very restricted job market for women, allowed many employers to pay only subsistence wages to women sewers. In some places and especially during depressions and wars, wages fell below subsistence levels. That these women were able to survive at all is amazing. They lived in the cheapest rooms, often sharing their quarters with other sewing women; they had their children help them sew or sent them into the streets to hawk small items, and almost all sewing women were dependent upon public or private charity during portions of the year. Some, of course, did not survive and died of the combined effects of overwork and malnutrition.[15]

As bad as conditions were for seamstresses in the first half of the nineteenth century, their situation worsened in the 1850s and 1860s. In part, this was caused by dramatic fluctuations in the economy: the depression of 1857, the skyrocketing inflation of the Civil War years, and the postwar recession leading to the depression of 1872. The already overcrowded labor market of the clothing industry was swollen by thousands of war widows, soldiers' wives, and southern refugees who gravitated to the cities looking for work during and after the war.[16] But on top of these serious dislocations came the introduction of the sewing machine. In the late 1850s each machine was estimated to perform the work of six hand sewers.[17] Alice Rhine calculated that there were 73,290 women displaced by the machines in New York City alone in 1862. This figure exaggerates unemployment since increased production absorbed much of this displaced labor. The result of these three factors was to reduce sewing women's wages after 1861 to levels nearly as low as those of the 1830s at a time when the cost of living was twice what it had been thirty years earlier.[18]

CAPITAL DEVELOPMENT AND THE TRANSFORMATION OF THE GARMENT INDUSTRY

Between 1830 and 1880 the making of clothing was "revolutionized." One aspect of this revolution was the development of the sewing machine. Thousands of patents were granted for sewing machines and sewing machine parts from 1842 to 1895 (see Table 1-1). The invention of the sewing machine followed changes in clothing manufacturing and the textile industry. The acceptance of the machine, and the definition for its use, were shaped not solely by technology, but also by the marketing techniques and selling strategies manufacturers of the sewing machine employed, and by the structure of the clothing industry.

The existence of an abundant supply of cheap cloth, the basic raw material, was the first step in the development of a clothing industry. Thus the transformation of garments into commodity production for profit was related to capital development in the textile industry. Textile production was the first industry to be transformed by both technological and capitalist domination of production. The invention of the flying shuttle in 1733 sped up the weaving process and created more demand for thread to weave. The inventions of the spinning

Table 1-1
Sewing Machine Patents, 1842–1895

Years	No. of Patents Granted in U.S.
1842–1855	70
1855–1867	843
1867–1877	2,144
1877–1887	2,496
1887–1895	1,886
Total, 1842–1895	7,439

Source: Frederick G. Bourne, "American Sewing Machines," in Chauncey Depew, *One Hundred Years of American Commerce, 1795–1895*, II (New York: D. O. Haynes, 1895), 533.

jenny and the water frame in the 1760s and 1770s allowed spinners to produce more thread than hand weavers could turn into cloth. In 1785 the power loom was invented, and soon thereafter, the bleaching and printing of textiles was mechanized. The cotton gin, developed in 1793, solved the problem of getting the cotton seed out of the fibers, and provided textile manufacturers with a bountiful supply of raw cotton.

By the late 1810s both cotton and woolen mills had been constructed near water power sources in New England, and by the 1820s other eastern states had become involved in the factory production of textiles.[19]

Textile manufacturers could then produce cheap cloth in large quantities. In the first third of the nineteenth century textile manufacturers sought, and obtained, protective tariffs, which reduced competition with better-quality foreign textiles, and alleviated problems created by an overabundance of goods. This political remedy to the oversupply of textiles was only temporary.[20] For profits to increase, new markets for textile products had to be found. These large quantities of cloth had to find a "home," for although cloth was the final product of the textile industry, it was not in and of itself useful to the consumer. It had to be made into something in order to have exchange value in the marketplace—sacks, sheets, tablecloths, and above all else, clothing.

Each of these final uses of cloth required sewing—everything from simple hemming (straight seams), to the elaborate tailoring, embroidery, and appliqué techniques of high fashion. The inefficient, time-consuming task of hand sewing became a bottleneck in the development of new markets for this abundance of cloth.

Thus the history of the garment industry entailed the development of "ready-made" clothing and the decline both of "customer goods"—garments made to the measure of specific individual customers by skilled tailors and dressmakers, mostly for the upper classes—and of homemade garments.[21]

The acceptability of ready-made garments for the "respectable" classes was part of the rise of Jacksonian Democracy, with its ideology of equality in all phases of life, including equal clothing for all. Clothing was no longer to serve as a sign of class distinction, for apparel was to be marketed to all at low cost. The definition of "respectable" clothing was revised to include ready-made apparel.[22] A 30-percent duty placed on imported ready-made clothing in the tariff of 1816, and the rise in the duty to 50 percent in the tariff of 1828, protected this growing industry.[23]

The abundant supply of cheap cloth produced by the developing textile industry found a "home" in the ready-made clothing industry, both for the poorer classes and for the new "respectable" classes of urban areas. The new white-collar employees—accountants, bookkeepers, clerks, salesmen—all required inexpensive suits and shirts. Therefore men's medium-grade clothing (primarily shirts) was the first to be manufactured and sold as "ready-made" rather than as custom-tailored garments.[24]

By the early 1830s this new industry was thriving. In 1831 Boston had tailoring shops employing 300 men, 100 children, and 1,300 women.[25] Ready-made clothing production was further expanded during the Civil War as uniforms were needed for soldiers, but the development of men's ready-made clothing had begun well before the outbreak of the war. In New York stores were advertising a large selection of ready-made garments by the early 1840s. This clothing was being distributed to other large cities in the West and the South.[26]

Women's clothing did not leave the home for commodity production at the same time as men's. Although there were some early manufacturers of women's cloaks prior to the Civil War, for the most part, women continued to obtain their garments as they had in the past. Upper-class women either imported fashionable clothes from

Europe, or employed dressmakers to copy European fashions. Most women of lesser means, however, continued to make their own less-fashionable clothes in the home.[27]

By 1860 women's outer garments (such as cloaks, coats, and mantillas), hoop skirts, and caps were being produced as commodities. Dresses and most underwear still were not a significant part of women's ready-made clothing. After 1860 production of this clothing began to expand rapidly; the number of wage earners employed in this sector of manufacturing doubled in the 1860s, and more than doubled in the 1870s. From 1860 to 1880 the value of the product in women's clothing increased from $7,000,000 to over $32,000,000; the number of establishments increased from 118 to 562; and the number of employees from 5,739 to 25,192.[28]

TRANSFORMATION OF THE TAILORING TRADE: THE INITIAL PROLETARIANIZATION OF SEWING

Preceding the technological changes brought by the sewing machine in the 1850s were changes that contributed to the development of the garment industry as a capital enterprise, changes that increased the labor supply, reduced labor costs, and transformed the craft work by increasing its profitability. Clothing became a commodity that attracted capital investment. Before the sewing machine came into widespread use, both the formal and real subjection of seamstresses to the capital mode of production had begun.[29] In selling "customer clothes" to the upper classes, the key concern of the tailor and dressmaker was not price but quality. As master tailors embraced ready-made clothing production, they were forced to become "cost conscious." By keeping their stores stocked with ready-made clothing year round, master tailors could increase trade and appeal to a new clientele of city workers who desired less-expensive, yet "respectable" clothing.[30]

Once the master tailors were involved in the production of ready-made garments, they further attempted to lower production costs by changing the work process. In the early development of the clothing industry the tools of production remained essentially the same as they had for the making of custom clothing. The important tools were still scissors, needles, and goose. The only addition made prior to the sewing machine was the inch tape measure, in 1820. The inch tape measure was the first step in the standardization of tailoring methods. Personal idiosyncratic systems of markings were gradually replaced by standardized rules and procedures for measurement and drafting, which could be predictably repeated, and which anyone could read. Standardized measurements allowed for the first detailed division of labor in the clothing industry—the separation of the drafter from the cutter of the pattern. Although the task of cutting itself still remained skilled work, the cutter now simply followed the pattern drafted by another.[31]

The development of a "proportional measurements" system in the 1830s and 1840s dramatically transformed the ready-made clothing industry. Based on the principle that the human body had set proportions, this system meant that by taking one measurement—the customer's chest, for example—and then consulting the table of proportional sizes, at least sixteen additional measurements could be eliminated. This reduced a portion of the tailor's and dressmaker's skill to some mathematical calculations. Ultimately this system was adopted for the ready-made clothing industry for it eliminated the need for direct measurement of individual customers altogether.[32] The development of a proportional system of measurements and then during the Civil War of a system of proportional sizes, shaped the cutting and drafting of garment pieces and hence reduced costs.

Further cost reductions were made by replacing skilled male and female workers with unskilled labor, primarily women who toiled long hours on each garment for a few cents. By 1820 women were already at work in their homes sewing straight seams on shirts, coats, trousers, and waistcoats for stores. The *Emigrants Dictionary of 1820* noted that New York tailors had been "much injured by the employment of women and boys who work from twenty-five to fifty percent cheaper than men." While the 300 men employed by Boston tailor shops earned $2 a day, the 100 boys and 1,300 women earned 50 cents.[33]

The development of standardized measurements for clothing not only eliminated the need for skilled custom tailors to take measurements of each individual customer, but also allowed for mass production of clothing for unknown consumers, as well as mass distribution for sale in the retailing "innovations"—the mid-nineteenth-century department store and the late nineteenth-century mail-order houses. The custom dressmaker or tailor who catered to individual customers became a less significant source of clothing. Although these skilled craftspeople were not altogether eliminated, their role in the production of clothing was transformed. The standardization of measurements contributed to the development of the ready-made clothing industry, which allowed for greater use of sewing machines in factories; it also contributed to the development of the pattern industry, and therefore to the greater use of the sewing machine in the home.[34]

THE SEWING MACHINE: TECHNOLOGICAL DEVELOPMENTS

Although the first recorded patent for any component of a sewing machine was granted in London in 1755, it took approximately a century for a practical, workable sewing machine to be developed. The slow development of the mechanization of sewing was in part due to the unavailability of cheap cloth before the early nineteenth century. Large numbers of unskilled workers were available in the growing cities. The master tailors had little motivation to mechanize when the labor of sewing women was so plentiful and so cheap.

Technological problems also delayed the development of the sewing machine. To mechanize the textile industry the relatively simple application of mechanical power to the actions of the hand was needed. In sewing, however, a machine could not duplicate the motions made by the human hand and work efficiently. Instead of replicating hand sewing, an entirely new process involving two threads, new stitches, needles with the eye at the head, feeding devices, and thread tension controls was developed. So complicated was the process that no one inventor made all the important innovations.

Early machines did attempt to replicate the hand motion. Such backstitch machines, as they were called, did not work effectively. By the mid-nineteenth century two other types of machines were developed: a chain-stitch machine and a lock-stitch machine, which was to become the most popular type.

The chain-stitch machine used one thread, catching each loop in the one following it, forming the stitch as in knitting. The major problem with this principle was that if one stitch tore, the entire seam would unravel.[35]

The lock-stitch machine used two spools of thread, one above the fabric and one below, forming a stitch by a shuttle that pushed the lower thread through a loop made by the upper one as the thread was pushed through the cloth by an eye-pointed needle. The first lock-stitch sewing machine using an eye-pointed needle was built by Walter Hunt in New York City around 1832–1834, but was never patented. Elias Howe, Jr., was granted the first United States patent for a lock-stitch sewing machine in 1846.[36]

Howe's machine also had functional problems. The "baster plate" used to hold the material in place limited the length of the seam which could be sewed at one operation. After a certain length was sewn, the fabric had to be unpinned from the baster plate and rehung and repinned.[37] Nor could the machine complete an entire garment, inasmuch as it could sew only straight seams. In spite of these drawbacks, in 1845 Howe demonstrated that the machine could complete five seams faster than a hand sewer could complete one seam.[38]

Refinements by other inventors in the next two decades solved most of the technical problems. The Singer machine, patented in 1851, replaced the handwheel with a foot treadle, thus freeing both hands for working with the fabric while sewing.[39] Eventually Singer acquired a patent for a machine that allowed the sewing of curved as well as straight seams and the sewing of any length seam without requiring readjustments,[40] and which did not lead to seam breakage or puckering.[41] Wheeler and Wilson soon added a small lightweight machine suited for lightweight fabrics, especially for household use.[42] It was cheaper, faster, easier to operate, and had fewer service problems than other machines on the market.[43]

In spite of all these advances in the development of the sewing machine in the 1850s, manufacture was not extensive in this decade. The I. M. Singer Company, the largest manufacturer of sewing machines in 1853, produced only 810 machines. Wheeler and Wilson, the second largest manufacturer, produced 799 machines. Grover and Baker Sewing Machine Company, the third largest, made 657 machines, while Blodgett and Lerow produced only 135.[44] Within two decades, however, sewing machine production increased enormously. In 1867 Wheeler and Wilson was producing 38,000 and Singer 43,000 a year.[45] By 1871, 700,000 machines were being produced.[46] Table 1-2 provides data on the growth of sewing machine production from 1853 to 1875.

Table 1-2
Number of Sewing Machines Sold: Selected Years, 1853–1875
Wheeler and Wilson Manufacturing Company and Singer Manufacturing
Company*

Year	Number of Machines Sold
1853	1,609
1855	2,054
1860	38,105
1865	65,497
1870	211,041
1875	353,592

*The records of the "Sewing Machine Combination" were partially destroyed by fire. Only the records of Wheeler and Wilson and Singer were available for the entire period. However, two years appear complete. In 1859 these two firms sold 70 percent of all sewing machines, while in 1871 they accounted for 44 percent of all sales. This data therefore underestimates the total volume of sales.

Source: Calculated from data in Frederick G. Bourne, "American Sewing Machines," in Chauncey Depew, *One Hundred Years of American Commerce, 1795–1895*, II (New York: D. O. Haynes, 1895), 530.

The first significant expansion of sewing machine manufacture occurred between 1858 and 1859 (see Figure 1). In part, this expansion of sewing machine production was an outgrowth of the further development of the ready-made clothing industry and the standardization of sizes. Primarily, however, sewing machine production expanded because of changes in the sewing machine industry itself, changes that transferred control from the inventors to capitalists who tried to make sewing machines a profitable enterprise. Thus capital expansion required transforming the system of production to reduce costs and finding new markets to increase sales.

Coinciding with the expansion of sewing machine manufacture, three developments in the industry allowed capital expansion: the production of machines in factories; the formation of the Sewing Machine "Combination," and the use of new sales and marketing approaches.

Until the late 1850s sewing machines were made by skilled machinists who handcrafted each machine. As a result each machine was different, and the component parts of each machine could fit only the machine for which they had been made, since none of the parts

Figure 1
Sewing Machine Sales, By Year, 1853–1876
Wheeler and Wilson Manufacturing Company and
Singer Manufacturing Company

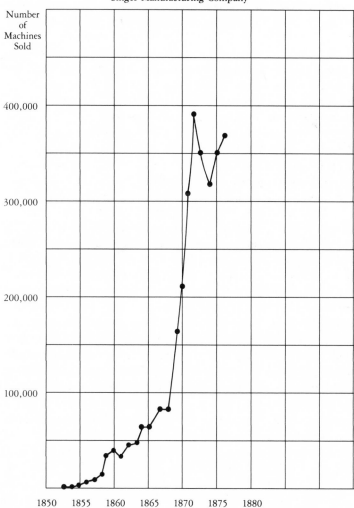

Number
of
Machines
Sold

400,000

300,000

200,000

100,000

1850   1855   1860   1865   1870   1875   1880

Source: Calculated from data in Frederick G. Bourne, "American Sewing Machines," in
Chauncey Depew, *One Hundred Years of American Commerce, 1795–1895*, II (New York:
D. O. Haynes, 1895), 530.

were exactly the same. With this method, each machine took a long time to make, labor costs were high because of the dependence on skilled craftsmen, and repairs were difficult. The system of interchangeable parts made it possible for manufacturers to considerably reduce the price of the sewing machines from about $300 to $125 by the late 1850s, and to $64 by 1870. However, the system of interchangeable parts required capital-intensive, specifically equipped factories. The Singer Company built the first such factory in 1857; other sewing machine manufacturers quickly followed suit in an effort to remain competitive with the Singer machines. These factories required the investments of huge sums of money.[47]

The formation of the Sewing Machine Combination in 1856 further advanced capitalization of sewing machine manufacture. Until that year most major manufacturers of sewing machines had been involved in law suits over patent infringements. As one writer stated: "Each company was suing all the others for one reason or another. The position was decidedly complicated and the lawyers were benefiting far more than the sewing machine manufacturers."[48] The Sewing Machine Combination pooled patents owned by Elias Howe, Wheeler and Wilson, Grover and Baker, and the I. M. Singer Company. The pool included such major patents as the eye-pointed needle, used with a shuttle to form a lockstitch (the Howe patent); the four-motion feed mechanism (Wilson patent); the vertical needle with a horizontal work plate, the continuous feed device, a yielding presser foot (Bachelder patent, bought by Singer); and the curved arm to hold cloth by yielding pressure, and the heart cam for moving the needle bar (Singer patent). Until 1877, when the extension for the Bachelder patent expired, sewing machine manufacturers bought a license from the Combination, and paid a fee for each machine produced.[49]

Because of the capital-intensive factories required for the manufacture of sewing machines and the legal battles over patent rights, three manufacturers of sewing machines came to dominate the market in this period—Wheeler and Wilson, Grover and Baker, and I. M. Singer.[50] Although the machines produced by each of these companies were orginally "invented" by mechanics and/or tailors, the business of making sewing machines now came into the hands of lawyers and businessmen.

Allen B. Wilson had originated the ideas that were patented and became part of the patent pool, but his business partner Nathaniel

Wheeler obtained financing for the factories from large capitalists in Connecticut.[51] W. D. Grover and W. E. Baker, two tailors, developed the machine technology, but Orlando Potter, a lawyer, became president of the company and handled its financial and business affairs. He had taken shares in the company as compensation for handling patent litigation. It was Edward Clark, the lawyer for the I. M. Singer Company during the patent infringement suits, who accepted shares in the company as payment for his legal fees. Clark first became partner and later president of the Singer Company. He aggressively expanded the company into new markets in the United States and abroad, and was the first to introduce factory production of sewing machines on the basis of interchangeable parts.[52]

It was these lawyers/businessmen, rather than the "inventors" of the machines, who dramatically transformed the business of manufacturing sewing machines and defined new uses for the machines. Together they were responsible for developing conditions under which sewing machine production could become enormously profitable. The Sewing Machine Combination ended the costly legal battles; this allowed sewing machine manufacturers to use financial resources for the construction of factories and machinery; it became easier to obtain financial backing from investors who previously were reluctant to place their money in such unstable production environments. The Combination also created monopoly conditions for the members, allowing them to keep prices relatively high. The production of sewing machines using interchangeable parts reduced the manufacturing cost far below the market price. Although machines sold for approximately $64 by 1870, they cost only $12 to produce.[53]

While seamstresses working at home were a potential market for the sewing machines, very few could afford machines in the 1850s and 1860s. Most of the earliest sewing machine models were heavy and expensive, suitable only for larger garment manufacturers and tailors' shops. Even when the price of machines dropped under $100, it was still too costly for most families since the average income was $500 per annum. Clark was the first to introduce an early version of installment buying, called the "hire-purchase" plan. The company rented or leased out machines on a monthly basis on "easy" payment terms. A customer thus could put $5 down, and pay between $3 and $5 per month with no obligation to buy the machine until the payments were complete. If the leasee did continue payments, which included interest charges, at the end of a certain period she would own the machine.[54]

The growth of the pattern industry in the 1860s significantly boosted the expansion of the home sewing machine market. The inexpensive, size-graded paper patterns along with changes in dress styles made it easier for women to produce fashionable clothes for themselves at home.[55]

By the late 1850s, the Singer Company and other sewing machine manufacturers began to pursue this potential market in earnest. Singer introduced its first "home" model, the "Turtle Back," in 1856, and a few years later the more successful home model, the "Transverse Shuttle" machine priced at $75.[56] Grover and Baker received the first patent for a sewing machine portable case in 1856.[57]

Such home and individual consumer markets required different sales and marketing strategies than those used with industries. Hire-purchase plans, then trade-in allowances for older models, were only part of selling American women on sewing machine ownership. Potential customers had to be convinced that the sewing machine was a "necessity" as a "labor saving device." According to one historian of the sewing machine, by the 1860s the Singer Company was spending $1 million a year on advertising.[58] The "poor sewing women" were a "natural" market for devices that increased production, but the major problem with this group was that they could not afford to buy the machines. On the other hand, the middle classes, who could afford to buy, had to be convinced that "domestic labor saving devices" were a necessity for the homemaker. There was considerable resistance to this idea.[59]

At first, the large sewing machine manufacturers—Wheeler and Wilson, Grover and Baker, and Singer—used independent agents who primarily worked on commission. As soon as large sewing machine manufacturers realized that this system was ineffective in capturing new home markets, they began to displace the independents, and established company owned and operated stores. These stores combined aggressive sales techniques with demonstrations on the use of the machine and repair service by trained personnel.[60] Grover and Baker was the first firm to establish such company "branch" stores in 1856, followed quickly by Singer and Wheeler and Wilson.[61] By 1860s the period of the franchised, independent agent had come to an end.[62]

To attract the middle-class homemaker, the larger sewing machine companies opened some of these branch offices, called "salons," in the business districts of major cities such as New York. These were fancy stores, with marble fronts, carpeting, and machines with silver plating in ornate rosewood cabinets displayed in a plate-glass window, surrounded by the latest women's fashions. Attractive young women were hired to demonstrate the machines; then saleswomen would escort the customer into a private "closing room" to "clinch the sale."[63]

Markets for the sewing machine continued to grow with continued improvements of the technology. By the late 1860s, basic refinements in the machine along with the development of various attachments and accessories simplified bobbin making, buttonholing, tucking, pleating, hemming, and numerous other processes. These devices were designed for both home and industrial sewing machines.[64]

THE HOME MARKET AND THE SEWING MACHINE

By the 1870s sewing machine manufacturers had developed a wide variety of marketing techniques including advertising, installment purchase plans, door-to-door canvasing, free lessons, discounts, and trade-in policies to vigorously exploit the home sewing machine market. The sewing machine became one of the first mass-marketed consumer durables, and a symbol of a family's middle-class respectability. The major selling point was that the sewing machine was a labor-saving device that would free women from the drudgery of hand sewing and allow them to devote more time to their families and to themselves. The sewing machine was widely touted as an agent of civilization, and *Godey's Lady's Book* was only one of many transmitters of this argument. In reality the sewing machine did not save time. Rather, as with other so-called labor-saving devices for the home, it increased expectations.[65] Women with sewing machines could produce more elaborate clothing with more seams, drapes, tucks, trimming, and ruffles than could women without a machine.[66] The lavishly illustrated women's fashion magazines of the period set the standards, while the development of the paper pattern industry in the 1860s provided the needed practical assistance to women who wished to become more fashionable.[67]

If the sewing machine did not save time, neither did it alter buying habits. Instead, an 1874 survey of the incomes and expenditures of 205 families of skilled workmen in Massachusetts showed that families with sewing machines spent a slightly greater proportion of their annual incomes on ready-made clothing and shoes than families without machines (12 percent against 11 percent). Both groups spent an additional 3 percent of their incomes on cloth, thread, and other trimmings for clothing to be made at home. The sewing machine was a symbol of middle-class respectability rather than either a practical investment or a function of wealth or income. While 50 percent of the families with annual incomes under $800 and 61 percent earning over $800 owned machines, there were higher correlations with, surprisingly enough, church attendance. Fifty-nine percent of the families who attended church owned machines, while only 24 percent of the families who did not attend church owned a sewing machine. The sewing machine represented the civilizing influence of women's values which helped make a home a haven. These families exhibited a hierarchy of values in which carpeting the floors held the highest place, followed by attending church, then keeping the children at home and out of the factory, purchasing a sewing machine, and, finally, buying a piano. Comfort, piety, and child-centered families were less related to income (especially since keeping the children at home involved a substantial loss of income) than to the influence of women over the home.[68] Some men saw the sewing machine as completely useless. As one wrote in the Chicago *Workingman's Advocate* in 1873, the sewing machine was "one of those stupid affairs / That stands in the corner with what-nots and chairs."[69] It was not the ownership of a machine but rather the growth of the ready-made clothing industry that finally reduced the amount of time housewives spent sewing.

THE DEVELOPMENT OF THE GARMENT INDUSTRY: "INSIDE" AND "OUTSIDE" PROCESSES

The history of the garment industry stands in stark contrast to the typical "textile paradigm" of industrialization. Unlike the textile industry which centralized production, the garment industry, even to date, has remained largely decentralized.[70] The history of the garment industry did not follow a simple, unilinear path of development, however. The diversity of the product, the differences between the needs and desires of consumers of men's and women's garments, and the contrast between work traditions of skilled craft tailors and unskilled seamstresses combined to produce multilinear paths of development resulting in different uses and consequences of the sewing machine. Two major tendencies existed in the nineteenth-century garment industry: centralized factory production ("inside" shops) on the one hand, and on the other hand, decentralized production, with an emphasis on "outside" shops (the "putting out system"), either in relatively small workshops operated by contractors or subcontractors or in the homes of individual seamstresses or tailors. The history of garment production and its various branches are best discussed in terms of the working out of these tendencies through combined uses of "inside" and "outside" *processes*, rather than in terms of the development of factories and "inside shops" per se. Both tendencies (centralization and decentralization) existed in greater or lesser degrees in the various branches of the industry, and as we shall see both became combined in a fashion peculiar to the garment industry.

Women's and men's garment production followed different paths of development. The men's clothing industry, especially the production of coats, began earlier than women's, and was chiefly influenced by skilled English male tailors who worked in their own shops or homes. Unskilled journeymen were paid by the piece to do the simpler tasks. Therefore production of men's clothing tended to remain decentralized. In contrast, the women's garment industry, which did not become important until after 1870, had its roots in the earlier manufacture of cloaks, and was influenced primarily by French (women) tailoresses.[71] This work tradition included hiring young, unskilled women who did not have their own workplaces. Therefore, production of women's clothing was more likely to involve primarily inside processes. As one historian wrote of the production of women's outer garments in the period 1860–1880: "The tendency was to bring together in one factory a considerable number of women. The employer furnished not only the workshop, but also the machines." In New York before the Civil War, there were several large cloak shops: one employed 100 workers, another 70, and a third 40. Boston, similarly, had a number of such large cloak shops: one shop with 100 workers, two others with 75 workers each.[72] Hoopskirts, one of the most important branches of the early women's ready-made garments, were made in large factories also, such as Wests, Bradley, and Carey's Hoop Skirt Works.[73]

In general, production in the decades 1860–1880 tended toward centralization and growth in firm size, although only in certain branches of the industry did centralization include all aspects of production. Large firms centralized only certain production processes, and let others be conducted "outside" the shop.[74] Just as before the invention of the sewing machine, the cutter would wrap the cut cloth into bundles, each containing the material for one garment. These bundles would then be sent to workers outside the shop to be completed, and then returned to the firm for sale.

One early form of this "putting out" or "contract system" was based on family production. Skilled journeymen tailors worked along with other family members on the bundles. A common practice in the eighteenth century, it continued throughout the nineteenth. According to a study by Christine Stansell, in one poor working-class New York City neighborhood in 1855, 16 percent of seamstresses were working for their husbands, brothers, or fathers.[75] A variation of family production in the "putting out" system developed in the 1850s. In this adapted form, unmarried journeymen hired women to work for them in their homes in place of wives and daughters. Still a third form of this "putting out" system was individual women seamstresses working in their homes. It was these women to whom Matthew Carey referred in his appeals to wealthy philanthropists in the 1830s and whose low wages have already been documented.

These different forms of the "putting out" system were the progenitors of the more exploitative system notorious in the industry in the later nineteenth and early twentieth centuries. Although all forms of the putting out system allowed the supplier of raw materials to make his profits from the sweat of the workers, be they relatives of journeymen or individual seamstresses, the "sweating system" based on contractors and later subcontractors was even more exploitative because each contractor had to make a profit as well.

Initially, the contractor acted as a middleman between the supplier of raw materials and the sewers who completed the garments. Gradually the contractor turned over the bundles to a subcontractor, who in turn distributed them among those who worked under his immediate supervision, in small workshops, usually "sweatshops."

Even as large firms developed in the garment industry after the 1840s, they continued to rely on the contractor and on outside work. Small firms generally had all work done on the outside, while large firms utilized a dual system of inside and outside processes. Utilizing outside work offered a number of advantages. It allowed the firm to keep overhead costs down, especially important since rents in the business districts of cities were high. Further, outside work did not require a large inside labor force, and therefore was more adaptable to the fluctuations in labor force needs arising from the seasonal nature of the garment industry. Even large firms tried to keep as much work as was practical an outside process. For example, Brooks Brothers, one of the large garment firms in New York City in 1860, employed 70 inside workers, and between 2,000 and 3,000 outside workers. Another large firm in New York employed 500 outside workers and 800 inside workers.[76]

The division of labor for inside work largely broke down to cutters and their overseers, inspectors, clerks, and sales personnel. For example, at Wanamaker and Brown's Department Store in Philadelphia in 1867, there were 600 employees: ten clerks and bookkeepers who purchased raw materials, inspected finished goods, and paid the workers; forty-one sales personnel and their assistants who handled the retail end of the business; and twenty-one cutters. The balance of the employees were outside workers, mostly "sewing hands" who picked up cut material at the store's cutting room, and finished the work at home.[77]

The proliferation of the contracting system and manufacturing under "sweating" conditions at the end of the nineteenth century did not mean the end of the large firm in the garment industry. Rather, large firms dominated the industry because they used contracting to their optimal economic advantage by combining it with the centralization of a few selected production processes.[78]

SEWING MACHINES AND THE FURTHER PROLETARIANIZATION OF SEWING

The contracting system, despite its advantages, presented problems for manufacturers. One major drawback was that outside work was not done in a uniform, standardized way, creating problems for standardized, unit pricing of garments.[79] To some extent the sewing

machine helped to resolve this problem. Contractors, therefore, began to require sewers, both seamstresses and tailors—whether working in contractors' shops or in their own homes or shops—to use
sewing machines. As one tailor who worked at home with the assistance of his wife and children recalled:

> In 1854 or 1855, and later, the sewing machine was invented and intro-
> duced, and it stitched very nicely—nicer than the tailor could do; and the
> bosses said, "We want you to use a sewing machine; *you have to buy one.*"
> Many of the tailors had a few dollars in the bank, and they took the money
> and bought machines. Many others had no money, but must help them-
> selves; so they brought their stitching, the coat or vest, to the other tailors
> who had sewing machines, and paid them a few cents for the stitching.[80]

Requiring workers to use sewing machines was only one method
devised by manufacturers to eliminate inconsistencies in production.
Another technique was to centralize all phases of garment construction in factories where close supervision of workers was possible.
Finally, manufacturers made the division of labor more detailed.
These methods of standardization were not mutually exclusive and in
some cases were used in conjunction.

The extent to which manufacturers could achieve standardization
depended to a great degree upon work traditions in different branches
of the garment industry. Men's coat production, based on the work
tradition of skilled English tailors, remained outside work. Contractors involved in coat manufacture were under less pressure to supply
either workplaces or machines because the skilled tailors they employed were relatively prosperous and could afford to purchase
machines. In the making of women's cloaks, large inside shops had
been established prior to the invention of the sewing machine, and
continued after the machine was introduced. Undergarments,
women's skirts, and to some extent men's shirts, which were made by
hand by women in their homes, were, after invention of the machine,
made in large inside shops. Since young women worked largely on
cloaks, undergarments, women's skirts, and men's shirts, employers
were under more pressure to supply sewers with machines since they
were less likely to be able to purchase their own. Women home
workers, especially shirtmakers, who had previously worked by hand,
could continue in the trade only if they bought or rented machines.[81]

In some cases home sewers subcontracted the machine work to others and a few specialized establishments arose in the late 1850s to assist these poorer workers. The W. H. Taylor Company in Philadelphia, for example, had sewing machines on the premises and did the machine work for those unable to purchase their own.[82]

The development of the sewing machine thus intensified the sweating system. Few tailors and fewer seamstresses could afford their own machines; but they could not afford to continue working in the garment trades without machines—hand labor could not compete effectively with machine labor because employers and contractors gave preference to sewing machine operators. With the switch to machines more seamstresses had to work for someone else in the sweating system rather than working for themselves and dealing directly with the supplier of the raw material.[83]

By the late 1870s sewing machine prices dropped dramatically following the development of interchangeable parts, the end of the patent Combination, and an increased use of the installment plan and monthly rental systems. Sewing machines became more easily accessible to contractors, and to workers. Some contractors rented machines to workers to use in their own homes;[84] others supplied sewers with machines to use in sweatshops but charged for their use. Contract shops in Boston in 1869 charged women $1 per week for the use of machines furnished by the employer.[85] After the price of machines dropped the number of subcontractors increased while the size of outside shops decreased.[86]

Just as the use of inside and outside processes varied in different branches of the industry, so too did the implementation of the sewing machine. The men's shirt and collar producers were the first to invest in machinery, but the ratio of workers to machines was still high in the 1850s. At the Edwin A. Kelley Company in Philadelphia in 1857, there were 600 hands but only 40 machines.[87] Machine work was confined to the sewing of collars and bosoms; the rest of the shirt was sewn by hand. By 1870, the ratio of hands to machines was much lower, yet there were still substantial differences among the branches of the garment industry (see Table 1-3). Only five firms, all in the shirt industry, utilized steam-powered machines. Since the shirt manufacturers had been the first to deskill labor through piecework and proportional sizing systems, these firms were in the best position to mechanize production. Also since the shirt industry, like the corset

Table 1-3
Ratio of Workers per Machine, Philadelphia, 1870

Branch of Garment Industry	Number of Workers per Machine	Number of Firms
Collars and shirts	2.7	74
Corsets	2.9	18
Men's and boys' clothing	4.1	420
Cloaks and ladies' garments	4.4	72
Shirts (women's)	5.9	25
Millinery and dressmaking	13.9	70

Source: Calculated from data in Philadephia Councils, *Manufactures of the City of Phila-delphia: Census of 1870* (Philadelphia, 1872).

industry, manufactured a standardized product, capital investment for manufacturers was more feasible.

Because the major advantage of the contracting system was its ability to deal with seasonal fluctuations by keeping capital costs and overhead low, most contractors remained organizers of labor rather than suppliers of capital. Workers who owned machines found they had an advantage in the labor market since they were given hiring preference.[88] This relieved the contractor from the burden of supplying the machine and having it lie dormant during off-seasons.

Generally contractors preferred to keep capital costs low. The operators usually had to supply their own machines, as well as thread and needles. They also had to supply their own power, for most machines continued to be operated by a foot treadle.[89] This tendency to keep overhead costs low and to require workers to absorb as much overhead as possible was not eliminated by inside shops. A large firm in Kentucky, for example, required their workers to "furnish their own stoves, fires, lights, and tools, the aggregate cost of which would diminish wages about 8 percent."[90]

Greater standardization of the product was also facilitated through the use of a detailed division of labor. To obtain greater product standardization from outwork, parts of garments, such as sleeves and collars, or distinct tasks, such as buttonhole making, were "put out." The finished pieces were then brought into the factory to be put together. Prior to the development of the machine some tasks had already been divided. Cutting and drafting the pattern first had become distinct operations, then with the cutting centralized in large inside shops and the development of standardized patterns, different classes of cutters emerged to perform different types of work.[91]

The use of the sewing machine made the division of labor in the garment industry more detailed, and work became increasingly routinized and repetitious. Sewing on buttons, buttonhole making, basting, felling, finishing, and pressing, were hand tasks done by other workers, sometimes in factories and sometimes as outwork. With the 1890s came an even more detailed division—each task mentioned above was further subdivided and skill levels were polarized. There were then different classes based on the skill required for each process—"second operators," "second basters," and "second finishers," for example, who did less difficult work.[92]

EFFECTS OF THE SEWING MACHINE: OCCUPATIONAL STRUCTURE
AND WAGES

The greatest change in the occupational structure of the garment industry after the development of the sewing machine was the creation of another unskilled category—the sewing machine operative.

The seamstresses who worked by hand and the custom dressmakers continued to work in the garment industry, but these occupations changed after the introduction of the sewing machine and the subsequent detailed division of labor in the industry. Because of the limitations of the early machines, only straight seams could be done by sewing machine operatives. And because these first machines were also expensive, most machine work took place in factories. The sewing machine operative usually was not a former seamstress. Just as the familial responsibilities of sewing women had kept them out of the better-paying jobs in the mills, so too did their need to be at home keep them out of the garment factories. Sewing machine operatives were young, unmarried women. In other words, they came from the same labor pool as other factory workers.

This factor largely explains the much higher wages received by the sewing machine operators—wages four to five times those paid to hand sewers.[93] While contemporary opinion held that the greater productivity of sewing machine operators accounted for their higher wages, it was labor supply, rather than productivity, which produced

the differential in average daily wages.[94] Women able to enter the
clothing shops and factories were also able to enter the shoe factories,
paper box factories, and mills. They had options that the home sewer
never had and therefore, at least in comparison to the seamstress, their
labor had a certain scarcity value. Employers had to compete with
other factories for their labor force.

The condition of factory workers was not good, nevertheless.
Women factory operatives were paid one-third to one-quarter the
wages of men. And many abuses of the putting-out system were
carried over into the garment factory. Sewing machine operatives
often had to absorb some costs of production overhead by purchasing
their own thread, paying "rent" for the use of the machine, or
supplying their own heat and light. Wages still were based on
piecework or a task system. In the majority of factories the tasks could
not be accomplished in the state-mandated ten-hour workday, so that
sewing machine operatives were forced to take bundles of clothing
home and sew for an additional two to four hours in the evening. Fines
for "shoddy" workmanship and payment in scrip or on account served
to reduce wages, and seasonal unemployment continued to plague the
garment industry. A new technique of exploitation even appeared
with the sewing machine, the so-called apprenticeship system. Manufacturers would take on young, inexperienced women for two months
without pay, promising to teach them to operate the machine and to
employ them at the end of their "apprenticeship." These women
would then be fired at the end of the two months.[95] The practice
occurred at the same time sewing machine companies claimed that
any woman could learn to operate a sewing machine in half an
hour.[96]

Yet factory work remained better paid only so long as machine
work was centralized. The cheap sewing machine allowed seamstresses to produce clothing at home on almost the same level as the
factory worker, so that it both revitalized the putting-out system and
encouraged the growth of subcontracted work. The cheap sewing
machine decentralized many branches of the garment industry, expanded the labor pool, and as a result reduced piece rates and average
daily wages in the late 1880s.[97]

Although the seamstresses who worked at home suffered from the
introduction of the sewing machine, facing reduced piece rates,
greater competition for work, and unemployment, they did not rise

up against the machine. Perhaps this was a result of their traditional lack of control over their work, or because this was not a case of the deskilling of a craft. The transformation of the garment industry occurred with little protest.[98]

The introduction of the sewing machine did not immediately displace all hand sewing. Some of the very cheapest grades of clothing continued to be made by hand as long as labor costs were low and the cost of capital investment in sewing machines high. Small items— men's underwear, ties, belts, infants' wear, handkerchiefs, artificial flowers and other trimmings—continued to be made by hand, perhaps because the sewing of many very short seams was not efficient on the machine. Tasks that could not be performed on the earliest machines, buttonholes and buttons, for example, were hand tasks until the 1870s. Much of the sewing of heavy materials was done by hand until the invention of the steam-powered machine in 1870. Other operations in garment construction were done by hand well into the twentieth century. The most important of these, basting and finishing, required too much manipulation of the material to be done efficiently on the machine.[99]

Over the course of the 1870s and 1880s, most remaining hand sewing was displaced by the use of the sewing machine. The putting-out system of garment construction was revitalized by the cheap sewing machine. Large and small manufacturers, labor contractors and subcontractors turned substantial portions of their work over to home workshops, where thousands of women toiled under miserable conditions for very low piece rates. In the 1890s this would be known as sweated labor, but naming the system did not mean it was new. The conditions of labor, the low piece rates, the methods of exploitation by employers had changed very little since they were first described by Matthew Carey in 1828. There were still thousands of women who worked at home. By the end of the nineteenth century, the needle trades were still the only occupations open to impoverished women heads of household (see Table 1–4).

For several decades after mass production techniques had been introduced into other branches of the garment industry, women's dresses were still made at home or by skilled dressmakers working for individual customers. As late as 1870, custom dressmaking existed and continued along traditional lines. Mother Jones described her experience in her autobiography:

I returned to Chicago [after the deaths of her husband and children] and went again into the dressmaking business with a partner. We were located on Washington Street near the lake [the central retail district]. We worked for the aristocrats of Chicago, and I had ample opportunity to observe the luxury and extravagance of their lives. Often while sewing for the lords and barons who lived in magnificent houses on the Lake Shore Drive, I would look out of the plate glass windows and see the poor, shivering wretches, jobless and hungry, walking along the frozen lake front. The contrast of their condition with that of the tropical comfort of the people for whom I sewed was painful to me. My employers seemed neither to notice nor to care.[100]

A survey of thirty-six businesses mass producing dresses in Boston in 1869 showed that they were in operation only sixteen weeks out of the year. The yearly demand for ready-made women's dresses in Boston could be met by 281 women working 10 or 12 hours a day for four months. In these circumstances there would be little motivation for the merchants who ran these establishments to increase productivity.[101]

Table 1–4
Conjugal Condition of Females Ten Years of Age and Over, 1890,
Selected Occupations

Occupation	Single	Married	Widowed	Divorced
Cotton-mill operatives	82.7	12.6	4.4	.3
Silk-mill operatives	92.8	4.6	2.5	.1
Woolen-mill operatives	86.3	9.2	4.1	.4
Seamstress	72.1	10.0	16.6	1.3
Dressmakers	74.9	12.1	11.6	1.4
Milliners	71.8	17.3	9.6	1.3

Source: Twelfth Census, 1900, in Helen L. Sumner, *History of Women in Industry in the United States*, vol. 9 of the *Report on the Condition of Woman and Child Wage Earners in the United States*, 61st Congress, 2d Session, Senate Document #645 (Washington, 1910), 248. (Some sewing women enumerated in this census worked in factories as sewing machine operatives, while others worked at home. Nineteenth-century census data almost never included information on place of work.)

In Philadelphia in 1860, for example, there were 308 dressmaking and millinery establishments employing over 1,138 workers. There was no production of women's clothing by machine. In the next decade nearly 80 percent of these businesses disappeared and over 80 percent of the workers were unemployed. By 1880 dressmaking and millinery trades had become so insignificant that they were no longer returned as separate categories in the manufacturing census. In the same twenty-year period the number of factories producing ladies' garments increased from 30 to 276 and the number of employees from 538 to 3,132 (see Table 1–5).

Not only were dressmakers thrown out of work by the growth of the ready-made ladies' garment trade, but those who remained in the business saw their daily wages considerably reduced. Dressmakers in the early 1850s could expect to earn $1.33 a day. By the 1860s the average daily wage had fallen to 93 cents, even though this was a period of rapid inflation caused by the Civil War. In the 1870s and

Table 1–5
Women's Clothing Production, Philadelphia, 1860–1880

Year	Number of Establishments	Number of Employees	Value of Product
	Millinery and Dressmaking		
1860	233 plus 75*	1,138	$1,334,964 plus $45,000
1870	70	222	242,904
1880	N.A.	——	——
	Cloaks and Ladies' Wear (Factory)		
1860	30	538	$ 689,580
1870	72	733	1,010,992
1880	276	3,132	3,138,333

*The Philadelphia Board of Trade used police files to correct the returns of the federal census of 1860 and uncovered 75 dressmakers and milliners missed in the census. The Board of Trade did not, however, include employment figures for these establishments. The low figure for value of product would indicate that these establishments did not employ help.

Sources: Philadelphia Board of Trade, Manufactures of Philadelphia: *Census of 1860* (Philadelphia, 1861); Philadelphia Councils, *Manufactures of the City of Philadelphia: Census of 1870* (Philadelphia, 1872): Lorin Blodgett, *Census of Manufactures of Philadelphia . . . for the Year 1882* (Philadelphia, 1883), 115.

through 1885, skilled dressmakers could expect only 87 cents a day. [102] This fifteen-year period was the low point of the dressmaking trade as the rapid expansion of the factory production of women's clothing forced the remaining dressmakers to compete for work. There was still some demand for custom-made women's clothing; wealthy women who wanted to be fashion trend setters had to have their clothing custom made, and other women continued to buy custom-made clothing for special events. Christening garments for infants, wedding dresses, ball gowns—all these required highly-skilled dressmakers. After 1885, the dressmaking trade stabilized. Wages for dressmakers began to rise, averaging $1.04 in the late 1880s and $1.10 in the 1890s. [103]

In the women's garment industry, skilled, highly paid women artisans were largely replaced by unskilled, poorly paid sewing machine operatives. This branch of the industry was transformed by not only the sewing machine but also the paper pattern industry and the standardization of sizes. Both of the latter developments eliminated the need for skilled sewers and allowed the mass production of dresses by machine.

CONCLUSION

Evidence has been provided to challenge some assumptions about technology and capital development. First, sewing technology was not the "cause" of a revolution in the garment industry. Rather, the development of the sewing machine was an outgrowth of the commodification of garment production. Economic and cultural changes that had occurred by the early decades of the nineteenth century— including the abundance of cheap cloth and the "democratization" of clothing—were preconditions for the development of the ready-made garment industry and for manufacturers' growing interest in a practical sewing machine. Thus while ideas for sewing machines had existed prior to the 1850s, clothing manufacturers' pursuit of such technology had not. The large pool of unskilled women laborers who were desperate for work in the cities allowed manufacturers to increase production without mechanization. In addition, developments within the sewing machine manufacturing industry, which made sewing machine manufacturing profitable, made the widespread use of sewing machines possible. Thus technology followed the path of capital development in textiles, garment production, and sewing machine manufacturing and was shaped by the characteristics of the labor market.

Further, it was not the sewing machine that created the detailed division of labor and deskilling of the tailoring trade. The trend toward the proletarianization of skilled sewing (both tailoring and dressmaking) preceded the implementation of sewing technology. The initial steps in this process included the standardization of measurements which replaced the need for tailor's skilled markings. The development of a system of proportional sizes and ultimately of standard-sized garments further reduced this need and contributed to the detailed division of labor. The standardization of measurements allowed for more effective use of sewing machines in factories; it also contributed to the development of the paper pattern industry, and therefore use of the sewing machine in the home. The invention of the sewing machine continued an established trend towards deskilling of garment production and helped to shape the structure of the garment industry, but it was not the cause of the process.

The study of the garment industry further documents that economies of scale are not always operative;[104] nor does technology necessarily lead toward increased firm size. Diseconomies of scale were especially pronounced in the garment industry. Although firm size appeared to increase in some branches after introduction of the machine, many aspects of production remained "outside" processes; and most workers were not strictly speaking employees but were piece workers who were managed by contractors or subcontractors. The major factors that had tended to centralize production—the cost of the early machines and the desire of manufacturers for greater product uniformity—were countered by the availability of inexpensive, mass-produced, more versatile sewing machines after 1870. These factors contributed to the decentralization of the garment industry by the late nineteenth century.

Last, the sewing machine cannot be blamed for the low wages and poor working conditions of needle-women in the late nineteenth and early twentieth centuries. Although wages and employment opportunities for skilled dressmakers in the women's garment industry were much reduced following the introduction of sewing machines, this was not the case for the majority of needle workers. Low piece rates, fines, and the assumption of some overhead production costs were the norm for both hand and machine workers.

The garment industry did not follow the textile paradigm of industrial development. The large factories with banks of machinery run by a few unskilled workers, common in the textile industry, were not characteristic of the clothing industry. In part this was a consequence of differences in technology, for while the sewing machine is a complex instrument it performs a very simple task—sewing a single operation on one garment at a time. Each machine requires its own operator. Production need not be centralized; it can take place in homes, sweatshops, large and small factories. The limitations of technological development in the industry combined with the seasonality of demand and the variety of the product to make most large-scale operations noncompetitive. Profit came not by reducing labor requirements but by seeking out cheap labor—the poor uneducated women of the American cities of the nineteenth century, the poor women of Latin America and Asia in the twentieth.

NOTES

1. "Grover, Baker, and Company's Sewing Machines," *Godey's Lady's Book and Magazine*, 50 (Aug. 1855), 185.

2. Caroline H. Dall, *The Right to Labor; or, Low Wages and Hard Work: In Three Lectures* (Boston: Walker, Wise, 1860), 156–157.

3. Jessica Daves, *Ready-Made Miracle: The Story of Fashion for the Millions* (New York: Putnam's, 1967), 21.

4. The terms in this chapter present ideal types. We have used the word "dressmaker" to describe skilled sewing women and the more generic term "seamstresses" to describe less-skilled sewing women. In the nineteenth century a number of different terms were applied: dressmakers, mantua makers, and tailoresses were generally skilled workers; seamstresses or sempstresses, needlewomen, shirtmakers were often less skilled. However, these terms were always loosely applied. Any sewing woman's work could include both skilled and unskilled labor processes, and many women did custom work or piecework depending upon the work available at a given time. While this chapter concentrates on sewing women in the garment industry, sewing women also worked in the manufacture of other products: hats and caps; leather and fur goods (and especially boots and shoes); gloves; trimmings; bags and sacks; sheets, towels, and other linens; lace; and pocketbooks. We are concerned here with the experiences of urban women in the eastern United States. Seamstresses in rural areas and in the

newly settled western states apparently were much less exploited largely because of their scarcity.

Louisa Frances Raymond gives a contemporary sketch of the dressmaker in "The Gilt Buttons; or, The Two Mantuamakers," *The Lady's Amaranth*, 4, no. 8 (1842), 192–193.

5. A good account of the working conditions of the seamstress can be found in Timothy Shay Arthur, *The Seamstress* (Philadelphia: Barrett and Jones, 1843). This short novel was republished many times—under different titles and with slight changes—over the following twenty years. While most fiction about sewing women reflected middle-class values and concerns, Arthur's treatment is more realistic in its descriptions even though the plot is melodramatic and the happy ending is contrived. Arthur had been a tailor's apprentice in his youth and knew the conditions of the trade from first-hand experience. See also his collection of short stories: *Woman's Trials; or, Tales and Sketches from the Life around Us* (Philadelphia: Collins, 1853).

6. "The Value of the Sewing Machine," *Godey's Lady's Book and Magazine*, 74 (Feb. 1867), 192.

7. Matthew Carey's many publications on sewing women are summarized in Helen L. Sumner, *History of Women in Industry in the United States*, vol. 9 of the *Report on the Condition of Woman and Child Wage Earners in the United States*, 61st Congress, 2d Session, Senate Document #645 (Washington, 1910), 123–133 (henceforth *Report*; Senate Document #645).

8. Sumner, *History*, 137–138.

9. George Rodgers Taylor, *The Transportation Revolution* (New York: Harper and Row, 1951), 297.

10. See Arthur, *The Seamstress*, 18–19; Sumner, *History*, 150–151.

11. "Women with half a dozen mouths around them, don't stand long to higgle about a few cents in a garment, when there are so many willing to step in and take their places" (a master tailor about to reduce piece rates by 4¢ in Arthur, *The Seamstress*, 27); see also Sumner, *History*, 130; and Ruth Brandon, *A Capitalist Romance: Singer and the Sewing Machine* (New York: Lippincott, 1977), 68–70. On the marital status of most women workers in the nineteenth century, see Carl Degler, *At Odds: Women and the Family in America from the Revolution to the Present* (New York: Oxford University Press, 1980), 375–394.

12. Sumner, *History*, 139–141. On prison labor see Mrs. M. Clarke, ed., *The Memoirs of the Celebrated and Beautiful Mrs. Ann Carson . . . Whose life Terminated in the Philadelphia Prison* (Philadelphia, 1838), II, 66. On poorhouse labor, George Ellington (pseud.), *The Women of New York, or The Under-World of the Great City* (New York: New York Book Company, 1869), 616–635. For farmwork see Charles P. Neill, *Men's Ready-Made Clothing*, vol. 2, *Report*, Senate Document #645, 492–493; and Sumner, *History*, 140–141. On charity work, Frances Trollope, *Domestic Manners of the Americans* (New York: Random House, 1949, repr. of 1832 ed.), 281–282.

13. Dall, *Right to Labor*, 104. There is also evidence that sewing, especially work on men's clothing, was not quite respectable. Frances Trollope reports that while women made shirts, it would have been "a symptom of absolute depravity"

to admit that fact to a man; *Domestic Manners*, 159. Mrs. Clarke attempted to convince Ann Carson to sew men's clothing and Carson replied that that was "employment only fit for the meanest and lowest females of the city." Clarke replied: "You, your mother, and all your sisters were glad to make soldiers' shirts, and give security for the fulfillment of the contract, here no security is required— Sam [Carson's son] can carry the work backward and forward, that we may not be exposed" (Clarke, *Memoirs*, II, 113–114).

14. Philip S. Foner, *Women and the American Labor Movement, from Colonial Times to the Eve of World War I* (New York: Free Press, 1979), 40–45, 113–121. Barbara Mayer Wertheimer, *We Were There: The Story of Working Women in America* (New York: Pantheon Books, 1977), 96–102; John B. Andrews and W. D. P. Bliss, *History of Women in Trade Unions*, vol. 10, *Report*, Senate Document #645 (Washington, 1911), 36–40, 58–60, 94–100.

15. There is little data on occupational mortality in the United States for the first half of the nineteenth century. However, data from England and later investigations by government and social work agencies in the United States point to high mortality among seamstresses.

16. Wertheimer, *We Were There*, 151–155.

17. Ibid., 102.

18. Alice Hyneman Rhine, "Woman in Industry," in Annie Nathan Meyer, ed., *Woman's Work in America* (New York: Holt, 1891), 285.

19. Claudia B. Kidwell and Margaret C. Christman, *Suiting Everyone: The Democratization of Clothing in America* (Washington: Smithsonian Institution, 1974), 37. Another of the many discussions of technology development in the textile industry is: Anthony F. C. Wallace, *Rockdale: The Growth of an American Village in the Early Industrial Revolution* (New York: Norton, 1978), esp. 124–242.

20. Yet textile manufacturers did not venture risk capital in an attempt to mechanize garment construction. They preferred the safer method of political solutions to the oversupply of textiles. Tailors and machinists were the major underwriters of the development of workable sewing machines. On tariffs and exports see United States Census Office, *Manufactures of the United States in 1860, Compiled from the Original Returns of the Eighth Census* (Washington: Government Printing Office, 1865), lxiii–lxiv.

21. Joel Seidman, *The Needle Trades* (New York: Farrar and Rinehart, 1942), 13.

22. Kidwell and Christman, *Suiting Everyone*, 39.

23. Seidman, *Needle Trades*, 14.

24. Ibid.; Daniel J. Boorstin, *The Americans: The Democratic Experience* (New York: Random House, 1973), 91–100.

25. Seidman, *Needle Trades*, 14; Sumner, *History*, 151–155.

26. Jesse E. Pope, *The Clothing Industry in New York*, University of Missouri, Social Science Studies, 1 (1905), 12; Kidwell and Christman, *Suiting Everyone*, 53–63.

27. Seidman, *Needle Trades*, 20; U.S. Census, *Manufactures in 1860*, lxxxii–lxxxv.

28. Seidman, *Needle Trades*, 20–21; U. S. Census, *Manufactures in 1860*,

lxxxv; Louis Levine, *The Women's Garment Workers* (New York: B. W. Huebsch, 1924), 8. These figures undoubtedly underestimate production, expecially for the manufacturing censuses prior to 1870.

29. The concept of proletarianization as used here refers to dual processes: the formal and real subjection of labor to the capitalist mode of production. In formal subjection labor power has been transformed into a commodity; in real subjection labor power is transformed into a technical means of production in the labor process. Ava Baron has argued elsewhere that these two aspects of proletarianization need not take place sequentially, and that both are ongoing processes shaped by workers' resistance to them and capitalists' responses to such resistance; see Ava Baron, "Women and the Making of the American Working Class: A Study of the Proletarianization of Printers," *Review of Radical Political Economics*, 14, no. 3 (Fall 1982), 23–42; and "Woman's 'Place' in Capitalist Production: A Study of Class Relations in the Nineteenth Century Newspaper Printing Industry," PhD diss., New York University, 1981.

30. Pope, *Clothing Industry*, 12; Kidwell and Christman, *Suiting Everyone*, 39.

31. Kidwell and Christman, *Suiting Everyone*, 42.

32. Ibid., 42–43; Boorstin, *The Americans*, 188–189.

33. United States Department of Labor, Bureau of Labor Statistics, *History of Wages in the United States from Colonial Times to 1928*, revision of Bulletin No. 499 with Supplement, 1929–1933 (Washington, 1934), 114–115. Kidwell and Christman, *Suiting Everyone*, 45.

34. Boorstin, *The Americans*, 89–156, 188–189; Margaret Walsh, "The Democratization of Fashion: The Emergence of the Women's Dress Pattern Industry," *Journal of American History*, 66 (Sept. 1979), 299–313.

35. Brandon, *Capitalist Romance*, 58.

36. Edward W. Byrn, *The Progress of Invention in the Nineteenth Century* (New York: Munn, 1900), 185. The story of the invention of Hunt's sewing machine is odd. Hunt supposedly invented a workable machine, but suppressed the knowledge of it when his daughter pointed out that many poor seamstresses would be unemployed as a result of this invention. This tale is often recounted as an example of workers' fear of labor-saving machinery. Yet the story did not surface until the 1850s, when Hunt was employed by I. M. Singer's lawyers in an attempt to break Elias Howe's patent, and it seems merely a fabrication designed to explain why Hunt never applied for a patent. While employed by Singer's lawyers, Hunt attempted to reconstruct his machine, but even with time, funds, and the many examples of working machines before him, he was unable to get his device to work (Brandon, *Capitalist Romance*, 93).

37. Frederick G. Bourne, "American Sewing Machines," in Chauncey Depew, *One Hundred Years of American Commerce, 1795–1895*, II (New York: D. O. Haynes, 1895), 526.

38. Frederick L. Lewton, "The Servant in the House: A Brief History of the Sewing Machine," *Annual Report, The Smithsonian Institution, 1929* (Washington: Smithsonian Institution, 1930), 566.

39. George Iles, *Leading American Inventors* (Freeport, N.Y.: Books for Libraries Press, 1968; repr. of 1912 ed.), 358.

40. Bourne, "American Sewing Machines," 526.

41. Andrew B. Jack, "The Channels of Distribution for an Innovation: The Sewing Machine Industry in America, 1860–1865," *Explorations in Entrepreneurial History*, 9 (1957), 136.

42. Ibid., 115.

43. The Job A. Davis machine was a vertical feed machine which was particularly popular in the "farm belt" because it could easily sew canvas, ducking, feed sacks, and any light leather goods. This company eventually supplied Sears, Roebuck and Co. with millions of machines. The Wilcox and Gibbs machines were sold for about $50, while most competitors sold for over $100. Although this machine never became popular with housewives because the seam formed by the chainstitch had a tendency to unravel, it did become popular for industrial use, especially for sewing seams on sugar, flour, or feed sacks. William Ewers and H. W. Baylor, *Sincere's History of the Sewing Machine* (Phoenix: Sincere Press, 1970), 77.

44. Brian Jewell, *Veteran Sewing Machines: A Collector's Guide* (New York: Barnes, 1975), 38.

45. Byrn, *Progress of Invention*, 188. These are conservative figures. Alfred D. Chandler, Jr., presents higher figures for sewing machine production in the 1860s in *The Visible Hand: The Managerial Revolution in American Business* (Cambridge, Mass.: Harvard University Press, 1977), 303.

46. Jewell, *Veteran Sewing Machines*, 46.

47. Brandon, *Capitalist Romance*, 101–102.

48. Jewell, *Veteran Sewing Machines*, 41.

49. Ewers and Baylor, *Sincere's History*, 123.

50. Chandler, *Visible Hand*, 303.

51. Bourne, "American Sewing Machines," 528.

52. Brandon, *Capitalist Romance*, 100–110.

53. Ibid., 101.

54. Ibid., 117.

55. Daves, *Ready-Made Miracle*, 26–27; Walsh, "Democratization," 299–313.

56. Brandon, *Capitalist Romance*, 116, 126.

57. Ewers and Baylor, *Sincere's History*, 65.

58. Ibid., 91.

59. Brandon, *Capitalist Romance*, 120–125.

60. See Jack, "Channels of Distribution," for a discussion of Singer stores.

61. Chandler, *Visible Hand*, 303.

62. Jack, "Channels of Distribution."

63. Ewers and Baylor, *Sincere's History*, 89.

64. Elizabeth Mickle Bacon, "The Growth of Household Conveniences in the United States from 1865 to 1900," PhD diss., Radcliffe College, 1942, 140–142, 244–247.

65. See Ruth Schwartz Cowan, "A Case Study of Technological and Social Change: The Washing Machine and the Working Wife," in Mary Hartman and Lois W. Banner, *Clio's Consciousness Raised: New Perspectives on the History of Women*

(New York: Harper & Row, 1974), 245–253; Bacon, "Household Conveniences," 137.

66. "Where is the woman who can say that her sewing is less a tax upon her time and strength than it was before the sewing machine came in? . . . As soon as lovely woman discovers that she can set ten stitches in the time that one used to require, a fury seizes her to put ten times as many stitches in every garment as she formerly did" (James Parton in 1867, quoted in Boorstin, *The Americans*, 96).

67. Walsh, "Democratization," 301 ff.

68. Calculated from data in Edward Young, *Labor in Europe and America; A Special Report* (Philadelphia: George, 1875), 822–826.

69. Quoted in Herbert G. Gutman, *Work, Culture, and Society in Industrializing America, 1815–1919* (New York: Random House, 1976), 7.

70. See Louise Lamphere, "Fighting the Piece-Rate System: New Dimensions of an Old Struggle in the Apparel Industry," in Andrew Zimbalist, ed., *Case Studies on the Labor Process* (New York: Monthly Review Press, 1979) 251–276.

71. Pope, *Clothing Industry*, 17–18. A description of these pieceworkers from London in 1747 sounds very like Carey's portrayal of women seamstresses in the 1830s in Philadelphia: "Not one in ten of them know how to cut out a pair of Breeches; They are employed only to sew the Seam, to cast the Button Holes, and prepare Work for the finisher. . . . They are as numerous as locusts, are out of business about three or four months in the year; and generally as poor as rats." These male tailors did however have a strong trade union whose origins dated back to the very early eighteenth century in England and the early nineteenth century in America. For this reason American manufacturers preferred to hire women workers: They did not have a craft tradition and did not strike. See C. R. Dobson, *Masters and Journeymen: A Prehistory of Industrial Relations, 1717–1800* (Totowa, N.J.: Rowman and Littlefield, 1980), esp. 60–73, quote on p. 39. Sumner documents this process of replacing male journeymen tailors with women workers in *History*, 120–121.

72. Levine, *Garment Workers*, 9–10.

73. Ibid., 6.

74. Ibid., 10.

75. Christine Stansell, "The Origins of the Sweatshop: Women and Early Industrialization in New York City," in Michael H. Frisch and Daniel J. Walkowitz, eds., *Working-Class America: Essays in Labor, Community, and American Society* (Urbana: University of Illinois Press, 1983), 92.

76. Ibid., 84.

77. Edwin T. Freedley, *Philadelphia and Its Manufactures: A Handbook of the Great Manufactories and Representative Mercantile Houses of Philadelphia in 1867* (Philadelphia: Edward Young, 1867), 616–620.

78. Levine, *Garment Workers*, 10.

79. Stansell, "Origins of the Sweatshop," 89.

80. Quoted in Edith Abbott, *Women in Industry: A Study in American Economic History* (New York: Arno, 1969; repr. of 1910 ed.), 222–223 (emphasis added).

81. See Pope, *Clothing Industry*, 15–21.

82. Edwin T. Freedley, *Philadelphia and Its Manufactures: A Handbook Ex-*

hibiting the Development, Variety, and Statistics of the Manufacturing Industry of Philadelphia in 1857 (Philadelphia, 1858), 225.

83. Stansell, "Origins of the Sweatshop," 94.

84. Pope, *Clothing Industry*, 30.

85. Massachusetts Senate, *Report of the Bureau of Statistics of Labor*, II (Boston, 1871), 221. The report states, "A good machine can be bought for $65, so that $1 per week, or $52 a year, *would be 80 per cent per annum. And for the thirty weeks would be 46 per cent.!!*" (emphasis in the original).

86. Levine, *Garment Workers Industry*, 14.

87. Freedley, *Philadelphia in 1857*, 224.

88. Pope, *Clothing Industry*, 30; Mass. Senate, *Report*, 221.

89. Levine, *Garment Workers*, 16. In Massachusetts, firms forced women to buy their thread from the company at a profit to the company of 67 percent (Mass. Senate, *Report*, 221). On the medical effects of treadle operation, see Azel Ames, Jr., *Sex in Industry: A Plea for the Working-Girl* (Boston: Osgood, 1875), 114–124.

90. United States Census Office, *Report on the Statistics of Wages in Manufacturing Industries*, by Jos. D. Weeks (Washington, 1886), 51. Wage data covers the period 1851–1880.

91. Pope, *Clothing Industry*, 23.

92. Ibid., 24, 66–67; United States Commissioner of Labor, *Thirteenth Annual Report: Hand and Machine Labor*, vol. 2, General Tables (Washington, 1899), 906–927.

93. U. S. Census, *Statistics of Wages*, 51–53; U. S. Dept. of Labor, *History of Wages*, 221–224.

94. For one expression of the contemporary view, see "The Results of the Invention of the Sewing-Machine," *Littell's Living Age*, 19, no. 1727 (July 21, 1877), 187–190.

95. Mass. Senate, *Report*, 210, 220–221.

96. Brandon, *Capitalist Romance*.

97. A final point on wages should be made. Data on hand sewers in the first half of the nineteenth century comes largely from charitable groups who saw only the most impoverished working women. Data on sewing machine operatives in the second half of the century comes from the government. Neither the Census Office nor the Commissioner of Labor had the authority to coerce employers to give wage information. Only the most reputable firms volunteered wage data. As Jos. D. Weeks of the Census Office remarked in 1886, "A few returns relating to the manufacture of clothing were received, but a disinclination to give facts was manifested" (U.S. Census, *Statistics of Wages*, 51). There are biases in the available data which exaggerate the differences between hand and machine labor. In spite of this, it is certain that factory work was better paid.

98. The futile and impractical wish of one seamstress, underemployed by the introduction of the sewing machine, suggests that viable avenues of protest were not available. This women said "that if she could, without destroying property, and thereby wronging others, she would burn every sewing machine in New York." This statement also reflects the desperate attempt by sewing women to cling to middle-class norms of respectability (quoted in Virginia Penny, *Think and Act: A Series of Articles Pertaining to Men and Women, Work and Wages* (New

York: Arno, 1971; repr. of 1869 ed.), 33. Some portion of the seamstresses were certainly thrown out of work by the invention of the sewing machine; the numbers involved and the fate of these women is not clear. The census of 1860 noted a loss of 7,303 women workers in the garment industry between 1850 and 1860 which was ascribed to the introduction of the sewing machine. These early manufacturing censuses were incomplete and undoubtedly underestimated job losses (U.S. Census, *Manufactures in 1860*, lxii). Many charitable organizations investigating the plight of sewing women had dissolved for lack of funds in the depression of 1857. The Civil War and Reconstruction absorbed the attention of the press during the 1860s and the first state bureaus of labor would not be established until the late 1860s. While there is data on sewing women prior to 1857 and after 1968, there is precious little for the crucial decade when the sewing machine came into widespread use. Still, one fact caught the attention of contemporaries—the dramatic rise in the number of prostitutes in the major cities. When William Sanger interviewed 2,000 of the estimated 6,000 prostitutes in New York City in 1858, one-quarter were sewing women. The anonymous author of the *Women of New York* (1869), who spent much of a 700-page book describing the varieties of commercial vice in the city, found low wages and scarcity of jobs in the sewing industry a factor in the recruitment of prostitutes. An estimated 10,000 streetwalkers in the city in 1870 grew to 40,000 in 1890. The introduction of the sewing machine increased unemployment in the sewing trades and seems to have forced some women into prostitution—one of the few options society offered to poor and unskilled women. Ellington, *Women of New York*, see as only one example, 311; Werthheimer, *We Were There*, 102–103.

99. Sumner, *History*, 144–151; U.S. Commissioner of Labor, *Hand and Machine Labor*, 906–927; Ellington, *Women of New York*, 579–581.

100. Mary Field Parton, ed., *The Autobiography of Mother Jones* (Chicago: Kerr, 1972), 12–13.

101. Mass. Senate, *Report*, 216.

102. Data computed from reports in U.S. Dept. of Labor, *History of Wages*, 219, 220, eastern U.S. only, excluding the Deep South.

103. Ibid.

104. For further discussion of diseconomies of scale see: Chandler, *Visible Hand*, and Bruce Laurie and Mark Schmitz, "Manufacture and Productivity: The Making of an Industrial Base, Philadelphia, 1850–1880," in Theodore Hershberg, ed., *Philadelphia: Work, Space, Family and Group Experience in the Nineteenth Century* (New York: Oxford University Press, 1981), 43–92.

CHAPTER 2

"A Paradise of Fashion": A. T. Stewart's Department Store, 1862–1875

Deborah S. Gardner

"IT IS not 'the common class of merchants,' whose goods are displayed on shabby counters, who grind their sewing women by ruinous rates and almost impossible requirements," proclaimed the feminist journal *The Revolution* in 1869, "it is rather the merchant whose self-satisfied features and established reputation stamp him a merchant prince among his peers." Editors Elizabeth Cady Stanton and Susan B. Anthony were referring explicitly to the labor practices of Alexander T. Stewart, the entrepreneur who created the department store that carried his name in nineteenth-century New York City.[1]

These unsentimental critics pointed to Stewart and his kind as prime examples of the vicious exploitation of industrial capitalism which laid a dual burden on working women. Their situation involved limited job opportunities and low pay created by the sexual division of labor, as well as heightened class conflicts engendered by the enormous disparities in wealth and lifestyle between wage earners and employers.[2] Anthony's radical critique, published in the pages of *The Revolution*, condemned the low wages paid to the "poor white slave girls" in Stewart's store as the "crime of a system not of an individual," a system in which labor, the source of wealth, was stolen from those who had created it.[3] On hearing that Stewart had ordered a large picture of the *Emancipation of American Slavery* from the French artist M. Yvon, *The Revolution* queried, "Who will one day paint the no less interesting picture of labor emancipated from capital?," thus equating wage slavery with chattel slavery as labor was appropriated by the capitalist.[4] The working millions saw their labor create an "aristocracy of wealth, a high priesthood of Mammon to which Alexander T. Stewart, the proprietor of the 'largest store in the world' pre-eminently belongs."[5] The concentration of great wealth in the hands of an elite was repugnant on its own terms and as a danger to democracy.

Stewart's department store represented new roles and lifestyles of urban Americans in a variety of ways. Its name alone, for some, "had pleasanter and tenderer associations than clung to any other store in the world, for it suggested the influence of women."[6] Lauded as the "most extensive and remarkable temple of business in the world," superior to the famed "Au bon marché" of Paris and the shops of London's Bond and Regent streets, it also represented a triumph of merchandising which eased the domestic burdens of New York's moneyed milieu, its social "upstairs."[7] The costs of these advances were carried by the women who worked at Stewart's and at other dry goods/department stores, comprising the "downstairs," whether they were physically located in a basement or an upper-floor workshop. Their low wages, long hours, and poor working conditions were to persist for many years.[8]

The department store's position at the nexus of major social and economic changes elicited both praise and blame, and the arguments of today's historians mirror the contradictions of a century ago. In current literature it is condemned as a "feminized monument to the interests of sentimental womanhood" which institutionalized woman's role as consumer and her lowly position in the labor force.[9] Yet it is also praised as the instrument which "introduced women as a new social force in city life," as it encouraged a public presence that could civilize the male business district, promote egalitarian behavior, and sustain communal life.[10] While the latter view makes claims that are too broad and generally unsupported, and the former is overly negative, these different perspectives evidence the tensions generated by feminist needs to interpret the lives of American urban women during the last hundred years. Department stores, particularly Stewart's, provide ample material for such an analysis.

THE POWER OF DRY GOODS

By 1865 New York was the largest city in the nation, with a population of nearly 900,000. It was a great commercial city, the major exchange and distribution center for the United States, as most domestic and transatlantic trade flowed through its port and wholesalers. Its retail sector was flourishing and diverse, with every kind of goods available in as many shops. Influential and central economically was the trade in dry goods, the various cloth materials produced by the industrialization of textile manufacture and used for clothing and home furnishings.[11] A decade earlier, a writer in *Putnam's Monthly* described dry goods as

> the great leading business of New York, that which gives employment to the vast fleets of sailing ships and steam vessels that continually crowd its magnificent harbor; which builds the superb hotels that ornament its streets; that creates banks, warehouses, extends its docks, attracts thousands of traders from all corners of the continent, and makes it the great wealthy, elegant and busy metropolis it is.[12]

Out of the extensive dimensions of the marketing of dry goods emerged the large concern combining wholesale and retail operations grossing millions of dollars annually, a business organization that came to be known as the department store. It was developed in America by Alexander T. Stewart (1801–1876), the acknowledged leader of the trade.[13]

Stewart was an Irish immigrant who prospered from both the general expansion of trade in the second quarter of the nineteenth century and his own innovative merchandising techniques. He was an importer, manufacturer, wholesaler, and retailer, and his business organization prefigured the vertical integration that was to characterize late nineteenth-century industrial corporations. The department store was a product of this structural change and of a unique combination of marketing and management practices: departmental sale of goods, buyer responsibility, and staff groups; fixed prices and payment in cash; small markup and rapid turnover in goods; and diverse merchandise offered for sale under one roof.[14] These practices evolved as his firm expanded from a small shop, opened in the early 1820s, to the grand emporium of the post–Civil War era.

Stewart also created the concept of an architectural program for department stores, a program that still influences retailing. His first store, the "Marble Palace," opened in 1846 at the corner of Broadway and Chambers Street. A four-story Italianate building, it was subsequently enlarged several times to accommodate the growing business.[15] Its large display windows and elegant domed interior were calculated to attract the middle-class and upper-class women who were finding more and more time to enjoy shopping. Whereas other stores of the period were deep and narrow, with floor-to-ceiling shelves behind display counters, Stewart introduced one vast selling room. His wares were divided among departments separated only by low storage and sales counters that did not interrupt the vista of alluring goods. The store quickly "created a great sensation in the fashionable circles, by the splendor of its decorations, and by its magnificent stock of dry goods and fancy articles."[16]

By 1855, Stewart's was the "richest dry goods house in the city" and Stewart's personal wealth was estimated at about two and one-quarter million dollars, a large fortune for the antebellum period.[17] As his profits increased from thriving wholesale and retail operations, Stewart decided to build a second store. His chosen site at Broadway and Ninth Street was considered far uptown from the rest of the dry goods trade; yet he was followed within a few years by his competitors. The building was designed by New York architect John Kellum and constructed in two major stages between 1859 and 1868. When completed, it occupied an entire city block, encompassed eight floors from subcellar to attic, and contained acres of sales and manufacturing space beneath its roof.

The store had a cast-iron facade and internal framework. Well aware of the advantages of cast iron, Stewart believed that "the material had in its favor unequalled advantages of lightness, durability, economy, incombustability [sic] and ready renovation."[18] Cast iron's superior compressive strength supported the large windows necessary for adequately lighting sales and manufacturing in the pre-electric age: Stewart again installed the oversize, imported plate glass windows that were a hallmark of his Marble Palace, the view of goods just beyond the sidewalk drawing customers quickly inside. Graceful and elegant cast-iron columns replaced space-consuming, internal weight-bearing walls, which resulted in spacious, open floors. Stewart was delighted with his $2,750,000 showpiece. The proud entrepreneur compared the white building to "puffs of white clouds, arch upon arch, rising eighty-five feet above the sidewalk."[19]

UPSTAIRS: WEALTHY DAME AND WORKING WOMAN

The store was an immense success with the shoppers who flocked to it on the opening day, November 10, 1862, and for years thereafter. The store was a magnet, "the centre of a lively and attractive scene, to be witnessed nowhere else in New York." Passersby could see

> on bright days, the rows of equipages lining the curb, the crowds of gayly dressed ladies entering and leaving the doors, the liveried coachman sitting dignifiedly upon the coachboxes, the button-emblazoned footman waiting by the coach-doors, and the stalwart private officers of the establishment, dressed in neat blue uniforms, pacing in front of the building.[20]

In the 1860s, fifteen to sixty thousand customers a day passed through the store. Upon entering, they encountered ushers who knew the location of all goods. The shopper might first descend from the street level and pass through a storage room filled with "great brown rolls of oilcloth" into the basement carpet department.[21] A reporter from *Godey's Lady's Book and Magazine*, a widely read fashion guide, described "the largest room in the world," with its great and varied stock:

> Carpets of every degree . . . from the cotton and woolen plaids still found upon the floor of the farmer's cheerful sitting room to the gorgeous velvet medallions, thick sewn with tropical blossoming on which the rich man kneels to pray . . . [and] the soft persian mats that muffle the footfalls of his chamber.[22]

The great diversity of the carpet selection typified Stewart's merchandising policy, which offered goods at various price levels in order to attract patrons from all income groups.

Ascending to the main or street floor, the customer could admire the complex organization of personnel and merchandise which Stewart had perfected. The range of goods was extraordinary, and journalists were awed by the plenty and by the "wonders achieved by industry and capital" in bringing together the "treasures of the world."[23] As one of them noted, "customers could be supplied with a paper of pins [or] a Tapestry Carpet," and all the accessories for a complete wardrobe, "from the neat valenciennes collar at two dollars and fifty cents to the Brussels point shawls at one hundred or one thousand dollars."[24] Journalists lyrically cataloged the multitude of fabrics on display:

> Hosiery of every make and description; linens from Belfast and Carrick-fergus; muslins, bleached and unbleached, from the mill-dams of New-England; silks from the looms of Italy and from China . . . satins and ribbons, Persian and Cashmere shawls running as high as . . . ten thousand dollars apiece; laces like the fabled gossamer of an angel's wings.[25]

Stewart relied on his international buyers to channel the most beautiful, the most exotic, and the best quality cloth from abroad, and trusted his American agents to negotiate the best deals on special orders for durable materials from American mills.

It was frequently claimed that the range of goods and prices made it possible for "the wealthy dame in quest of rich silks and velvet, and the poor working woman in want of a cheap calico dress [to meet] on a common level," with each served individually with no distinctions as to social rank.[26] In the same way that journalists of the period delighted in reporting on the democratic mixture of classes in the great public spaces of Central Park, so they provided evidence of such juxtapositions in Stewart's store. A writer from *Hearth and Home* observed the Italian actress

> Ristori leaning her magnificent body across the counter. . . . She was negotiating for a robe that would cost over two thousand dollars. Her dense luminous eyes gleamed as she handled the gauze-like texture of lace. . . . At the other side of the great classical tragideen [sic] sat a poor German woman who was purchasing a couple of yards of white muslin.[27]

Less-affluent women were believed to find satisfaction in the remnant counter, used by Stewart to move slow items.[28] While it was true that these sales practices, as well as the fixed prices, would physically lessen the social distance that normally separated women of different classes by bringing them into one shared space, the actual impact on

behavior and attitudes is debatable. The apparent democracy of the
selling floor was superficial, and for many shoppers proximity to
conspicuous wealth could only intensify disparity between want and
plenty. The middle-class editors of *Godey's* counseled their poorer
readers to resist the temptation to anger; rather, it was argued, they
should accept their status and not envy the expenditures of wealthier
women at Stewart's:

> Let us be content, my sisters, with our neat muslins, our simple marinoes,
> and admire Mrs. Smith and Mrs. Jones in their simple *moirés* and cashmeres.
> Let us repress the bitter slander of "extravagance" and "wordliness" when
> we speak of them. It is not extravagance for them, but proper expenditure of
> ample means.[29]

Implicit in such remarks was the role of purchasing—one of the
dynamic forces of capitalism—to create demand for goods, encourage
production, and generate jobs.

The purchases of expensive, lush materials, of the dazzling and
delicate "silks of the Indies," were often quite substantial. *Leslie's
Weekly* suggested in 1865 that during a typical morning at a high-
class emporium such as Stewart's or Lord and Taylor, "a lady could not
expect to get anything to wear short of . . . a bill of two or three
thousand dollars."[30] The amount of fabric needed by a dressmaker to
create current fashions was stupendous compared to modern dress.
The graceful looking, though awkward, hoop skirt of the 1860s was
supported on a steel cage which might measure five and one-half to six
yards of material at the hem. For an extremely elegant evening dress
with several overskirts, each with fancy trim, some 1100 yards of tulle
would be used![31] Complicated wardrobes decreed by reigning fashion
contained prescribed costumes for every conceivable occasion, from
watching a horse race or playing croquet, to breakfasting and dining.
And every article of clothing had its comparable variations. At
Stewart's, for example, one could purchase kid gloves, silk gloves,
chamois gloves, riding and walking gloves, and fur gloves, imported
from all over Europe.[32]

The American woman's devotion to fashion sustained the dry-
goods trade. Demand for fabric and accessories was constantly stimulated as fashions changed, requiring that high-class dressmakers follow European styles closely. They were guided by the plates, patterns,

and advice found in such magazines as *Godey's* (founded 1830), *Madame Demorest's Quarterly Mirror of Fashions* (founded 1860), and *Harper's Bazaar* (founded 1867).[33] As the *Nation* suggested in a biographical portrait, Stewart was the great innovator in the marketing of dry goods, a trade whose "pre-eminence and attractiveness . . . in this country is due mainly to the great purchasing power and varied requirements of American women."[34] Stewart's success was attributable to his brilliant analysis of the relevant social and economic trends which reflected a rising standard of living as well as the powerful forces of the cult of domesticity which assigned separate spheres of activity and interest to men and women. Stewart was, according to the *Nation*,

> the first shopkeeper who perceived the position which the two sexes on this continent were destined to occupy with regard to dress. Fifty years ago his keen insight into dry goods taught him that in the bright future which was opening for the race in America, the money devoted to dress would be mainly devoted to the clothes of women; that toil and labor hitherto so selfishly imposed upon them, would now be mainly assumed by men whose monotonous and ill-dressed lives would be made happy by the spectacle of the gorgeous dresses and bonnets and trimmings displayed by their wives and daughters.[35]

The enormous market for fashionable merchandise was to some degree a reflection of the prescribed female role as ornament in a masculine world. One writer of the period observed that the only worth of the "modern fashionable wife" was as a "figure piece for the house."[36] Upper-class women in the mid-nineteenth century already exhibited what Thorstein Veblen later described as "conspicuous consumption."[37] Such women were "walking frames" for the display of possessions, who did "little but don and doff dry goods." In the nation's large cities, most notably in New York, they had ample opportunity to display themselves, "not tamely at home, but in the streets, in horse-cars, omnibuses, excursion boats, railroad trains, and hotel corridors," and in the many theaters, concert halls, and promenades.[38]

Household goods, clothing, and special services were located on the second floor of Stewart's. Patrons reached the upper level in three "beautifully upholstered" elevators or by climbing two flights of stairs in the older section of the store. From this vantage shoppers could admire the frescoed walls and ceilings, the splendid gilt gas chandeliers, and the dramatic skylit rotunda rising up the full height of the building. Similar features were soon emulated in department-store architecture around the nation. The second floor contained retail departments for housekeeping goods, including upholstery, blankets, table linens, and all curtain materials, from the simplest gingham to "cloth of gold" at fifty dollars a yard. Some ready-made men's clothing was available also, and an abundance of women's outer garments: furs, shawls, and myriad others, "from the street wrap to the delicate cloth or cashmere opera cloaks, snowy white, crimson-lined, and gaily tasselled that hang in the convenient wardrobes with sliding doors [lining] the walls."[39]

Nearby were washrooms and "saloons" or parlors for the female customers.[40] These were another Stewart innovation which made hours of chatting, browsing, and shopping amid the vast displays of merchandise comfortable for customers who came from uptown residential neighborhoods or commuted in from nearby suburbs. There were few other socially acceptable public places or spaces in the city where respectable women could congregate. Tea rooms, church gatherings, and the department store were about the only such places until the last quarter of the nineteenth century. Then libraries and museums would provide cultural centers for the fashionable. For women who felt a pietistic or social sense of noblesse oblige, the club movement and philanthropic organizations provided additional respectable meeting places. Under their sponsorship, activities were undertaken which would eventually modify the spatial segregation of the female domestic world and the male sphere of business and politics.[41] In this sense, for middle-class women at least, the department store did indeed encourage a public presence. The "downstairs," or working areas of the department store, presented quite a different picture.

DOWNSTAIRS: CASH BOYS AND SEWING WOMEN

The dry goods were examined and purchased at Stewart's at low counters where some five hundred male clerks presented, measured, and cut them, and handed the customer's payment over to a cash boy. He whisked the money to one of several cashier's desks enclosed behind a white iron filigree screen to have the purchase checked and to receive change. The cashier's cage was the heart of the cash system which Stewart had introduced at the Marble Palace, eliminating the credit system that had prevailed until then.[42] Cash boys could aspire, if they were quick and good looking, to the better-paying position of sales clerk.

Sales positions in dry goods stores had been urged for women since the 1830s; it was considered wasteful for men to hold such jobs when they could be doing more "significant" work. The following comment from a *New York Daily Tribune* article of 1845 offered a typical opinion:

> It is a shame that fine, hearty lads, who might clear their fifty acres each of western forest in a short time, and have a house, a farm, a wife, and boys about them in the course of ten years, should be holed up in hot salesrooms, handing down tapes and ribbons and cramping their genius over chintzes and delaines.[43]

Despite the prevalence of such sentiments, women did not begin to enter sales positions until the mid-1860s and then only in small numbers and due to the labor shortages caused by the Civil War. Women were most likely to find work in the dry goods trade as seamstresses and dressmakers; only 5 percent of New York's 86,000 working women in 1870 were employed as "clerks, salesmen, and accountants" in the city's retail stores.[44]

Working women were all but invisible to the customers. Out of sight but adjacent to the carpet salesroom was an area where floor coverings were assembled for individual orders, whether a modest row house, a large hotel, or a passenger ship. Women worked on the floor, matching cut pieces of carpet which were then laid out on forty-foot-long tables to be sewn by steam-powered machines operated by men. As uncomfortable as kneeling for many hours a day was for the women, at least mechanized cutters and sewing machines relieved them of some of the most unpleasant aspects of such work, which still prevailed in old-fashioned establishments, where hands blistered from struggling with the stiff carpet fabric.[45] The carpet department exemplified Stewart's shrewd investment in the most advanced technology, as well as his commitment to the inequities of the prevailing labor system. Throughout his stores, the better-paying and more skilled jobs were reserved for men; women earned lower wages, often on the exploitative piecework system, and had little chance for advancement.

The remaining floors of the building symbolized this same order of spatial segregation, dividing the consuming women from the producing women. On these upper levels, hidden from public view, worked most of the store's thousand seamstresses, dressmakers, and laundresses. In their workshops, many of the items sold on the lower floors were manufactured, and the requests of the wholesale and special-order trade were filled. Animal hair was unpacked and prepared for the manufacture of mattresses, and household furnishings "from blankets to kitchen towels" by the "hundreds of dozens" were hemmed and packed for delivery in wicker crates in a "light and cheerful saloon . . . full of work tables and busy groups."[46] The sewing women made "walking dresses, mantillas, underskirts . . . millinery . . . robes . . . and material of every description that can be mentioned in the house-furnishings or dry goods line."[47] Like many other dry goods establishments, Stewart's produced ready-made children's and women's clothing—relatively new apparel lines—as well as lower grade men's ready-made clothes.[48]

Stewart's workrooms were considered among the finest in the city—spacious, adequately ventilated, and well lighted. Located on the fourth and fifth floors, the sewing rooms looked out over the rooftops of the surrounding area and the busy street below. At the long rows of tables where the hand-sewing women sat facing one another, each had ample space for her workbasket and tools. The pleasant surroundings at Stewart's contrasted with the foul air and dark spaces of other workshops, where sewing women in "myriads of marble palaces" fought "poverty with the point of a needle," and were not even permitted to look out of their windows.[49] Stewart's also provided a dining room, where tea and coffee could be prepared to accompany the lunches the women brought for their half-hour meal break.[50]

In spite of Stewart's relatively generous amenities, however, the women employed to sew there suffered from the difficult labor conditions created by changes in the clothing industry and labor market. The cumulative impact of these changes, which dated from the late eighteenth century, were realized in a glut of unorganized and semi-skilled women workers drawn from the increasing ranks of immigrants and, with the inflation and tragedy of the Civil War, from the ranks of native-born women too. The result was the familiar pattern: the depression of wages as too many women entered the job market in the previously male-dominated sewing trade. By 1850 over four thousand workshops in New York were coordinating and conducting clothing manufacture; two-thirds of the ninety-six thousand workers involved were women.[51] The city was the leading producer in the United States of ready-made clothing just as the sewing machine was introduced, an invention that considerably expanded production and changed the nature of the clothing industry itself.

By the early 1860s it was estimated that 400 sewing machines and their operators would replace 2000 hand sewers, with comparable savings in cost and increases in production.[52] The Wheeler and Wilson Company, for example, ran experiments that graphically demonstrated the validity of these statements. In one, the number of stitches per minute taken by a sewer was 23; a machine made 640 stitches. A second experiment revealed how much time could be saved in manufacturing a garment: a calico dress was completed in 57 minutes by machine whereas a seamstress needed 6½ hours to sew it by hand. A man's shirt was completed in just over an hour by machine compared to 14 hours by hand.[53] Small wonder that by the end of the Civil War 63,000 industrial sewing machines were in use, and the thousands of sewers thrown out of work were competing for handwork at extraordinarily low wages.[54]

The sewing machines were operated, more often than not, by women workers. Whether it was "an instrument . . . peculiarly calculated for female operatives," as one newspaper had asserted in 1853, the skills women had and the nature of the labor market insured their employment in such light manufacturing.[55]

The machine also influenced fashion. It made possible the elaborate trim on women's clothing because of the ease with which it could be sewn on, and thus enlarged the market for such wear. The yards of material needed to cover hoop skirts were quickly ornamented by machine, whether braiding, pleating, or tucking was required. And the machine contributed to the popularity of certain fashions by reducing their costs. Women's ready-made cloaks, "mantillas," cost 50 to 80 percent less when manufactured by machine. These cloaks and other apparel were made by Stewart's four hundred seamstresses working at sewing machines powered by steam engines located in the building's subbasement. This mechanized assist not only led to increased productivity and hence profit for Stewart but also, it was observed, relieved "the operatives of much tedious labor."[56]

Supervised by a female superintendent, the needleworkers in the store earned from five to nine dollars a week if they were consistent, depending on their piecework scale and the difficulty of their tasks.[57] Such wages were much superior to those of women working in other large-scale manufacturing shops or under the dismal conditions of home piecework where 12 to 18 hours of labor a day paid only for the meanest tenement lodging and poor food. For these unfavored women, ninety dollars a year might be wrested from shirt finishing at four to eight cents a garment, seventy-five cents a dozen for overalls, or twenty cents for a day's hand stitching of pantaloons.[58] Too many women workers made the manufacture of clothing cheaper and more widely available while their economic status declined precipitously.

Stewart used such women as part of his system. The women workers who called at the store for take-home work often had to leave a deposit for the value of the goods. It was also the custom to require that they provide their own threads, needles, and machines.[59] The outwork required by Stewart's was varied, including branding patterns to be embroidered and fashioning such accessories as artificial flowers, umbrellas, and straw hats.[60] The pay for this work was extremely low, and the profits commensurately high. After an investigation of the Stewart store, *The Revolution* reported that for seven days of embroidery on a single dress, a seamstress received $3.75; the cloth of the dress cost the store about $20.00 and the finished product sold for $85.00. The journal's exposé concluded: "It is no wonder that dry goods are sold in marble palaces."[61] At the time this article was published, Stewart's total annual sales were about fifty million dollars.[62]

Some journalists believed that "ruinous rates" drove sewing women to apply to benevolent societies for aid to avoid having to supplement their pitiful wages by resort to the "social evil." For those who did not have this option, one writer asked, "Is it a wonder that so many of the working women and girls glide into sin, with the hope of bettering their hard lot?"[63] The contrast between the everyday conditions of Stewart's employees and the lot of many Stewart customers was representative of the widespread socioeconomic split among women of the period.[64] Life was grueling, impoverished, and unhealthy for female workers at a time when industrialization and the availability of servants freed many middle-class and upper-class women from domestic chores, permitting them to spend numerous hours shopping.

The use of this wealth for "conspicuous consumption" also elicited comment, notably in relation to Stewart's mansion on Fifth Avenue and Thirty-fourth Street. Its size and decor made it the first "millionaire's mansion" (as did its price tag), predecessor to the palatial residences of the Gilded Age. In 1868 *The Revolution* noted that "we hear much about what Mr. Stewart is going to do for the New York poor, but we know nothing he has done as yet to benefit them, and we fear he never will. Philanthropy would be a far nobler monument to his money than a needless marble mansion."[65] Stewart's one attempt to make a grand philanthropic gesture for women—to whom he owed his fortune—was a hotel for working women. Finished after his death, its purpose was subverted by his executor and the venture failed.[66]

The Revolution's critique and rage was directed at Stewart as the personification of the new industrial capitalism which affected the working conditions and lives of not only his 1000 women workers but all 2000 employees. Departmental managers and their assistants exercised continuous supervision throughout the twelve-hour workdays that began at seven o'clock in the morning. There were also various checks on customer sales, a system of fines for lateness, mistakes, and improper conduct, as well as bonuses based on merit and good work. No different from the management of factories of the period, this strict regimen marked the modernization of work habits and behavior imposed by the industrial revolution and the functional requirements of large, complex firms. Stewart's attitude toward his employees was summarized by a contemporary publication—in which the generalized male references should be understood to apply equally to female employees:

> He regards his employees as cogs in the complicated machinery of his establishment. . . . The men are numbered and fined. . . . There is a penalty attached to all delinquencies. It takes all a man can earn for the first few months or so to pay his fines . . . if he exceeds the few minutes allotted for dinner . . . if he eats on the premises . . . if he sits during business hours . . . comes late or goes early . . . if he misdirects a bundle . . . mistakes a street or number, if he miscounts money, or gives the wrong change.[67]

The differential between the appearance and the reality of working at Stewart's was also considered in the *Woman's Journal*: "The women who worked for Stewart have been supposed to be the best cared for in the city but this idea has since been discovered to be fallacious, since the fines for every trivial shortcoming materially reduced the earnings of all Stewart's employees."[68]

The exploitation of sewing women thus accompanied emerging industrial capitalism in the mid-nineteenth century and would continue for decades thereafter. Only if the conditions under which the sewing women worked are ignored can one conclude that the department stores were an unalloyed benefit for women. And that said, the value of the department store, even for middle-class and upper-class women, is still open to debate.

NOTES

1. "The Sewing Women," *The Revolution*, 1 (Feb. 26, 1868), 117. The phrase "a paradise of fashion" comes from W. Frothingham, "Stewart and the Dry Goods Trade of New York," *Continental Monthly*, 2 (1862), 531. For a wider discussion see Deborah S. Gardner, "The Architecture of Commercial Capitalism: John Kellum and the Development of New York, 1840–1875," PhD diss., Columbia University, 1979.

2. My understanding of Anthony's criticism of Stewart in *The Revolution* was considerably strengthened by Ellen Carol DuBois, *Feminism and Suffrage: The Emergence of an Independent Women's Suffrage Movement in America, 1848–1869* (Ithaca and London: Cornell University Press, 1978), chaps. 4 and 5.

3. *The Revolution*, 1 (Sept. 3, 1868), 136.

4. "Patronizing Art," *The Revolution*, 1 (Dec. 17, 1868), 380.

5. *The Revolution*, 1 (Sept. 3, 1868), 136. Two years later, the journal wrote, "It takes the toil, tears, brains, sinews, souls of thousands like these poor wharf rats to make a Peabody, an Astor, a Stewart" (3 [Feb. 3, 1870], 73).

6. Bayrd Still, *Urban America* (Boston: Little, Brown, 1974), 148.

7. "An Hour in A. T. Stewart's Retail Store," *Frank Leslie's Illustrated Newspaper*, 40 (Apr. 24, 1875), 107.

8. A number of investigatory articles at the end of the nineteenth and the beginning of the twentieth centuries documented these persistent problems. See, for example, surveys on working conditions and wages in big department stores in *The Arena*, 22 (Aug. and Sept. 1899), 290–291, 165–186, 320–321; *The Survey*, in 1913 and 1915; "Labor Conditions in the Department Stores," *Municipal Affairs*, 3 (June 1899), 361–362; and *History of Women in Industry* (Washington: Government Printing Office, 1909), vol. 9. See also Sarah S. Malino, "Faces Across the Counter: A Social History of Female Department Store Employees, 1870–1920," PhD diss., Columbia University, 1982.

9. William Leach, *True Love and Perfect Union: The Feminist Reform of Sex and Society* (New York: Basic Books, 1980), 213. Chapter 9 is devoted to the topic "The Bee and the Butterfly: Fashion and the Dress Reform Critique of Fashion," 213–260.

10. Gunther Barth, *City People: The Rise of Modern City Culture in Nineteenth Century America* (New York: Oxford University Press, 1980), 144. See chap. 4, "The Department Store," 110–147.

11. The general discussions of urban commerce and the dry goods trade are based on the following studies: Alfred D. Chandler, Jr., *Strategy and Structure: Chapters in the History of an Industrial Enterprise* (Cambridge, Mass.: MIT Press, 1962; Garden City, N.Y.: Doubleday, 1966), and *The Visible Hand: The Managerial Revolution in American Business* (Cambridge, Mass.: Harvard University Press, 1977); Thomas C. Cochran, *Two Hundred Years of American Business* (New York: Basic Books, 1977); Elisha P. Douglas, *The Coming of Age of American Business* (Chapel Hill: University of North Carolina, 1971); Herman E. Kroos and Charles Gilbert, *American Business History* (Englewood Cliffs, N.J.: Prentice-Hall, 1972); and Glenn Porter and Harold C. Livesay, *Merchants and Manufacturers: Studies in the Changing Structure of Nineteenth Century Marketing* (Baltimore: The Johns Hopkins University Press, 1971).

12. "New York Daguerreotyped, 2. Business Streets, Mercantile Blocks, Stores, and Banks," *Putnam's Monthly*, 1 (Apr. 1853), 356. In 1850, there were 139 dry goods importers serving a comparable number of retail firms (Cochran, *Two Hundred Years*, 87).

13. Stewart's life and business activities are reconstructed from contemporary sources as no personal papers have survived. Supplemental material was provided by an unpublished biography, and notes on the development of the department store ("The Ladies Paradise, 1830–1880") in the Harry E. Resseguie Collection, Baker Library Division of Archives and Manuscripts, Harvard Business School. Several articles written by Resseguie were also useful: "The Decline and Fall of the Commercial Empire of A. T. Stewart," *Business History Review*, 36 (Autumn 1962), 255–286; "A. T. Stewart's Marble Palace—Cradle of the Department Store," New-York Historical Society *Quarterly*, 48 (Apr. 1964), 131–162; and "Alexander Turney Stewart and the Development of the Department Store, 1823–1876," *Business History Review*, 39 (Autumn 1965), 300–322.

14. While there will always be scholarly arguments to decide the first person to invent a new technology, or devise a new means of marketing, or in this instance create the department store, clearly the management as well as the economic and physical organization of the Stewart stores were the prototypes for the modern department store, evolving from the same social and economic developments that were shaping similar retail ventures in England and France during the mid-nineteenth century. Resseguie argues convincingly (1965) that Stewart originated the department store *system*, for its salient characteristics were all present in his organization: central location (in the business district), many departments under one roof, "free" services (exchanges and refunds, delivery, rest rooms), one price, low mark-up, cash sales, aggressive advertising, large volume, centralization of nonselling functions, buying for cash, "free" entrance, maintenance of a clean stock (clearance sales), and an efficient, disciplined store organiza-

tion. Chandler (*Visible Hand*, 225) concurs with Resseguie's assessment, suggesting that Stewart's became a full-fledged department store about 1862 when it added more lines: "The department store appeared when an establishment which retailed dry goods or clothing began to add new lines such as furniture, jewelry, and glassware." The evolution of the department store in America after Stewart is traced in Chandler, *Visible Hand*, 225 ff.; John William Ferry, *A History of the Department Store* (New York: Macmillan, 1960); Leach, *True Love*, 227 ff.; and Sheila M. Rothman and David J. Rothman, *Sources of the American Social Tradition* (New York: Basic Books, 1975), II, 3–17.

15. The store is discussed in Resseguie, "A. T. Stewart's Marble Palace,"; Mary Ann Smith, "John Snook and the Design of A. T. Stewart's Store," New-York Historical Society *Quarterly*, 58 (Jan. 1974), 18–33; and Winston Weisman, "Commercial Palaces of New York: 1845–1875," *Art Bulletin*, 36 (Dec. 1954), 285–307. Stewart's architectural innovations can be appreciated by contrast with previous American practice and contemporaneous European stores in Nikolaus Pevsner, *A History of Building Types* (Princeton: Princeton University Press, 1976), chap. 16, "Shops, Stores and Department Stores," esp. 261–266. A major difference between Europe and America was evident to Stewart's peers: "One peculiarity of the New York stores which distinguishes them from their London and Paris rivals is the fact that they generally occupy the whole of the building for purposes connected with their business, and are not confined to the first stories" (*Putnam's Monthly*, 1853, 129).

16. *New York Herald*, Sept. 26, 1846, 1.

17. Baker Library Division of Archives and Manuscripts, R. G. Dun & Co., *Credit Ledgers*, 197:026 (1855).

18. For a detailed discussion of the aesthetic and technological attributes of cast iron, John Kellum's (1809–1871) career and experience in the medium, and the Stewart store, see Gardner, "Architecture of Commercial Capitalism," 21–49, 62–69, passim. Stewart's opinion is quoted in "Men Who Have Assisted in the Development of Architectural Resources, No. 1. John B. Cornell," *Architectural Record* (Dec. 1891), 245. Resseguie ("Biography," 85) suggests that cast iron was a desirable medium because its use lowered insurance costs by 25 percent.

19. "Men Who Have Assisted," 245.

20. *Frank Leslie's Illustrated*, 40 (Apr. 24, 1875), 107.

21. Alice B. Haven, "A Morning at Stewart's," *Godey's Lady's Book and Magazine*, May 1863, 430.

22. Ibid.

23. D. J. K., "Shopping at Stewart's," *Hearth and Home*, 1 (Jan. 9, 1869), 43.

24. R. G. Dun & Co., *Credit Ledgers*, 204:778 (1863), and Haven, "A Morning," 431.

25. D. J. K., "Shopping," 43.

26. Edward Crapsey, "A Monument of Trade," *Galaxy*, 8 (Jan. 1870), 98.

27. D. J. K., "Shopping," 43.

28. Haven, "A Morning," 431.

29. Ibid.

30. "Rich and Poor of New York," *Frank Leslie's Illustrated Newspaper*, Nov. 18, 1865, 135.

31. Alison Gernsheim, *Victorian and Edwardian Fashion* (orig. pub. 1963; New York: Dover, 1981), 45–46, 48. The crinoline or structurally supported skirt dated from the seventeenth century. The heavy petticoats and other stiffening materials were replaced in the 1850s by a French invention consisting of a separate cage of steel springs in hoops of increasing diameter to the bottom, connected with tapes or curved steel ribs. It was quickly adopted in Europe and America.

32. D. J. K., "Shopping," 43, reported that Stewart's sold a thousand pairs of gloves in a day.

33. Margaret Walsh, "The Democratization of Fashion: The Emergence of the Women's Dress Pattern Industry," *Journal of American History*, 66 (Sept. 1979), 300; see also Stella Blum, ed., *Victorian Fashions & Costumes from Harper's Bazaar: 1867–1898* (New York: Dover, 1974), Introduction.

34. "Stewart's," *Nation*, 34 (Apr. 20, 1882), 332.

35. Ibid. The occasion for the *Nation* article was the closing of Stewart's. When A. T. Stewart died in 1876, his close friend and executor Henry Hilton bought the firm (building, factories, cash assets) with his million-dollar bequest from Stewart. Lacking Stewart's acumen, he overextended the firm and was forced to dissolve it by 1882. The firm failed also because he embezzled from it.

36. George Ellington (pseud.), *The Women of New York, or the Underworld of the Great City* (New York: New York Book Company, 1869; New York: Arno, 1972), 69.

37. Veblen elaborated this concept in *The Theory of the Leisure Class: An Economic Study of Institutions* (1899 and 1912; New York: Modern Library, 1961), chap. 4.

38. Ellington, *Women of New York*, 28, 37; *Nation*, 1882, 332.

39. Haven, "A Morning," 431–432.

40. *New York Times*, Sept. 19, 1868, 2; Haven, "A Morning," 430, "a neatly decorated ladies' dressing room of good dimensions." When John Kellum designed a new store for Charles L. Tiffany, famous purveyor of jewelry and elegant household effects, he included a "retiring room for ladies and children." As the *New York Times* noted, "very many ladies residing in the country, or in towns adjacent to New York, come here to purchase their holiday goods, and almost invariably they bring their children with them, and such toilet rooms become an absolute necessity" (Nov. 12, 1870, 2). The cast-iron Tiffany store was located on Union Square. See Gardner, "Architecture of Commercial Capitalism," 93–98.

41. See Marlene Stein Wortman, "Domesticating the Nineteenth-Century American City," *Prospects*, 3 (1977), 531–572.

42. "The New Store of A. T. Stewart," *New York Times* (Sept. 19, 1868), 2; James McCabe, Jr., *Lights and Shadows of New York* (1872; facs. New York: Farrar, Strauss and Giroux, 1970), 381; Crapsey, "Monument of Trade," 95, 98; Haven, "A Morning," 430–431; and R. G. Dun & Co., *Credit Ledgers*, 204:377–378 (July 1862).

43. The *Tribune* of Mar. 7, 1845, was quoted in *History of Women in Industry*,

vol. 9, 34. The male clerk, according to Resseguie ("Biography," 25) and the *Herald* (1835) played an important role in attracting customers. Stewart's men were long known as "handsome, polite and well bred." See Ellington, (*Women of New York*, 343–344): "It is a fact that most women had rather be attended upon by a polite, handsome man, who will smile upon them and say pretty things than by the cleverest girls that can be found. . . . This is one of the reasons why shopping becomes such a passion with the women, and is such a bore to the men. What fun or interest could there be for a man to purchase a dozen yards of silk from a man? But for a woman the case is entirely different." Even the male clerks at Stewart's had some cause of complaint about their salaries during the Civil War which, some felt, had not kept pace with inflation. See *New York Times*, July 29 and 31, 1864, 8 and 8.

44. According to Seymour Mandelbaum, *Boss Tweed's New York* (New York: John Wiley, 1965), 31. See also *History of Women in Industry*, vol. 9, 238–240. There were not enough women dry goods clerks to form an association to better their working conditions until 1870, when they were assisted by the existing male organization. See *The Revolution* (July 21, 1870), 42–43. Leach reports that Stewart employed some Englishwomen as salesclerks (*True Love*, 223). In hiring foreigners he may have been following the example of Arnold Constable who hired women salesclerks (at lower wages) after a trip to Paris where he observed that young educated women added "class" (Barbara Wertheimer, *We Were There: The Story of Working Women in America* [New York: Pantheon Books, 1977], 156).

45. Haven, "A Morning," 430. On conditions in the "old fashioned establishments" see McCabe, *Lights and Shadows*, 379–380, and "Working Women's Association Meeting," *The Revolution*, 1 (Oct. 1, 1868), 198. The carpet department is a good example of Stewart's mixture of wholesale and retail business. Carpet factories sold through agents or commission houses who, in turn, "disposed of goods to the wholesalers or large jobbers in New York, Boston or Philadelphia—to a house like A. T. Stewart & Co.—who in turn, supplied the retailers throughout the country" (Arthur H. Cole and Harold F. Williamson, *The American Carpet Manufacture: A History and Analysis* [Cambridge, Mass.: Harvard University Press, 1941]), 53.

46. Haven, "A Morning," 431–432.

47. D. J. K., "Shopping," 43.

48. Lower-grade men's ready-made clothing had held an important place in the domestic market since the 1820s (Resseguie, manuscript notes on the men's clothing industry).

49. See Haven, "A Morning," 432–433; *New York Daily Tribune*, Sept. 18, 1868, 2; McCabe, *Lights and Shadows*, 827; "The Working Women of New York," 2 and 3, and "The Sewing Women," in *The Revolution* (Feb. 26 and Mar. 12, 1868), 117, 148–149.

50. "Notes and News," *The Woman's Journal*, 8 (Nov. 3, 1877), 349.

51. Grace Rogers Cooper, *The Sewing Machine: Its Invention and Development* (Washington: Smithsonian Institution, 1976), 101.

52. Ibid., 58.

53. Ibid. For other contests between hand and machine sewers, see James Parton, *History of the Sewing-Machine* (Lancaster, 1868), 7 ff. (repr. of an article in the *Atlantic Monthly*, 19 [May 1867], 527–544). Parton reported that the victory

of Elias Howe and his one machine over five seamstresses in an 1845 encounter elicited the following comment from journeymen tailors, "320 stitches a minute at first trial. Death to sewing machines or death to tailors!"

54. Wertheimer, *We Were There*, 155. For an analysis of the impact of the sewing machine on female labor, wages, and occupational segregation within the context of industrializing America, see the excellent survey by Joan Wallach Scott, "The Mechanization of Women's Work," *Scientific American*, 247 (Sept. 1982), 136–151.

55. Cooper, *Sewing Machine*, 30. Cooper notes that Singer merchandised his light-weight family machine to women, 33–34, 47, 158. The potential for its home use was realized by the pattern industry, according to Walsh.

56. Walsh, "Democratization," 301 ff.; Cooper, *Sewing Machine*, 59. *Frank Leslie's Illustrated*, April 24, 1875, 107.

57. Haven, "A Morning," and "A. T. Stewart and William B. Astor," *Belfast News-Letter*, July 15, 1876, cited in *The Posthumous Relatives of the Late Alexander T. Stewart* (New York, 1876). The wage figures appear somewhat inflated as they would compute to a yearly income of $250 to $450. This compares favorably with incomes of highly skilled dressmakers catering to the wealthy at $3.50 to $6.00 a week. The *New York Times* (July 31, 1864, 8) reported that male clerks at Stewart's earned $400 a year while the average annual sewing woman's wages there were $100 to $250.

58. "The Working Women of New York," *The Revolution*, 1 (Feb. 19, 1868), 99–100, and "The Needle Again," *Hearth and Home*, 1 (May 15, 1869), 320–330. On the sewing industry, see *History of Women in Industry*, vol. 9, 115–145, and McCabe, *Lights and Shadows*, 822–828.

59. Wertheimer reports that early sewing machines were unreliable and often tore the fabric of a garment. Home workers were charged for these damaged goods (*We Were There*, 101).

60. Lace collars earned 22 cents a dozen, and ladies' cloth cloaks, sewn in a day, $2; see Haven, "A Morning," 432; McCabe, *Lights and Shadows*, 824–825; *History of Women in Industry*, vol. 9, 23, 160 ff.; "Working Women's Association Meeting," *The Revolution*, 1 (Oct. 1, 1868), 198.

61. H. M. Shepherd, "Experiences," *The Revolution*, 1 (Apr. 23, 1868), 117. *The Revolution*, 1 (Jan. 15, 1868), 21, quoting the *New York Sun*, a workingmen's paper, gave another example of a woman being paid $4 for an infant's cape which took her fourteen days of labor; the store sold it for $70.

62. Resseguie, "Alexander Turney Stewart," 320, estimates that the total value of retail and wholesale transactions in 1865 was over fifty million dollars; eight million dollars of this sum was retail sales.

63. McCabe, *Lights and Shadows*, 282. See also *Hearth and Home*, 1 (May 15, 1869), 329–330, wherein readers are exhorted to assist in the organization of protective unions, cooperatives, and emigration societies (to send women west for better opportunities) and to patronize homeworkers themselves. The New York Working Women's Protective Union was founded in 1868 to act as an employment agency and give legal assistance in the collection of wages withheld by unscrupulous employers. The Workingwomen's Association was founded by Susan B. Anthony in 1868 to organize women for better wages and job conditions. Neither organization had the resources to really tackle the severe wage

problems. See Rosalyn Baxandall et al., eds., *America's Working Women* (New York: Random House, 1976), 82–84, 117–119; DuBois, *Feminism and Suffrage*, chap. 4; and *History of Women in Industry*, vol. 9.

64. On the shift in lifestyles, see Gerda Lerner, "The Lady and the Mill Girl: Changes in the Status of Women in the Age of Jackson," in Jean E. Friedman and William G. Shade, eds., *Our American Sisters*, 2d ed. (Boston: Allyn & Bacon, 1976), 120–132.

65. *The Revolution*, 1 (Feb. 12, 1868), 89. See Gardner, "Architecture of Commercial Capitalism," 211–216, on the history and design of the mansion.

66. On the history, design, and problems of the hotel, see Gardner, "Architecture of Commercial Capitalism," chap. 5, "The Commercial City: Wealth and Welfare," 216–260.

67. Frothingham, "Stewart," 532–533; McCabe, *Lights and Shadows*, 59, 383; Crapsey, "A Monument of Trade," 99. This mechanistic imagery was popular; "Stewart, plain, earnest and industrious . . . amid this army of clerks and bustle of external traffic, drives the secret machinery with wonderful precision," Frothingham, 533.

68. "News and Notes," *The Woman's Journal*, 7 (June 24, 1876), 205.

PART II

THE
GREAT
UPRISINGS:
1900–1920

THE GREAT UPRISINGS: 1900–1920

Joan M. Jensen

B ETWEEN 1905 and 1915 a hundred thousand women in the clothing factories of New York City, Rochester, Chicago, Philadelphia, and Cleveland walked off their jobs, demanding higher wages, better working conditions, and an end to subcontracting. Owners fought back with all the weapons at their command: police control, undercover agents, bootlegged garments, and strikebreakers. Women took their cause to middle-class women, asking for solidarity in their efforts. Militant Jewish and Italian immigrant women moved into new positions of leadership in speaking, organizing, and planning strategy. It was an incredible decade, with thousands of working women in the streets demanding economic justice. New leaders emerged—and new martyrs. The uprisings culminated in the movement of women into unions and in the beginning of the runaway shops.

Women emerged as militant workers at the same time that clothing workers as a whole moved out of the sweatshops into factories and into the forefront of American organized labor. In fact, women's organizing activities not only made the clothing industry unique; they also accounted for the particular interest by the public accorded to the conflicts over the wages and work conditions of needleworkers. The flood of women who burst onto the streets and into the organizations of previously male workers, gave the needlework industry a particular importance to the era of reform from 1890–1920. The militance and organizational strength of women often encouraged their male comrades to join in demands for better working conditions. These women wanted bread and roses—increased wages and a better way of life. For two decades, women workers in America—like the women in revolutionary Russia—were a catalyst for worker discontent.

The garment districts, as they became known, were areas in the middle of cities devoted almost exclusively to the manufacture of clothing. While heavy industry and other types of manufacturing usually moved to the periphery of the growing nineteenth-century cities, clothing manufacturing remained centrally located. New York City's garment district eventually centered in Manhattan, clustered from 34th to 40th streets between Sixth and Ninth avenues. Chicago's district was centered between Halsted Street and the Chicago River and south to 22nd Street. Baltimore, Rochester, Cleveland, Boston, and Philadelphia had similar districts where most manufacturing centered, developing out of the commercial city and surviving into the twentieth-century industrial city. The districts were composed of multi-story manufacturing establishments and nearby subcontracting shops in which women manufactured such accessories as artificial flowers and belts, or did special trimming, hand sewing, and embroidery. Nearby were working-class residential areas, usually close enough for women to walk to the factories. Some workers came to work on the new municipal transportation systems being created to get workers from their homes to the more distant heavy industry, but most lived within a mile of work and usually walked. This arrangement allowed close physical proximity of workers, shops, and factories. Often in the cities where garment districts were located, the industry accounted for a large portion of the work force. The pattern developed early. By 1860 Baltimore already had one-third of its work force involved in manufacturing ready-to-wear. By 1910 the men's clothing industry was Chicago's largest employer, larger than the much described stockyards. New York City by 1914 had 62 percent of all wage earners manufacturing women's clothing.[1] These garment districts were enclaves where immigrants found supportive relatives, abundant work, easy job entry, and a community culture that provided them with a transition point to the New World.

While some employees walked to the garment district factories and worked there, others returned home with piles of cut clothing to be sewn at home. Still others worked in the tenements at the small subcontracting shops, where they toiled at discrete sewing tasks, some performed by hand, some by foot-powered machines. There is no way of knowing exactly how many women worked at these tasks, for this cottage industry employed thousands each year, usually for only part of the year, without leaving records on individual workers. The factories by the 1880s were usually under some sort of primitive municipal laws that governed health, housing, and age of workers. Subcontracting shops were not.

Subcontractors were often known as "sweaters" because of the system of lowering bids in periods of extreme competition and then "sweating" the difference out of the workers. The term "sweatshop" came to describe the environment of this highly competitive enterprise. The rooms were often small and crowded, sometimes located in the homes of subcontractors, where the sewing work went forward amid the daily tasks of cooking, cleaning, and child rearing. Sweatshops attracted a great deal of attention between 1890 and 1920 because they exemplified the uncontrolled conditions of manufacturing. Jacob Riis, the famous New York photographer, recorded the crowded conditions of the sweatshops on Hester, Division, and Ludlow streets, which he visited in 1889. His memorable description of the end of a day in the New York sweatshop district revealed the sweatshop to middle-class people, who knew little of the conditions under which their own garments were being made. "The thousands of lighted windows in the tenements glow like dull red eyes in a huge stone wall," he wrote in *How the Other Half Lives*. "From every door multitudes of tired men and women pour forth for a half-hour's rest in the open air before sleep closes the eyes weary with incessant working." Riis saw no solution but teaching manual trades and the English language to the young.[2]

The sweatshops Riis described and the criticism of them were soon dwarfed by the new manufacturing lofts of Manhattan, large buildings where hundreds of women workers stitched at machines. There was strong public support for the establishment of factories, because subcontracting had joined the home-and-work lives of immigrant clothing workers in a way that middle-class reformers saw as a threat to family life. But factories were scarcely more healthy for workers than crowded homes. Factories simply created new problems. They brought thousands of young women out of their homes and into shops where they worked alongside male workers. Most of the married women remained at home sewing in cottage industries, but their daughters crowded into the new factories, providing the first really mass-production proletarian labor force in the clothing industry. Factories provided not only a new physical space within which young women worked, but also further segmentation of their work. The older task system of constructing an entire garment now gave way to complete fragmentation of process where women always worked on only one part of a garment—a seam, a sleeve, a buttonhole. Behind the rows of sewing machines, or at work in rows of hand basters, they repeated the same process over, and over, and over again. No longer could a worker keep track of the number of garments completed in one day. Instead, she had a pile of tickets that she received in return for each piece of garment finished. With steam to power the sewing machines, women could work faster and faster on smaller and smaller units in the construction of garments. They could replace men at lower wages. By 1913, 70 percent of all clothing workers were women.[3]

Women joined an industry already divided by conflict. During the last two decades of the nineteenth century and the first two decades of the twentieth, the clothing industry was one of the labor sectors most affected by strikes. While labor historians have traditionally focused on the predominantly male industries of mining and building—two sectors with the largest number of strikes and striking workers from 1880 to 1920—they have usually neglected the third most strike-prone industry, the needle trades. The needle trades rivaled the two male-dominated industries in conflict during the period when increasing numbers of women were moving into the factories of those trades. There are no systematic statistics for the years 1905 to 1914, the years in which women first became visible in large clothing strikes, but the unrest in the industry can be seen in the overall figures. From 1881 to 1905, over two and one half million mine workers were involved in strikes, over one million building workers, and over eight hundred and fifty thousand in the needle trades—including clothing, hats and caps, hosiery and knit goods, and millinery. These workers engaged in over 2500 strikes and lockouts. During the period from 1914 to 1926, the number of strikes involving needle workers would increase to 3563, surpassed only by strikes in the building trades.[4]

Confrontation between capital and labor was a constant theme between 1880 and 1920. Employers, government officials, middle-class reformers, and many organizers sought solutions that would decrease the growing conflict. Welfarism and scientific management were favorite employer solutions. But in the clothing industry, collective bargaining emerged as the solution favored by workers, and accepted by employers, in the face of increased disruptions of production due to strikes. One historian has estimated a 400 percent increase in unionism during the period 1897 to 1903. Mine workers were the first to move toward industrial unions, in which strict trade autonomy was replaced by unions joining together the various crafts in one industry and, in some cases, drawing skilled and unskilled together in one union. The panic of 1907 created a financial crisis that lasted until World War I revived production. During these years of retrenchment, the clothing industry attempted to reduce operating costs by introducing new efficiency schemes, by encouraging the expansion of immigration to form a reserve of low-paid workers, and by hiring increasing numbers of young women who were at the bottom of the wage scale. When tapped by employers, this huge reserve of women workers became a crucial element in labor-capital conflicts. Their role determined who would emerge victorious in the conflict over power.[5]

Women became the new proletariat in this rationalization of the work place. Previously, women, like unskilled males, were peripheral to the work process. Skilled males dominated labor-capital relations. Now, older male unionists had to successfully incorporate into their strategy both the immigrant male and the woman worker, or lose the place they had carved out for themselves in the economic order. The deteriorating working conditions of the women who became mass-production workers set the stage for their revolt. That revolt propelled union membership forward in the clothing industry even after 1915, when the growth of unionism had been checked in other sectors, and employers no longer felt the need to compromise with labor on collective bargaining issues. The force of organizing was the only weapon workers had, as manufacturers appeared less and less willing to meet their demands. With the growing violence of the period between 1910 and 1915, middle-class reformers—alarmed by death, injury, and arrest of female as well as male workers—pressured employers to meet some worker demands. Under these pressures, manufacturers became more conciliatory. Needleworkers in New York and Chicago emerged with the strongest union base, buttressed by a preferential shop and collective bargaining. In other cities, even where unions were less successful, organizing and strikes resulted in establishment of common workplace standards, elimination of sweatshops and subcontracting, and a measure of stability in the strike-torn clothing industry.[6]

Four unions participated in the organization of clothing workers during this era of the great uprisings—the United Garment Workers of America (UGWA), the International Ladies Garment Workers Union (ILGWU), the Amalgamated Clothing Workers of America (ACWA), and the Industrial Workers of the World (IWW). The first two became affiliated with the American Federation of Labor—the UGWA primarily organizing the men's clothing trade, the ILGWU the women's clothing trade, but both remaining within the circle of older craft-based unions. The ACWA and the IWW operated outside the federation, the ACWA carving out its own place among skilled and unskilled clothing workers, primarily in the men's clothing industry, and the IWW attempting to organize entire industries regardless of industry or skill. A brief history of these unions, their ideology, and their tactics, will help to explain their interactions during this period of industrial upheaval and mass organizing.

The UGWA, oldest of the clothing unions, was founded in 1891 by skilled male workers, and was the most traditional. By 1900, women scattered and isolated in rural factories comprised 30 percent of the membership. The UGWA, oriented to workers producing men's clothing (mainly overalls and shirts), used the union label as an organizing device, allowing employers to display the label in return for recognition. As some employers began to specialize in producing better-quality men's clothing, the label became less important. Middle-class males in general were not interested in knowing whether the workers producing their clothing were unionized or not. Moreover, the UGWA had difficulty in organizing urban shops, in which a majority or a large minority were skilled male workers, who could rely on their skills in negotiating favorable contracts. The UGWA also had particular difficulty in organizing the Jewish needleworkers of New York City, who supported an aggressive strike strategy rather than negotiation alone.[7]

The ILGWU came into being in 1900 to organize the rapidly expanding women's ready-to-wear industry. From the beginning the ILGWU was much more ideologically oriented than the UGWA, although the leadership was often at odds with its militant members. Its revised 1912 constitution explicitly stated that its aim was to organize into a "class-conscious trade union" to bring about a "system of society wherein the workers shall receive the full value of their product." The preamble of the constitution also provided for support of the "political party whose aim is the abolition of the capitalist system." Still, the organizational structure was the same as that of a craft union, with leaders merely more committed to careful listening to rank-and-file attitudes. Locals organized single crafts, ethnic groups from all crafts, and women. Because of both political traditions and cross-craft solidarity, ethnic and women's locals became some of the most militant in the ILGWU. The ILGWU was unique—a strongly socialist union that maintained close ties to the AFL and its middle-of-the-road president Samuel Gompers.[8]

From the beginning, women were a large minority in the ILGWU. By 1903 over one-third of its 10,000 members were women. The depression of 1903, and a simultaneous switch to more conservative leadership, combined to decimate the ranks of the new union to 300. Officials even contemplated merging with the UGWA, but the more radical rank and file rejected the merger. Within a few years, however, workers again began moving into the union. Although the women shirtwaist makers spontaneously walked out in 1909, the union mobilized strikers because it was convinced that the organization of women was crucial to union survival. Successful strikes in New York in 1910 gave the ILGWU a commanding place in the growing clothing industry and recognition as the bargaining agent for most workers in women's clothing. By 1912 the union had 50,000 members, approximately one-half women, and had spread from New York to other centers of the women's clothing industry in Chicago, Philadelphia, and Cleveland. By 1920 it was the sixth largest union in the AFL with over 100,000 members.[9]

The UGWA, meanwhile, lost most of its remaining support among the male clothing workers when, in 1913, it announced the settlement of a New York strike without consulting the strikers. The workers continued the strike, and won additional concessions. The UGWA also lost support in Rochester by its lack of ability to organize women, immigrants, and more militant workers.[10] Out of the failure of the UGWA to retain the loyalty of its urban, female, and militant workers, came secession in 1914 and the formation of a more radical union, the ACWA. The ACWA was much more explicit in its radicalism than even the ILGWU. In its constitution it recognized class divisions caused by the ownership of the means of production by one class and the labor power by the other, and a "constant and increasing struggle" between the classes. The leaders of the new union believed that modern industrial methods had wiped out the old craft demarcations and that conditions dictated organizing along industrial lines. An industrial organization based on class consciousness would "put the organized working class in actual control of the system of production." The AFL refused admission to the ACWA, calling it a dual union, and continuing to recognize only the UGWA. Workers in men's ready-to-wear industries poured into the new union which, despite its radical rhetoric and interest in mass organizing, also gradually settled into an emphasis on negotiations rather than on strikes, and collective bargaining to avoid work stoppages that caused loss of wages to workers and loss of profits to employers. Still, the ACWA remained the most militant of the three major unions, much more receptive to women than the UGWA, and willing to recognize women as officials and organizers.[11]

The IWW was formed in 1905 by radical dissidents from the AFL, who seceded to form a union based entirely on industrial principles and dedicated to organizing masses of workers. The IWW had a shadowy existence among the clothing workers in the early years of its existence. It appealed to Italian syndicalists and Jewish revolutionaries who migrated from Russia after the abortive 1905 uprising. A number of ILGWU locals went over to the IWW in the first years of its existence, helping to organize a number of strikes. ILGWU wooed many of the dissident locals back into its ranks during 1908 and 1909, but the IWW remained a left-wing force among garment workers, pushing the other unions farther to the left in an attempt to keep the militant and active workers within their organizations. The IWW continued to support strike independence by the rank and file, and opposed a number of compromises hammered out by the ILGWU and ACWA leaders in the years between 1905 and 1916. The IWW was suppressed by the federal government with the acquiesence of the AFL during World War I. From that time on, the ILGWU and the ACWA led the organized forces of needleworkers against radicals to their left, and against employers to their right. Jewish leadership remained firmly in control of both unions.[12]

While these four unions were becoming the vehicles for organizing working-class women in the needle trades, middle-class women were also becoming active in supporting working women's move into these unions. The main organization for this support was the National Women's Trade Union League (WTUL), formed in 1903 and headed by a group of dynamic reformers. Although the WTUL had a national membership, the New York state organization, headed by Margaret Dreier from 1905 to 1915, remained the driving force in organizing middle-class and working-class women into alliances. Historians who have studied the WTUL have concluded that these coalitions of women never completely reconciled unionism and feminism, but that although cross-class alliances remained fragile, the WTUL provided a framework for support and networking. Most of these alliances disintegrated under the pressure of the 1919 Red scare. As one consequence of government efforts to suppress radicals in the spring of 1919, many middle-class women refused to work with Socialists or radical unionists. Meanwhile, the ILGWU journal, *Justice*, warned: "The interests of the women of the working classes are diametrically opposed to those of the middle classes."[13]

While these alliances flourished, however, they provided middle-class support for working-class women strikers and working-class support for social reformers. The peculiar blend of social legislation and union organization which emerged in the early decades of the twentieth century was reflected clearly in the activities of the WTUL. After the uprising of 1909, the WTUL helped organize ILGWU locals; and after the Triangle Shirtwaist Factory fire in 1911, it began lobbying the state legislature to establish an investigating committee to examine safety and health standards. The Triangle fire of 1911 remains one of the most powerful symbols of the oppression endured by sewing women in America. Trapped in the building where they worked with fire-escape doors locked, almost one hundred and fifty women jumped and fell to their deaths, or were incinerated inside the multi-story building. The grief and outrage of the survivors' coworkers and families, combined with the horror of middle-class women, led both to increased unionization and to protective legislation for women. By late 1912 the state of New York had renewed its efforts to control the health and safety of its young women workers, and to protect "future generations" by means of a bill limiting the hours women could work to fifty-four a week between 6 A.M. and 9 P.M.[14]

Both working-class and middle-class women in the WTUL also compaigned for suffrage. As Nancy Schrom Dye has observed, however, WTUL women never proceeded to an analysis of American conditions which came to terms with the exploitation of women as workers and as women. Although such union organizers as Pauline

Newman found a home in the WTUL in the 1910s, working-class women often felt alienated by the teas and social events planned by the "ladies" for the working class "girls." The labor crisis of 1919, then, released women from the necessity of bridging classes with their coalitions. [15]

The WTUL continued to support protective legislation in the 1920s, but the promise of sisterly solidarity faded before the rise of class consciousness following World War I. For most women the political stress of that period led back to class-based organizing. Feminism could function as a unifying theme only when that unity seemed essential to both groups. Women clothing workers entered the decade of the 1920s essentially on their own. In an era when middle-class women increasingly feared that social reform might lead to more radical social change, working women found their allies among working-class males. The sewing women were now almost entirely dependent upon efforts of unions to stabilize production and control the migration of clothing shops to unorganized areas, as employers faced another escalation of economic competition. The 1920s witnessed the flooding of eastern sewing women into the ILGWU and the ACWA in an attempt to control their deteriorating working conditions, and the movement of union organizers west in an effort to protect eastern workers from the competition of western women workers. [16]

NOTES

1. Edward K. Muller and Paul A. Groves, "The Emergence of Industrial Districts in Mid-Nineteenth Century Baltimore," *The Geographical Review*, 69 (April 1979), 159–178; Edward K. Muller and Paul A. Groves, "The Changing Location of the Clothing Industry: A Link to the Social Geography of Baltimore in the Nineteenth Century," *Maryland Historical Magazine*, 71 (Fall 1976), 403–420; and Max Hall, ed., *Made in New York: Case Studies in Metropolitan Manufacturing* (Cambridge: Harvard University Press, 1959), 22, 68.

2. Jacob A. Riis, *How the Other Half Lives: Studies Among the Tenements of New York* (New York: Dover, 1971), 97–107.

3. Alice Kessler-Harris, "Organizing the Unorganizable: Three Jewish Women and Their Union," *Labor History*, 17 (Winter 1976), 6, n. 1.

4. Florence Peterson, *Strikes in the United States, 1880–1936* (Washington: Government Printing Office, 1938), 30, 38.

5. Bruno Ramirez, *When Workers Fight: the Politics of Industrial Relations in the*

Progressive Era, 1898–1916 (Westport, Conn.: Greenwood, 1978), provides the best discussion of this period although he barely mentions women. See also Melvyn Dubofsky, *When Workers Organize: New York City in the Progressive Era* (Amherst: University of Massachusetts Press, 1968).

6. Ibid., 135–138.

7. Joel Seidman, *The Needle Trades* (New York: Farrar and Rinehart, 1942), 88–124.

8. J. M. Budish and George Soule, *The New Unionism in the Clothing Industry* (New York: Russell & Russell, 1968; repr. of 1920 ed.), 169–175.

9. John Laslett, *Labor and the Left* (New York: Basic Books, 1970), 98–143.

10. Benjamin Stolberg, *Tailor's Progress: The Story of a Famous Union and the Men Who Made It* (Garden City, N.Y.: Doubleday, 1944), 49, 53.

11. Seidman, *Needle Trades*, 122.

12. Budish and Soule, *New Unionism*, 169–170.

13. Louis Levine, *The Women's Garment Workers* (New York: B. W. Huebsch, 1924), 126, 226, 274.

14. Kessler-Harris, "Organizing," 17.

15. A selection of eyewitness and contemporary writings is in Leon Stein, ed., *Out of the Sweatshop: The Struggle for Industrial Democracy* (New York: Quadrangle, 1977), 188–197.

16. Robin Miller Jacoby, "The Women's Trade Union League and American Feminism," *Feminist Studies*, 3 (Fall 1975), 126–140, and Nancy Schrom Dye, "Creating a Feminist Alliance: Sisterhood and Class Conflict in the New York Women's Trade Union League, 1903–1914," *Feminist Studies*, 2 (Spring 1975), 24–36, and *As Equals and As Sisters: Feminism, Unionism, and the Women's Trade Union League of New York* (Columbia: University of Missouri Press, 1980).

CHAPTER 3

The Great Uprising in Rochester

Joan M. Jensen

THE "great struggle of the Garment Workers of Rochester," as the strike of 1913 came to be known, for the first time in Rochester history drew thousands of women out of the factories and into the streets to demand changes in their working conditions. The strike began in January 1913. It ended two months later, after one woman striker had been killed by an employer, several others seriously injured, and at least sixteen arrested. Although few of the Rochester women workers who spontaneously walked off their jobs in mid-January of 1913 were union members, many were active, a good number were militant, and a few were effective strike organizers. Women were prominent in the 1913 strike from its beginning. In the first parade by strikers, women who were not on strike risked losing their own jobs to march in solidarity with the women strikers.

This strike, the largest in the history of Rochester's 150-year-old clothing industry, provides an excellent case to begin study of the interrelationship of women workers, their employers, and the unions in the early twentieth century. During this period, women in garment districts all over the northeastern United States were rebelling against the oppressive conditions that had developed in the industrialization of the highly competitive clothing industry. Rochester women were part of that great uprising.

For a few months in early 1913, the streets were filled with young women marching, singing, protesting, and fighting. Flags, banners, clubs, and guns were the external manifestations of conflict deeply rooted in the long struggle of Rochester's sewing women to control the conditions of their labor. The lives of women clothing workers, their struggle for better working conditions, the attempts of male union members to organize women workers, the support offered by middle-class reformers, and the response of Rochester employers—all these key elements in Rochester's labor history were brought into sharp focus by the 1913 strike.

Rochester had a much smaller and more geographically concentrated clothing industry than New York City. By 1910 Rochester ranked fifth—after New York City, Baltimore, Philadelphia, and Chicago—among cities producing 68 percent of men's ready-made clothing. It had the largest proportion of women workers in the men's clothing industry of any of these cities—61 percent. Over 3,000 women were employed in factories, shops, and homes making clothing.[1]

While numbers are less significant than the actions of the women in the strike, this number of 3,000 is a rough minimum estimate of women involved in the clothing industry. The number of women actually sewing for the Rochester clothing establishments was never accurately recorded during that city's rise as a clothing center. Early in the nineteenth century, when male tailors began to employ increasing numbers of seamstresses and to send out clothes to surrounding farm women for finishing, no official records were kept. The 1860 census counted only 745 women in the industry because neither farm women nor women sewing at home were included. By 1879 one local estimate was that three-fourths of the 2700 clothing workers were women and children. The census of 1910 listed about 5,000 women tailors, seamstresses, and semiskilled factory workers, but one local study of the clothing industry estimated that of 12,000 to 15,000 workers, over half were women. Another local study, in 1912, estimated 12,000 women in clothing, millinary, and laundry, with clothing accounting for the largest percentage. In 1912 no one seemed sure exactly how many women were at work with their needles and sewing machines. The best estimate was that over 3,000 women were accounted for, but recognized that women in outside shops of subcontractors and at home often escaped the attention of census takers. An estimated 60 percent of sewing women worked in factories; 32 percent worked in outside shops of subcontractors; and 8 percent worked at home.[2] Whatever the exact number, the needlework industry touched a large percentage of working-class women. They or their female relatives worked, or had at some time worked, at the trade; and factories, subcontracting shops, and home sewing operations were visible in most working-class neighborhoods.

Wages for Rochester women clothing workers in 1912 were estimated by social workers to be higher than the wages of women clothing workers in New York City. German women made the highest wages, followed in decending order by the wages of Italian, Jewish, and Polish women. Despite the relatively high wages, Rochester women earned proportionately less than did the female clothing workers of other cities compared to male clothing workers. Rochester women received about 60 percent of the wages earned by men in the same work, while Chicago women made 70 percent of men's wages. Thus, the high wages of women did not match the high wages of men, over 40 percent of whom made over $12 a week, while over 50 percent of the women made between $4 and $8 a week.[3]

Records of garment companies are still difficult to find, but books for the Michael Stern Company for the years 1909 to 1912 confirm the low and unstable place of women in the clothing industry's hierarchy. Of 114 women listed in one set of books, seventy-five made $5 to $7 a week, most as "ticket girls." Less than one-half of these women ever advanced in wages. One "ticket girl" after three years had advanced to $9 a week. Most of the remaining women quit after short periods of time. The top pay of any of the women listed in these books was $18 a week, paid to a stenographer. Male supervisors sometimes earned as much as $50 and $60 a week.[4]

The low wages of women were a reflection of the historical development of Rochester's garment industry. The men's clothing industry passed through three discernable stages. First, in the 1820s, a few tailors, principally German, developed a retail trade, as the new canal brought to the city itinerant men needing ready-made men's clothing. The trade was local, confined to small shops, and overshadowed by the growing prominence of gristmills, which were Rochester's principal form of capitalist investment. In the late 1840s, local markets gave way to regional markets, as railroads allowed wholesalers to develop broader distribution networks. To maintain a place in the more competitive regional markets, shop owners mechanized, introducing sewing machines and buttonhole makers, as well as specialization of work processes. Rochester shops also converted to manufacture of men's dress clothes (suits and coats as opposed to work pants and shirts), which sold for high prices and allowed them to employ skilled tailors at high wages. Finally, in the 1890s, large factories displaced small shops, and the sewing women performed at home for the market—a transition almost completed by the 1913 strike.[5]

Each stage in the evolution of Rochester's clothing industry involved more women in the labor force, because labor remained the crucial element in clothing making, even with the introduction of mechanization, and women could be hired for lower wages than the men. Early expansion in the 1820s resulted in women being employed as tailor's helpers, primarily as finishers. As employers responded to the pressures of wholesalers for competitive products, more seamstresses were employed, their wages kept low by the large number of women who needed to make a living and who had few job alternatives in Rochester.

The introduction of machines increased productivity, reduced the number of workers needed, raised factory wages, and lowered the retail cost of the garment. According to an 1899 survey by the United States Commissioner of Labor, the use of machine-made buttonholes instead of hand-sewn buttonholes could reduce labor time as much as 95 to 96 percent in buttonhole making, and 88 to 91 percent in buttonhole cutting. For every one buttonhole machine operator, there were fourteen sewing machine operators who reduced labor time from 77 to 93 percent. To sew one of the popular Prince Albert coats would have taken an estimated 100 hours by hand, but required less than 40 minutes by the machine process. The cost of producing a vicuña worsted Prince Albert coat could be reduced at least 66 percent, from $5.91 to $2.00; the cost of vicuña worsted single-breasted vests by 64 percent, from $1.37 to 50 cents; and the cost of cassimere (woolen twill) trousers by 74 percent, from $1.97 to 51 cents.[6]

While a few women may have purchased sewing machines of their own in Rochester, the highly competitive contractors quickly captured the market for machine work. Establishing small two-story shops, often behind their homes, these subcontractors to large firms in turn hired women to finish garments in their homes after the machine work was completed.[7]

The introduction of large factories into Rochester during the 1890s began the elimination of work in subcontracting shops and homes. Along St. Paul and Mill streets, capitalists erected large five-story factories, and further rationalized work processes. In the large factories, women received higher pay than in the smaller shops, but were worked harder and pushed to produce more. By 1913, almost all homework, as well as much of the work in the smaller shops, had been eliminated. The strike of 1913 would, in the main, put an end to the subcontracting system in Rochester.

As employers made greater profits and skilled male workers made higher wages, the wages of females remained depressed. At the Second Woman's Suffrage Convention meeting in Rochester, in 1848, a convention member reported that seamstresses were working fourteen to fifteen hours a day for 31 to 38 cents a day. Two weeks later women made an attempt to increase their wages. Seamstresses met in Mechanic's Hall to form a Women's Protective Union which demanded equal rights with men, cash wages, and regular house- and piecework. This organization foundered after a year. Five years later, women formed a Seamstresses Protective Association with more success. The women issued an appeal for wage increases, mobilized public support, and obtained an increase of 60 cents a week.[8]

Working conditions thereafter remained relatively unchanged. A decade later seamstresses still averaged $1.50 to $3.00 a week, while unskilled and home workers made far less. An attempt to increase wages in 1864 was unsuccessful.[9] This defeat left women clothing workers unorganized until the Knights of Labor began their organizing drive in Rochester in the 1880s.

The very skilled male tailors and cutters became highly unionized under the Knights. The wages of men subsequently became among the highest in the country for clothing workers. Employers, however, kept the wages of the female majority of the work force down, by utilizing sex segregation in the workplace and by keeping many women workers unorganized in subcontracting shops or in the home. The main technological invention of the nineteenth century in the clothing industry, the sewing machine, could be adapted to the existing labor force, while affording an expansion of production and profit. The sewing machine was introduced into Rochester for the same reasons that it was introduced into the garment industries of other cities at about the same time. It increased productivity, reduced the number of workers needed, raised wages, and lowered the retail cost of the item. Karl Marx, viewing a similar process of industrialization in Europe, would label this process the surplus labor theory of capital. The productivity of each woman was increased five times with the sewing machine, but her income increased only by one-third. The surplus labor of each woman paid for the machines, which remained under the control of the factory owner along with the surplus profits from her work. [10] The only way to counteract the loss of profits to the workers was to organize. The women soon did, following the men into the Knights of Labor.

Women formed two locals of the Knights of Labor in Rochester, one a sewing local and the other a women tailors' local. While the Knights encouraged the formation of women's locals in the 1880s, they were unable to exercise responsible leadership for the women workers. Knights acquiesced in the blacklisting and firing of striking women tailors who, as a consequence, went back to work. [11] Women workers indicated a continued interest in organizing, but the Knights had disintegrated to such an extent that they would not respond to the needs of the Rochester women. Male garment workers, meanwhile, had moved into the United Garment Workers, a union affiliated with the American Federation of Labor which began in 1890 as an all-male union. By the late 1890s a few women had followed the men into the UGWA. Women's locals soon formed within the UGWA, and women joined its general executive board. By 1909 the national UGWA had 17,212 women, organized in 133 locals representing 40 percent of the total membership. Almost 24 percent of all women in the men's clothing industry had been organized. [12] Unionization of women spread first in small towns where men, outnumbered greatly by women in small shops, needed the women to organize any union at all. [13] In such cities as Rochester and New York, men were either in a majority or close to it in the factories, and thus had less need to admit women into the unions. As factories became larger, however, more women became involved in strikes when men struck; and as employers began to cooperate with each other on a regional level by supplying garments to strike-bound factories, men became more interested that women become union members. At the same time, women workers were beginning to react to the increased exploitation of their labor power.

That exploitation was increasing as women moved out of subcontracting shops into the large factories where their pay was better, but where they were pressured to produce more, under more structured working conditions. After 1890 the generation of power from Niagara Falls was adapted to industrial power in Rochester, and the largest companies began to supervise increasing operations in large five-story buildings. The expansion of the market in the 1880s allowed capital previously used for supplies to be invested in buildings, and in the last decades of the nineteenth century a few large firms emerged to dominate the Rochester clothing market. By 1893 one-third to one-half of all clothing was produced in factories. By the time of the 1913 strike, almost all of it was produced in factories; nevertheless, the elimination of the remaining subcontractors led the list of strike demands. [14]

By 1907 an estimated 15,396 working people of the 75,000 workers in Rochester were unionized. Only 268 of these members were women, however; apparently a few of them were in the garment union, the existence of which was being tolerated by the new large companies because of their need for skilled male workers. While factory women in Rochester engaged in small strikes to improve working conditions between 1890 and 1907, they remained unsuccessful in their organizing efforts. Among the organized Rochester workers, strikes during these years were only about 58 percent wholly or partially successful, at a time when clothing workers' strikes nationally were achieving greater success.

A strike in 1903–1904 had revealed the major weakness of organizing only men and of keeping the shops open to nonunion employees. When new cutting machines were introduced, reducing the number of working days per year, Rochester men struck for an eight-hour day. The largest shops opposed the unions, broke the back of the strike, and kept the shops open. That same year, when New York clothing workers went on strike, the Rochester firms supplied clothing to the struck New York employers. Previously, employers had primarily competed on the national market. The 1905 strike showed workers that employers were helping each other by supplying clothing to strike-bound factories. Because of the open shops in Rochester and the weakness of the United Garment Workers, factory workers in Rochester were forced to perform what amounted to strike breaking. [15]

The lesson of 1905 was a harsh one, and not forgotten. From that time on, New York unions became increasingly concerned about the health of unions in Rochester, and Rochester unions became increasingly concerned about moving women out of subcontracting and homework into factories, and into the unions. A national competitive labor market was demanding coordinated and broadened efforts to organize clothing workers on a national scale, both men and women. While records do not exist to show how many Rochester women actually joined the United Garment Workers, the union more often received the support of women in the strikes, and offered them support in turn. By 1913 women were a large percentage of the workers in clothing factories, and unions could not ignore them. In the 1913 strike, women emerged as active and effective strike organizers.

Abolition of subcontracting was the first of five formal demands issued by a strike committee formed after an estimated 3,000 strikers walked off their jobs in mid-January of 1913. In addition, workers demanded a 48-hour work week, overtime and holiday pay, a wage increase, no discrimination against union members, and a shop committee and an arbitration committee comprised of one union representative, one employer, and a third representative selected by the two. The strike committee printed these formal demands in four languages—English, German, Yiddish, and Italian. Women publicized other grievances as well. The primary one was sexual harassment by male supervisors. John A. Flett, general organizer representing the strikers for the AFL said, "The women and girls are treated brutally by foremen in their [the manufacturers] employ." At one point in the strike, newspapers hinted that women strikers might air these grievances at a public meeting, and discuss the "lack of decency" on the part of the foremen. Libbie Alpern, a strike leader, told workers, "The foreman used to pinch and tease me. He asked me to go out to dinner with him and tell my mother that I was going to stay at a girl friend's house." The women deeply resented this kind of treatment by supervisors, yet these complaints formed only an undercurrent to the formal demands. The grievances did, however, motivate and strengthen the militance and solidarity of the women.[16]

Alpern was one of the young Jewish women to emerge as a leader of union organizing efforts. Alpern was born in Bialystok, Russia, and emigrated with her mother in 1911. At seventeen Alpern became a militant strike leader known as "Captain Libbie." She spoke daily at union halls, describing her oppressive factory experiences and urging support for the strike in both English and Yiddish. Between talks, she and other women searched out independent subcontracting shops that were still operating. Returning with groups of predominantly women strikers, they would call the nonstriking women out and attempt to close the shops. Under the leadership and discipline of Alpern, groups closed twelve shops in the first three weeks of the strike.[17]

Alpern was sick the day a group of strikers visited the shop of Valentine Sauer and precipitated the confrontation that was to martyr Ida Brayman, another young Jewish clothing worker. Brayman, also seventeen, had come from Kiev eight months before the strike began. After narrowly escaping two pogroms in Russia, the Brayman family decided that Ida and her father should go to the United States in order to earn the money needed to bring the rest of the family to the new world. The father went to work in New York; the daughter found work in Rochester, where an uncle already lived.

At dusk on the afternoon of February 5, Brayman was with a group of strikers that visited Sauer's shop. At the head of the group was Fannie Gordon, a friend of Brayman's, and an organizer who had been working with Alpern. The strikers surrounded the small shop, calling on the forty women inside to leave their machines and join the strikers. The specific causes of the violence that ensued are not clear. The crowd outside may have been in an angry, impatient mood; the shop owner may have intended to make a show of defiance. It was, however, more than a show. Sauer fired a gun into the crowd, wounding Gordon and killing Brayman.[18] A few days later, women marched by the thousands to the small Jewish cemetery outside of Rochester, where Brayman was buried.

Women strikers became increasingly bitter after Brayman's death. Their criticism of employers sharpened. One woman who had worked as a buttonhole maker for the ten preceeding years, never averaging more than $8 a week, wrote a paper entitled "Why I Am Out on Strike." She listed low wages, poor working conditions, and harassment by foremen as the women worker's main grievances.

> The cry of the Rochester clothing manufacturers that their employees have no cause to strike, and that the strike is a result of agitation among the workers by outsiders is more than an effrontery on their part; it is an insult to the strikers. . . . In one of the [big factories] seven of us had to work at one table with only two lights about us. When we asked for an additional light, the so called "system man," whom that firm employs for the purpose

of cutting out expenses, came up to us and said that we ought not to ask for more lights, as expenses are too large. They actually removed one of the lights that very day, and moved the single light to the center of the table.

The small shops, according to this worker, did not seem to encourage personal mistreatment, but in the larger factories, foremen abused the women in every way, from using insulting language to firing the women at will. "There was not a day," she wrote of one foreman, "that some people were not fired by him, some of them having worked for that firm a number of years." Or they might hire too much help, and "thereby crush the old piece workers' spirit. . . . They pick and choose," she concluded, "just as if we were cattle in the market, without regard to our loss of time and feelings."[19]

Brayman's death occurred during the second week of the strike. There was little violence for the next few weeks, but as the strike entered its second month with no resolution of the conflict, clashes began to occur between groups of strikers and police and between individual women strikers and nonstrikers. Employers seemed to become more stubborn in their refusal to settle the strike by compromise. They employed strike breakers, and their associations encouraged intransigence by the mayor and the police. At the same time, the workers drew on outside supporters to help publicize their cause. The Rochester Socialist Party was active in support of the strike—Norman Thomas marched in one parade and Ella Reeve Bloor spoke to a special meeting of women workers. But as the strike dragged on, Socialists seemed unable to do more than serve free lunches to the strikers and encourage them to hold out. The Industrial Workers of the World also surfaced during the strike. Although there is little documentation of IWW participation, its members did attend strike meetings, and they encouraged Italian women to speak to their coworkers in Italian. The IWW continued to oppose the strike settlement when the United Garment Workers began to compromise. In the end, only the IWW opposed the final settlement, and only the Italian workers voted against going back to work.[20]

Italian women were among those arrested in the police-striker conflicts. Most of the women arrested in these altercations were between the ages of seventeen and twenty-five, but two were in their forties. The militant women were often less than gentle. One woman spat in the face of a scab (strike-breaker) and gave her a punch in the jaw. Some broke shop windows, and a number of women beat up employees who refused to leave their jobs. Others hurled insults, hissed, or gathered in groups at the factories to criticize the women who refused to quit work. On a number of occasions police used clubs to disperse crowds. Women retaliated against police with fists and umbrellas, and one woman bit a policeman's finger. One group of strikers marched from the union hall to a factory, where they refused an order to return to the hall. Police began clubbing them. They retreated singing, "the land of the free and the home of the brave." Newspapers reported that a delegation of women workers had told stories of police brutality to a society women's meeting, and that the middle-class women planned to support the strikers by going into the clothing district to monitor trouble between women pickets and the police.[21]

This meeting, held in the home of one of Rochester's well-known society women, pointed to a growing middle-class concern that the strike might foster increasingly militant worker action, thus intensifying the conflict, rather than leading toward compromise. In other cities, middle-class women had formed women's trade union leagues to encourage and support unionism. In Rochester, there existed no equivalent of those feminist unions of working-class women and their middle-class allies who supported both trade unionism and suffrage. No Women's Trade Union League was organized in Rochester, nor did any of its well-known New York leaders appear there to support strikers or to help organize middle-class Rochester women into a support network. Only one WTUL member, Leonora O'Reilly, and the head of one New York suffrage organization, Anna Cadogan Etz, spoke to women strikers. While Rochester was the home of Susan B. Anthony and had a strong middle-class female reform tradition, the women seemed unable or unwilling to take part in working-class women's struggles in their own backyard. Or across the canal, as the case was in Rochester, for the canal served as a dividing line between the wealthy and the working classes—with factories and the dwellings of workers on one side, and the homes of the well-to-do on the other. Newspapers recorded only the single meeting referred to above, estimating that about fifty women attended. In addition, newspapers mentioned by name ten middle-class women who became active in the strike after police brutality escalated in early March.[22]

The most active organizer among these women was Catherine Rumball. Her husband, Edwin A. Rumball, minister of the First Unitarian Church and member of the Socialist Party, would become increasingly important in strike negotiations during late March. The Rumballs were both known as independent progressives, active in the publication of a small reform magazine called *The Common Good*.

The Common Good devoted much attention to the living conditions of the workers and the social injustices they suffered. The concern of the reformers whose writing filled the pages of the magazine was focused particularly on the destiny of working-class children, who were dependent upon the conditions in their homes. Factory conditions of women workers became an extension of this concern, since a significant number of young working-class women would be expected to work in Rochester's factories prior to marriage and child rearing. The reforms advocated in the pages of *The Common Good* attempted to fit together the various pieces of working women's lives into a comprehensive whole whose center was the home.

Given the assumption that the home and child rearing should be central to the lives of women, it followed that workers' housing should be a preoccupation of the reformers. Single-family dwellings, owned or rented, followed by multi-family houses, tenements, and last, rooming houses, represented the housing hierarchy from desirable to undesirable. One change that Edwin Rumball opposed in the pages of the little reform magazine was a large 200-family tenement proposed in 1911 and supported by such businessmen as George Eastman, head of Kodak Company. The complex was planned with playgrounds, a common laundry and bathing area, drying chambers for clothes, and various common amenities. Even in contemporary times, it is difficult for civic officials to deal satisfactorily with all the problems raised by urban housing complexes. It is therefore not surprising that early twentieth-century reformers cast a skeptical eye on this new proposal. But the philosophy that undergirded the reformers' opposition held special implications for women, emphasizing their societal role as a stabilizing influence, and seeking assurance of their isolation in the nuclear family. Tenements, according to Rumball, by their very nature should be considered evil, because "democracy" could not survive there. "It is useless to expect a conservative point of view in the working man if his home is but three or

four rooms in some huge building, and this home only his from
month to month," Rumball quoted, with approval, from another
housing critic. Such housing would break up the sanctity and privacy
of home life and the loyalty of children to the home, thereby creating
group life in place of family life. Only detached homes offered the
stable, orderly life desirable for the working-class family. Rumball
helped kill the proposal, supporting instead more stringent health
laws and housing legislation to address the problems of the poor living
conditions of the working class.[23]

Studies of infant mortality, the results of which were published in
The Common Good, came to similar conclusions: that the only hope for
reduced mortality lay in individual homes with mothers present
inside. The founding of Mothers' Clubs (forerunners of later Parent
Teacher Associations), the training of young girls for their maternal
duties, the establishment of child welfare stations and an infants'
summer hospital, the improvement of the public milk supply—all
these measures could help. But, mainly, women had to be educated to
their home duties. Although it was desirable that females be educated
in the schools, the schools should reinforce the female's domestic and
maternal role. Churches and the settlement houses could also be
useful in providing proper models for the working class. In addition,
the enforcement of existing municipal laws could solve many problems associated with the living conditions of the working class.[24]

Concern about children led to concern about women's working
conditions. Reformers argued that poor working conditions sapped
the vigor of young working women who, as a consequence, would be
unhealthy mothers, neglecting their children. The children thus
became a public care, thrusting the community into an area of
responsibility where it did not belong. Progressive reformers sought
to get at the root of the problem by examining and exposing the
condition of working women. *The Common Good* gave considerable
attention to the "factory girl." One account by a girl described a work
life which had begun with a part-time job in a pin factory at age
eleven, full-time work at age fourteen, and graduation to custom
hand sewing fifty-six hours a week at seventeen. Her shop was dirty,
there was no cafeteria, and she stayed inside all day. In the evenings,
she learned buttonhole making. By the end of her third year at this
job, the young woman was feeling run down; she therefore switched
to a large factory where she could make more money, but there she was

forced to work even harder. Twenty-two years old, the worker told her interviewer: "So many years I have worked and doing skilled work, and am earning only nine dollars. And then I have such terrible headaches, and my mind keeps working all the time. But then I am better off than most other factory girls, I have better wages and I have more ambition."[25]

According to reformers, the poor health of these "factory girls" led to infant mortality. During the strike, Catherine and Edwin Rumball published an extensive study of "The Working Girls and Women of Rochester" in *The Common Good*. They argued that the districts with the highest infant mortality rates were those where women were factory girls before marriage. The community, they argued, was paying the costs of exploitation by the factory owners. In 1911 the magazine had favored factory welfare: a warm lunch, pleasant eating place, hospital rooms for sick employees, recreational activities, training schools, profit sharing, and insurance benefits. Only a few clothing factories—the Adler Brothers, for example—practiced this type of welfare capitalism, or, as it was then called, "the social spirit." Now, however, the Rumballs also advocated a more active role for the workers and collective bargaining as a necessity for the working women of Rochester. Organized labor was the only way to progress, they argued. Women needed to insist on the same wage as men for the same work, and to unite with men to demand a maximum wage. Women workers must organize. "The woman's cause is not only man's," they concluded, "it is the cause of all of us together."[26]

Catherine Rumball was the most visible middle-class ally in the strike. She spoke to women strikers at workers' halls, inviting them to address meetings of middle-class women; she did picket duty and urged women to bargain collectively to prevent further deterioration. She was joined in her efforts by Mary Thorn Lewis Gannett, a wealthy Unitarian with Quaker antecedents, as well as by the daughter of a Presbyterian minister, the daughter of a stockholder in one of the strike-bound factories, and by a handful of other prominent women who joined the pickets as observers to prevent police brutality. But unless private correspondence can be found to indicate further cross-class activity, these efforts apparently were all that the sisterhood across the canal could provide for the women strikers. Rumball talked of sisterhood and promised that sentiment in support of the women strikers was growing, but she could never mobilize more than a few

other women in the worker's support. Whatever pressure women may
have exerted in traditional private ways to help end the strike, they
were only slightly visible publicly and, even then, not as an organized
force.[27]

At the end of the strike the working women did ask their union
representative to express their thanks to six of these women for their
work with the pickets and for their support, but no evidence exists
that sisterhood flourished or that it outlasted the strike. The women
Rumball described as having "time and influence at their disposal"
may have decreased police violence, but they were unable to exert any
major influence on the strike. The working women had to rely on
themselves and other working-class women in their struggle.

Italian women emerged from the Rochester strike displaying what
at first might seem surprising militance. Researchers have long characterized Italian parents, especially patriarchal fathers, as opposed to
daughters working outside the home. Were Rochester families
unique, with the daughters somehow more militant than their parents, or were their parents somehow different? Researchers apparently have projected later ideology back into the early period and have
deemphasized early militant rhetoric and employment practices. As
Miriam Cohen's study of New York Italians shows, these immigrant
families valued the paid labor of their daughters so much that they
favored their daughters' working over their going to school. Because
wages of Italian males were low, the most rational family strategy was
to encourage daughters to work. Mothers took in boarders and did
finishing work—often brought home by daughters who worked in
factories. Daughters working in factories were thus valuable contributors to the household income. Moreover, Cohen has shown that this
was the best family strategy, for education made absolutely no difference in the earnings of women in the garment industry.[28] The pattern
in Rochester seems similar to that in New York, and would offer some
explanation for the militance of the young Italian daughters.

Beyond the street militance of Italian women strikers, some
Italian women spoke to other workers, and a number apparently
joined the IWW, the organization representative of the most militant
ideology. In Rochester Italian women never moved into prominent
strike leadership, as the Jewish women did, but they helped make up
the most militant strike forces, and some were among those few
hundred garment workers who opposed the settlement of the strike on

the grounds that it gained too little from the employers. The activities of the young women from the Italian garment communities of Rochester may not have been unique, but rather part of a pattern of labor, community, and family militancy still inadequately studied by labor historians. They had the most to gain from a favorable wage settlement, the least to lose from militant demands.

The Jewish daughters, on the other hand, while also displaying militant organizing actions and moving to the forefront in strike leadership, had more to gain from peaceful settlement. While one should not forget that Emma Goldman had her first taste of wage slavery in the garment district of Rochester in the 1870s, she also found more congenial radical networks in New York—to which she removed herself with her sewing machine in 1889. The main difference between Italian and Jewish communities may have been the relatively greater security of Jewish immigrants because of their greater number of skilled workers. While Italian daughters came from relatively homogeneous unskilled (at least in terms of earning power) communities of workers, Jewish daughters came from mixed economic communities. This mixture of skilled and unskilled work community gave Jewish leaders an edge in recognizing the possibilities and the necessity of organizing broad-based industrial unions that included both skilled and unskilled workers.

Again, Cohen's research in New York hints at differences that seem to have existed in the Rochester Jewish community. Jewish males had entered the expanding garment industry before the Italians, using their previous experience in small-scale mercantile operations to set up shops in the garment districts of each major clothing center. Lower infant mortality rates among the Jewish community— perhaps because of better access to health care as well as to economic advantages—meant Jewish families could educate their daughters. They also could, and did, move from homework into factory work in the first decade of the twentieth century, thus finding healthier working conditions. As a consequence, Jewish workers were less tied to subcontracting and homework than the workers of some other ethnic groups. When the Rochester strikers demanded an end to low-paying practices, the Jewish community could more easily support these demands, because it was less dependent on this lowest paying work. The Jewish daughters were also more literate upon their arrival in the United States, and increased their literacy once they were settled. Literacy gave these women greater social, if not employment, opportunities. Thus, the leadership of Jewish daughters emerged in the more moderate wing of the Rochester movement, which voted for settlement of the strike once subcontracting had been eliminated.[29]

As the strike continued into late March, the middle class seemed to abandon its support for collective bargaining. Edwin Rumball proposed a board composed of employers, workers, and public representatives to monitor complaints and correct abuses through private conferences with employers and publication of facts where abuses were not corrected. State mediators hammered out a compromise that both union and employer could claim as a victory. The strike itself had already forced employers to abolish subcontracts and to establish a 52-hour week. Workers were also granted overtime and work-free holidays. There was no overall increase in wages; workers were merely compensated for time lost in hourly reductions. Employers did agree not to discriminate against union members and to meet with committees of employees; but there was no official union representation on these employee committees.[30] Strikers appointed Edwin Rumball, along with a second minister and two union officials, to see that the new agreement was lived up to, but clearly the union did not have an accepted place at the bargaining table. Rumball advised the workers to return to work and, with the exception of the more militant Italian workers, they returned.[31]

The agreement finally accepted by the majority of the strikers under the guidance of the United Garment Workers was far from the type of collective bargaining most workers wanted. The Rochester strike did not achieve a protocol like that achieved by the New York garment workers, with union-employer arbitration and grievance committees. What then did the workers receive for the million and a half dollars lost in wages?

Most important for women workers came recognition by the male-dominated unions. During the strike of 1913, Rochester women workers became a major part of a previously male union movement. The willingness of women to organize, to risk physical injury as symbolized by the death of Ida Brayman, and to follow female leaders won much support for women workers and for unionism. The solidarity of male and female workers reached a new level.

In fact, this new militance of the women and the new worker gender solidarity could not be contained within the United Garment Workers once the strikers had returned to work. As a result of their strike experiences, women workers became more insistent that they maintain a permanent presence in the union. When the UGWA refused to recognize women as a permanent and active part of the union structure, as shop chairwomen, as business agents, and as organizers, Rochester union women led the movement of clothing workers away from the old UGWA to form a new, more militant Amalgamated Clothing Workers. Women in the ACWA had to continue their struggle within that union for recognition and control, but their place was now within rather than outside a dynamic, growing, militant labor movement.

The decade of 1910 to 1920 marked a gain in women union membership all over the country, especially among clothing workers. But the increase in the city of Rochester was particularly impressive. From a total of 348 women union members in 1909, membership grew to 9,515 in 1920. This was 25 percent of the women gainfully employed in Rochester, a higher percentage than the nationwide average of all organized wage earners. More than 70 percent of these women—nearly 7,000—were in the clothing trades.[32] It was the beginning of a new era.

NOTES

1. For recent studies see especially Alice Kessler-Harris, "Organizing the Unorganizable: Three Jewish Women and Their Union," *Labor History*, 17 (Winter 1976), 5–23; and Kessler-Harris, " 'Where are the Organized Women Workers?' " *Feminist Studies*, 3 (Fall 1975), 92–110; and Nancy Shrom Dye, "Feminism or Unionism? The New York Women's Trade Union League and the Labor Movement," *Feminist Studies*, 3 (Fall 1975), 111–125.

2. Statistics on women in the Rochester clothing industry can be found scattered throughout Charles P. Neill, *Men's Ready-Made Clothing*, vol. 2, *Report on Conditions of Women ad Child Wage Earners in the United States* (61st Congress, 2d Session, Senate Document 645, Washington, 1911), and summarized in Edwin Rumball and Catherine Rumball, "The Working Girls and Women of Rochester," *The Common Good*, 6 (Feb. 1913), 133–157.

3. Boutelle E. Lowe, *Representative Industry and Trade Unionism of an American City* (New York: Gray, 1912); and Alan H. Gleason, "The History of Labor in Rochester, 1820–1880," Master's thesis, University of Rochester, 1941.

4. Records of the Stein Company, University of Rochester.

5. Blake McKelvey, "The Men's Clothing Industry in Rochester's History," *Rochester History*, 22 (July 1960), 1–32; Elmer Adler, "Notes on the Early History of Rochester Industries, I: Clothing," *The Common Good*, 5 (Oct. 1911), 18–21.

6. United States Commissioner of Labor, *Report on Hand and Machine Labor* (2 vols., Washington, 1899), I, 197–204; II, 906–911, 914–919, 923–927.

7. "My Work in Rochester," by a Factory Girl, *The Common Good*, 6 (Dec. 1912), 71–74.

8. Lowe, *Representative Industry*, 45.

9. Blake McKelvey, *Rochester: The Water Power City, 1812–1854* (Cambridge: Harvard University Press, 1945), 287, 349; and Blake McKelvey, *Rochester: The Flower City, 1855–1890* (Cambridge: Harvard University Press, 1949), 76.

10. McKelvey, *Flower City*, 76.

11. Ibid., 18; Natalie F. Hawley, "The Labor Movement in Rochester, 1880–1898," Master's thesis, University of Rochester, 1949, 205–206, 217, 235; and John Andrews and W. D. P. Bliss, *History of Women in Trade Unions*, vol. 10 of U.S. Labor Bureau, *Report on Conditions of Women and Child Wage Earners*, 129. Philip S. Foner, *Women and the American Labor Movement: From the First Trade Unions to the Present* (New York: Free Press, 1979), 70–97, relates numerous instances of the reluctance of Knights to support militant strike activity of sewing women.

12. Ibid., 136.

13. The total number of union women in Rochester in all industries was only 348 in 1909, Lowe, *Representative Industry*, 21. The spread of UGWA among women workers in the men's garment industry is described in Andrews and Bliss, *Women in Trade Unions*, 161.

14. See printed strike demands and "Why I Am Out on Strike," in the E. A. Rumball Papers, University of Rochester.

15. Supplying garments to strike-bound factories in other towns was mentioned as a grievance in *Rochester Democrat and Chronicle*, Feb. 7, 1913.

16. *Rochester Democrat and Chronicle*, Feb. 13, 1913; Mar. 6, 1913.

17. *Rochester Democrat and Chronicle*, Feb. 13, 1913.

18. The most complete accounts of the shooting are in the *Rochester Democrat and Chronicle*, Feb. 6 and 7, 1913, and *Rochester Union and Advertiser*, Feb. 7, 1913. Sauer was never indicted but was released shortly after his arrest and left town, *Rochester Evening Times*, Feb. 20, 1913.

19. "Why I Am Out on Strike," Rumball Papers, University of Rochester.

20. Newspaper clipping file of the garment worker's strike in the Rumball Papers, University of Rochester.

21. *Rochester Post Express*, Mar. 17, 1913, reported on the society women.

22. Their names were Mrs. Cogswell Bentley, Gertrude C. Blackall, Mrs. Clements, Mrs. W. C. Gannett, Laura Griesheimer, Mrs. Florence Cross Kitchett, Alida Lattimore, Mrs. Edwin A. Rumball, Mrs. Joseph Talling, and Louise Taylor.

23. Edwin Rumball and Catherine Rumball, "Working Girls," 137–138, 155–156; "Rochester Factories and the Social Spirit," *Common Good*, 4 (Mar.

1911), 10–12; John R. Williams, "A Study in Rochester's Infant Mortality," *The Common Good*, 5 (Jan. 1912), 14–22; Wm. Channing Gannett, "The Abdication of the Parent," *The Common Good*, 5 (Apr. 1912), 20–23; Edwin Alfred Rumball, "Shall Rochester Have a 200-Family Tenement," *The Common Good*, 5 (May 1912), 18–29; and "Model Tenements and the Alternative," *The Common Good*, 5 (July 1912), 6; and Mrs. George W. Moore, "Rochester's 3,500 Rooming Girls," *The Common Good*, 6 (July 1913), 301–302.

24. Edwin A. Rumball, "The Fourth Ward Survey," *The Common Good*, 5 (Oct. 1911) 22–24.

25. "My Work in Rochester," *The Common Good*, 6 (Dec. 1912), 71–74.

26. Rumball and Rumball, "Working Girls," 156.

27. *Rochester Democrat*, Mar. 7, 1913.

28. Miriam Cohen, "Changing Educational Strategies among Immigrant Generations: New York Italians in Comparative Perspective," *Journal of Social History*, 15 (Spring 1982), 443–466.

29. Ibid.

30. McKelvey, "Men's Clothing Industry," 20.

31. See *Rochester Post Exchange, Rochester Herald, New York Evening Journal*, and *Rochester Evening Journal*, for Mar. 20, 1913.

32. Alice Henry, *Women and the Labor Movement* (New York: Arno, 1971; repr. of 1923 ed.), 83; Leo Wolman, *The Growth of American Trade Unions, 1880–1923* (New York: Arno, 1975; repr. of 1924 ed.), 105, 108.

CHAPTER 4

The Uprising in Chicago: The Men's Garment Workers Strike, 1910–1911

N. Sue Weiler

> A lull in the struggle,
> A truce in the fight,
> The whirr of machines
> And the dearly bought right,
> Just to labor for bread,
> Just to work and be fed.[1]

ON SEPTEMBER 22, 1910, Hannah Shapiro decided she could not accept three and three-fourths cents (a reduction from four cents) to sew a pocket into a pair of men's trousers. Hannah and sixteen other young women picked up their scissors and walked out of Shop No. 5 at 18th and Halsted streets, one of the forty-eight tailor shops owned by the Chicago firm of Hart, Schaffner & Marx. Thus began a strike that would last four and one-half months, enlist strong support from progressive trade unionists and reformers, and bring about an investigation by the Illinois Senate.

Reprinted from an article entitled, "Walkout: The Chicago Men's Garment Workers' Strike: 1910–1911," *Chicago History*, 8, no. 4 (Winter 1979–1980), by permission of the publisher, Chicago Historical Society.

Although the Chicago strike of 1910–1911 has been cited as a breakthrough because of the resulting agreement between the garment workers and a major firm, Hart, Schaffner & Marx, it has rarely been given the attention of the "Uprising of the 20,000" in New York City the previous year. While the importance of New York's garment industry is commonly understood, the significance of the garment industry to the Chicago economy continues to be relatively unrecognized. At the turn of the century, the garment trades vied with the stockyards as the city of Chicago's major employers. New York's trade was dominated by the struggling women's garment industry and its corresponding fledging union, the International Ladies Garment Workers, whereas the major producers of the more traditional men's garment industry were located in Chicago.

The Chicago walkout also affords an opportunity to analyze the collaboration among the Women's Trade Union League, the Chicago Federation of Labor, and some immigrant workers. (The cooperation of these three groups was much more effective than in the New York strike.) A group of young working women came to the WTUL shortly after the walkout occurred, and received invaluable assistance. But the feminist alliance between middle-class and working women was not equal.[2] The older, well-educated, affluent allies took charge of the proceedings. The wage-earning women proved themselves eager to cooperate and willing to become loyal union members, but the young men who also were aided in the strike were to break away from the alliance. Margaret Dreier Robins, president of the Women's Trade Union League, considered the collaborative experience "one of the most splendid demonstrations of the courage, endurance and fraternity in the human heart . . . on the battlefields of American industry."[3] Sidney Hillman, president of the Amalgamated Clothing Workers, on the other hand—while expressing gratitude for the Hull House training, especially for the support necessary in a strike—felt humiliated at being forced "to beg for charity outside the labor movement."[4]

The men's garment industry began in Chicago in small workshops, following the Great Fire of 1871. The industry grew rapidly during the next forty years. By the turn of the century, two types of manufacturing existed side by side in the city. A market for quality clothes had compelled the larger manufactures to combine small shops into large factories as a way of assuring a standard product. At the same time, a growing market for ready-made clothes and the seasonal nature of the industry encouraged the continued proliferation of contract or sweatshops. The contract system continued to flourish alongside the large, fully integrated concerns, primarily because of its elasticity. The existence of contractors meant that large manufacturers did not have to add employees during the busy season; they simply contracted for extra work. Sweaters continued to compete by providing small orders directly to retailers.

Whether the garment was produced from start to finish in a factory or partially made by contract labor, the initial stages of production were the same. The designing and cutting of the garments took place in the factory. If contractors were involved, the cut cloth was packed in bundles and delivered to the sweatshops. Here a succession of specialized machine operators (each doing a specified portion of the garment) did the sewing, helped by basters, who basted the unsewn pieces and removed the bastings from the sewn ones. Next, the garments went to the buttonholer (usually a subcontractor), and, finally, to the presser back in the factory in which the production process had begun.

The needle, the sewing machine, the pressing iron, and the sheers dictated the primary division of labor into hand sewers, machine operators, pressers and trimmers. Occupations performed exclusively by men were those that required standing all day—pressing coats and pants, basting coats on table tops—and those that required the skills of a tailor, trained to make up an entire garment. On the other hand, "woman's knowledge of hand sewing, her deftness and speed with the needle, as also her acceptance of wages which a man cannot afford to accept," determined the domain left exclusively to women—hand sewing, buttonholes, and sewing buttons on garments. In machine sewing, nationality and availability of men generally determined whether men or women were hired. German, Scandinavian, and Bohemian shops hired women exclusively as machine operators. Shops operated by Jews, Lithuanians, and Italians almost always used men as machine operators. Less-demanding basting on coats was done by men in New York, but elsewhere, including Chicago, by women.[5] With the elaborate refinement in the division of labor, the sewing of a coat could be broken down into approximately 150 separate operations.

This division of the manufacturing process into self-contained operations was highly conducive to sweatshop production. Moreover, with fifty dollars in capital and some knowledge of tailoring, a contractor could establish his own business. A typical entrepreneur might buy half a dozen sewing machines, set them up in his apartment, and hire neighbors to operate them. Such tenement sweatshops dotted Chicago's West Side. So did the workshops of the country's largest clothing manufacturer, Hart, Schaffner & Marx.[6]

This manufacturing firm had been organized in Chicago in 1887 by a family of Bavarian immigrants who wanted to produce suits for their own retail stores. At first, the company contracted orders to tenement sweatshops, which employed an average of fifteen persons per shop. By 1905 the firm had purchased forty-eight of these sweatshops, bringing production under its direct supervision. The contractors sold their equipment to the company and became foremen, while the workers continued to perform their customary tasks for a new employer.[7]

Other large manufacturers of men's clothing in Chicago were the House of Kuppenheimer (founded in 1876 as a retail store); the Scotch Woolen Mills, Royal Tailors, and Society Brand. These Chicago clothing firms became pioneers in mass merchandising, associating their trade names with quality clothing through advertisements in such national magazines as *Colliers* and the *Saturday Evening Post*.[8]

By 1910 the men's clothing industry had become Chicago's largest employer—even larger than the stockyards—with a work force of 38,000 (not including home workers).[9] Sixty-five percent of these clothing workers were foreign born, with another 32 percent having foreign-born fathers.[10] The two largest ethnic groups were Polish Catholics and Bohemians, with substantial numbers of Italians and Eastern European Jews also working in the industry. Approximately half of these workers were women.[11] Employers furnishing information to the Immigration Commission of 1910 explained that, "To a certain extent immigrants have been employed in the clothing trades of Chicago, because of their peculiar skill. This is more especially true of the Bohemians, who are considered the best coat makers in the world; of the Scandinavians, who are the best workers on pants and vests; and of the Italians, who are the best hand sewers." After this lavish praise of foreign expertise, the report continued, "The chief explanation . . . given by the manufacturers . . . that American employees were not available was that . . . the Americans had a very marked prejudice against the business and refused to work at it."[12]

In Chicago, as in other cities, the industry was concentrated in several distinct districts. The sales and general offices and the cutting and shipping rooms were usually located in the same building, close to the central business district. The contract shops were located in surrounding areas near the workers' homes, in ethnic enclaves. Italian workers, who did most of the handwork, were squeezed into the West Side. Close by, thousands of Russian Jews operated some of the most crowded sweatshops in the city, specializing in coats and pants. Bohemians, located further west, produced coats. Sprinkled among them were Germans and Scandinavians, although these groups had almost disappeared from the industry by 1910. To the northwest was the large Polish district, whose garment workers specialized in pants.[13]

Sporadic attempts to organize garment workers in large cities had been only partially successful. The United Garment Workers of America was formed in 1891, at a convention called by the United Hebrew Trades and the Knights of Labor to combine organizations serving the men's garment industry. The delegates of cutters' locals, representing conservative American workmen, dominated the proceedings, and soon affiliated with the craft-oriented American Federation of Labor. By 1896 the officers of the UGWA had turned their attention to the union label as a way of discouraging purchase of clothing produced by nonunionized workers, a practice that discouraged and angered more radical tailors. The union label, while effective in influencing sales of overalls and work shirts that were produced in rural areas, scarcely touched the urban industry that specialized in fashionable male clothing.[14] In spite of its weaknesses the UGWA managed to organize some women. Three of the original twenty-four chapters were given to unions composed wholly of women, and mixed locals were common. The executive board usually had one or two women members. Chiefly, the UGWA factories were scattered in small towns, often formed on the initiative of employers desiring a union label.[15] The UGWA, which portrayed immigrants as a menace to American trade unions, dragging the native laborer down to an un-American level, could hardly have been enthusiastically organizing a work force composed primarily of immigrants.[16]

Disgusted with the prevailing attitude, a group of workers in Chicago formed a new organization in the late 1890s, the Special Order Clothing Makers' Union—a short-lived example of a successful women's union. Ellen Lindstrom led an active local of 850 skilled and Americanized Scandinavian women operators. The women's local persuaded the male pressmen's local to include the Swedish and Italian hand finishers in their successful wage negotiations of 1900. The American Federation of Labor subsequently acceded to pressure by the United Garment Workers to revoke the Special Order charter, but the independent union refused to join the UGWA because the Chicago group had been rebuffed in its earlier struggle by the UGWA. Because of its acceptance by the skilled tailors, however, the UGWA was able to pressure the women into signing a wage contract. When the agreement was later broken, and a lockout and strike of eight and one-half months followed, the women's union died.[17] The strike, and subsequent policy of employers not to hire union members or sympathizers, decimated the ranks of the United Garment Workers in the city. Only two UGWA cutters locals, with men working in a few of Chicago's small shops, survived between 1904 and 1910.[18] But the UGWA still retained the recognition of the AFL and the authority to speak for organized garment workers.

Employers, meanwhile, suffering from intense competition, consolidated and built cooperative organizations, one purpose of which was to resist the organization of unions. Louis Kuppenheimer, one of the founders of the Chicago Wholesale Clothiers' Association, described its objectives as exchanging credit information and facilitating the sale of goods. But the Chicago Wholesale Clothiers' Association (WCA), and the two national associations with which it was affiliated—the National Association of Clothiers and the National Association of Manufacturers—were also dedicated to resisting labor unions. A Chicago Labor Bureau constructed an elaborate blacklisting system, exposed by an Illinois Senate Committee investigating the garment workers' strike in 1911.[19] Although the firm of Hart, Schaffner & Marx did not join these organizations, it shared their attitude toward unions, refusing to hire anyone suspected of union sympathies.[20]

As the men's garment industry was consolidating, the workforce also was changing. A Chicago newspaper reporter lamented the passing of "the bright, healthy looking Scandinavian girl," replaced by Italian girls carrying big bundles from the workshop to their homes.

> Where the union workers were paid 15 cents for finishing a pair of pants, these Italian girls are doing the same work for 8 or 10 cents a pair . . . this is what the blessed open shop brings about in the clothing industry. . . . Thus do we see a race of people who have high ideals of a standard of life, supplanted by a race content to live on a lower scale."[21]

This was the atmosphere in which Hannah Shapiro (also known as Annie) and her coworkers decided to protest their employer's action—one that was by no means uncommon in the industry—to lower the piece rate agreed upon at the start of the season.

At eighteen, Hannah Shapiro was a veteran of Chicago's garment industry. The oldest child of a Russian immigrant family, she had gone to work in a small shop making bow ties when she was thirteen. Two years later, she moved on to Hart, Schaffner & Marx, where she earned $3 a week, for ten-hour days, pulling out bastings on coats. At one point she operated a pocket-cutting machine, receiving her highest weekly wage of $12. But the rates on that task had also been reduced. In September of 1910 she was earning $7 a week by seaming pockets.

In a 1976 interview, Hannah Shapiro Glick recalled that period of her life. In spite of her strike experience, she did not remember the Hart, Schaffner & Marx workshop as a terrible place. She noted the advantage of being allowed passes to leave early on Friday and of not being forced to work on Saturday, which pleased her father, an orthodox Jew. Nor did she mind walking to the fifth floor, or the petty fines, which she was skilled enough to avoid. But inevitably, there were grievances, and because she was friendly with many of her coworkers—Polish, Rumanian, and Italian, as well as Jewish—and also high spirited, Hannah often carried both their complaints and her own to the bosses. The cut in the piece rate was strongly resented. Despite fear of the consequences, Hannah Glick recalled: "We all went out; we had to be recognized as people."[22]

Three weeks elapsed between the first walkout and the time that most Hart, Schaffner & Marx workers were on strike. Communications were slow—there were no leaders to make decisions, no mechanism to call a strike. Spontaneous walkouts by angry workers in sweatshops were common. Usually the contractor either met their demands or fired the few involved. Employment in larger factories gave workers a better opportunity to communicate with each other, but much of the work was still done in shops scattered throughout the area.

Within a week, people from seven of the ten West Side pants shops refused the work from Shop No. 5.[23] Sidney Hillman, another recent arrival from Russia who worked in one of these shops, later recalled that at first these girls were a joke to the men, until finally some "bold spirits" decided to join them.[24] Another Jewish immigrant, Jacob Potofsky, attended a meeting of more than 500 people at Hull House, where workers aired their grievances. The next day he talked about the meeting to the Bohemian, Polish, and Jewish women with whom he worked. When the 300 people in the workshop started to leave the room, the foreman shut the doors in a vain effort to stop them.[25] After three weeks, at least 2,200 "bold spirits" were attending daily meetings.[26] Hart, Schaffner & Marx reacted to the walkout in a variety of ways. First the firm insisted that there was no strike. At the same time, Harry Hart authorized a rate adjustment in the shop in which the trouble had started. But by then things had gone too far, and there was no stopping the strike. Three weeks after the walkout the firm admitted that it had been forced to hire private detectives "to protect the weak and foreign born employees from intimidation by strike agitators."[27]

By the middle of October, Hart, Schaffner & Marx strikers were being joined by workers from Kuppenheimer's, Hirsch-Wickwire, and other clothing firms. Spokesmen for the Chicago Wholesale Clothiers' Association claimed that their workers had no grievances and were only striking out of sympathy for Hart, Schaffner & Marx workers, or because they feared violence from agitators—a position from which these spokesmen never deviated.

Although their workers were harassed by insults and by bricks hurled at them through the factory's windows, Kuppenheimer managed to maintain production throughout the strike. Louis Kuppenheimer prided himself on the "moral" atmosphere of his factory, in which there was no mixing of girls and boys. Indeed, he claimed that many parents appealed to him to hire their daughters because of the protection thus afforded them. Like most industrialists, Kuppenheimer refused to deal with a union because he claimed that workers were better off contracting as individuals. Furthermore, he considered open shops more American. As the strike continued, in addition to advertising for workers, he hired a New York agent to recruit strikebreakers. One entire floor of the factory was converted into sleeping and kitchen facilities to protect and isolate strikebreakers.[28]

Nevertheless, the walkout continued to spread. Strikers paraded past shops blowing whistles, a signal to workers to join them. One of the strikers, Clara Masilotti, recalled that, having heard about the signal, she told the other workers in her shop: "The first whistle we hear . . . means for us to strike. You cannot work for twelve cents a coat and I cannot baste 35 coats a day." One day 200 people appeared under the shop window. Masilotti was the first to respond to the whistles, and the "greenhorns" followed.[29]

Born in the United States, Clara Masilotti had been taken back to Italy by her family as an infant. She returned to Chicago in time to attend school for several years. At the age of thirteen she went to work in a date factory for thirty-two cents a day. Later she basted coats in a number of small shops, usually quitting after a disagreement with a foreman. In 1910 she was asked to be a forewoman and to teach the "greenhorns." She remembered that "the boss preferred Italians, Jews, all nationalities who can't speak English. They work like the devil for less wages." Masilotti lost her position as a forewoman when she refused to tell the workers that their wages had been cut. She returned to doing piecework. In the course of the 1910 strike, she became a leader in the Women's Trade Union League and a union organizer.[30]

At the time of the walkout, the strikers had approached Robert Noren, Chicago district president of the United Garment Workers of America. After consulting Thomas Rickert, the national president, Noren turned down their request for support. Rickert's reluctance stemmed from a "lack of faith in the possibilities of organizing these people," and the conviction that "it was just an over-night strike."[31]

Not until one month after the walkout did the UGWA finally issue a general strike call. Within a week of that call, on November 5, Thomas Rickert and Harry Hart signed a document agreeing on the selection of three persons to take up alleged grievances. The agreement also guaranteed that former employees could return to work without discrimination should they affiliate with UGWA. It specifically excluded the question of any shop organization.[32] When the agreement was submitted to strikers at a meeting at Hod Carriers' Hall, it was overwhelmingly rejected. The cutters—the aristocrats of the industry—had elected Sidney Hillman to explain why the settlement was unsatisfactory. Rickert was hooted with cries of "sold out," "betrayed," "traitor," and was forced to flee from the hall.[33] This episode was followed by a near riot when the UGWA was unable to honor 10,000 of its strike benefit vouchers.[34]

In the meantime the strikers were seeking support from a variety of sources. A delegation of women had approached the Women's Trade Union League, founded in 1903 by social reformers and settlement-house workers to support the efforts of working women. Members of the WTUL, moved by what they heard, promised to help if the Chicago Federation of Labor (CFL) would endorse the strike.[35] The WTUL would provide aid to pickets, speakers for meetings, relief aid, and contact with the general public, which encouraged much favorable publicity.

After listening to an appeal by the strikers, the Chicago Federation of Labor delegates were moved to declare that "this firm [Hart, Schaffner & Marx] and others of like character were nothing more or less than slave driving institutions of the worst imaginable kind, and . . . gradually but surely, getting worse year by year." The day after the strikers rejected the Hart-Rickert agreement, the CFL declared its support of the garment workers.[36]

A Joint Strike Conference Board assumed leadership of the garment worker's strike. The CFL's president, John Fitzpatrick, became chairman; Edward Nockles, the CFL vice-president, vice-chairman; Agnes Nestor, a glove worker and president of the Chicago WTUL, and Margaret Dreier Robins, president of the National WTUL and a member of the CFL Board, represented the WTUL; and Robert Noren and Samuel Landers represented the UGWA. A committee of thirty-five strikers met with the board to maintain liason between it and the ranks. The board unanimously adopted an agreement stipulating the need for a union shop, minimum hours with time and a half paid for overtime, and the establishment of grievance procedures.[37]

Several other community groups rallied to support the struggling clothing workers, including the city's socialist organizations and a Citizens Committee. The *Chicago Daily Socialist* strongly supported the strikers; two special strike editions were sold, earning over $3,000 for the strike fund as well as spreading the workers' story.[38] The Socialist Women's Strike Committee raised an additional $5,400.[39]

Chicago's prominent reformers established a Citizens Committee chaired by Rabbi Emil Hirsch, whose congregation included some of the clothing manufacturers. A report prepared by the committee and given widespread attention by the press "revealed serious difficulties in all of the shops." The report denied that union agitators were responsible for the walkout and declared that the strike was justified. It went on to recommend some form of shop organization.[40] Citizens Committee members, often behind the scenes, became active in attempts to mediate the strike.

Jane Addams attended the first conference between Harry Hart and Thomas Rickert. Harry Hart, a Hull House supporter, became embittered by the role of Hull House women and the Citizens Committee. Jane Addams continued her role of mediator although she stated in a letter written November 22: "I do not believe that there is the least chance for arbitration now and of course no chance that the strikers will win." She also expressed concern over the heavy involvement of Ellen Gates Starr, cofounder of Hull House, who refused to accept any prospect of the strikers' defeat.[41]

To sustain the strike through an especially cold and blustery Chicago winter, the Joint Conference Board commenced a massive fund drive, ultimately collecting $110,000. Approximately 65 percent of the funds came from organized labor, 10 percent from socialist organizations, and the remainder from appeals organized by the Women's Trade Union League. In addition to financial aid, the Jewish Labor Federation donated $36,000 worth of meal tickets, while the Bakers Union contributed 60,000 loaves of bread.[42]

Gertrude Barnum, Margaret Dreier Robins, and other WTUL members took "girl strikers" to meetings all over Chicago to plead for support. A breakfast meeting across the street from the old Chicago Daily News building was well attended by newspapermen who frequented the restaurant. "Over a simple little breakfast the girls talked their hearts out and explained their problems in a natural fashion to a few friends."[43] One reporter wrote that "Annie Shapiro . . . told her story in such a dramatic manner in broken English that her hearers were moved to tears." Clara Masilotti revealed that she had been coerced into working faster for less pay. Bessie Abramovitz explained that during rush periods she was often forced to work twelve or thirteen hours without extra pay, despite the Illinois ten-hour law, while during the slack periods she had to stay in the workshop all day for only one or two hours' pay. Anna Cassetteri carried additional material home to earn nine or ten dollars a week. Sixteen-year-old Anna Rudnitsky had been forced to sew slowly, in order to keep her pay low. In spite of intimidation by the foreman, she led 300 young women out of Hart, Schaffner & Marx Shop No. 11. Bina Wool testified that she had gone from place to place looking for better conditions, but found them all the same.[44]

Hannah Shapiro did not confine herself to addressing society women and reporters. For the first time in her life she entered saloons to plead for her cause. One bartender contributed fifty cents saying: "That's all I've got, little girl, for since the strike started nobody pays for a drink."[45]

The most successful undertaking of the board was the operation of six commissary stores that provided appropriate fare for the different ethnic neighborhoods. Shop chairmen were responsible for distributing tickets for prepackaged weekly supplies. Reformers took advantage of the opportunity to educate the immigrants. Among these reformers were Zelie P. Emerson and Katharine Coman, who noted: "Many foreigners learned the nutritive value of articles of food hitherto unknown, such as beans and oatmeal. Hereafter, they will probably demand a higher class of ordinary groceries."[46] Tickets for fifteen-cent meals were distributed to single men and women without family support. A special fund of two dollars a week was set aside for some Jewish and Polish girls who came to Margaret Dreier Robins in tears because it would be indecent for them to go into a restaurant with strange people. Robins was less sympathetic when a group of boys requested laundry money. They were told to wash their own laundry like the girls.[47] Twenty-two carloads of food and 200,000 loaves of bread were distributed to over 11,000 families a week.[48]

Of special concern were the 5,000 babies whose families were now unemployed. "Strike babies"—1,250 were born during the strike—received layettes and milk through settlement houses. Appeals for financial aid were sent on postcards carrying the heading, "Sacred Motherhood," and picturing a woman nursing a baby and working on a sewing machine while several small children played among unfinished garments.[49]

The reformers were less successful in controlling the streets. Early efforts by the strikers to induce all the workers to join them were relatively calm. But as the weeks dragged on, and employers began to import strikebreakers, violence escalated on the part of strikers, nonstrikers, and the Chicago police.[50]

A Women's Trade Union League picket committee chaired by Emma Steghagen "undertook the twofold task of picketing with the girls and of patrolling the streets for their protection."[51] After being handled roughly by the police, Steghagen and Ellen Gates Starr protested publicly as well as officially. Starr had been grabbed insolently and told that if she did not go away, she would be sent to the police station, even if she was a social worker. Steghagen was given more explicit instructions: "Go home and wash your dishes."[52]

A daily pattern was set by the end of the first month. Meetings were held in at least thirty-four halls scattered throughout the garment district. Speakers orated in several languages, sending cheering strikers to the streets, where they marched past tailor shops, blew whistles, and enjoined other workers to abandon their machines.

Strikers pouring out of meeting halls encountered 200 regular policemen and 50 mounted police—called Cossacks by the Socialists—as well as private detectives hired by the manufacturers to guard their establishments.[53] Newspapers portrayed the women as being more violent than the men in resisting efforts of bluecoats to disperse mobs.[54] One riot erupted when fourteen-year-old Josie Mielewski and her chief lieutenant led a mob of 200 against police blocking the entrance to Kuh, Nathan, Fisher & Company. Accounts varied as to whether the police were forced by armed rioters to use revolvers, or whether the police took the initiative in setting upon hundreds of workers.[55] The dispersal of women complicated matters for police used to handling crowds of men. A study of policing of labor disputes in Chicago states that the police were cowed by women who "often fought and scratched and bit and pulled hair like demons—and no man likes to hit a woman."[56]

Just before Thanksgiving, strikebreakers attracted to the city by employers' agents and advertisements began to arrive in Chicago in large numbers. Pickets were sent to guard the railroad depots and clashes increased. Occasionally appeals to potential strikebreakers to go home succeeded—in one case the United Garment Workers paid the return fares of thirty-five arrivals. But more often the outcome was less peaceful.[57] The Chicago Railroad Company appealed to the police for protection after twenty women set upon nonunion Italians inside a streetcar.[58]

Out-of-town strikebreakers were not the only source of trouble. A substantial number of garment workers had never joined the strikers. As the tension mounted, many workers were chased and attacked by strikers on their way home. Private guards were hired by employers to escort strikebreakers to elevated stations and to their homes.[59]

Alarmed by the mounting violence, City Council member and social reformer Charles E. Merriam of the University of Chicago proposed that the City Council, headed by Mayor Fred Busse, mediate the strike. The Joint Conference Board—with approval by the Chicago Federation of Labor and the strikers' committee—and Hart, Schaffner & Marx cooperated with these efforts. All these parties believed that if a settlement could be reached with the largest manufacturer, the others would follow. But the representatives of the Chicago Wholesale Clothiers' Association tenaciously refused to meet with union representatives; nor would they talk with arbitrators appointed by the Illinois Board of Arbitration.[60]

Joseph Schaffner and his partner, Harry Hart, appear to have been genuinely shocked by the outbreak of the strike. They had prided themselves on their modern, sanitary workshops, offering conditions that compared favorably with those prevailing in the sweatshops. As the strike progressed, however, it became clear that many of the oppressive conditions typical of the sweatshops had persisted. In 1916, testifying before the United States Industrial Regulations Commission, while insisting that the strikers' grievances were minor in character, Schaffner admitted that they had been allowed to accumulate to the point of creating in workers "a feeling of distrust and enmity toward their immediate superiors." Schaffner confessed that he had been "so badly informed of the conditions . . . that he had concluded that the strike should have occurred much sooner."[61] The owners were too absorbed in the merchandising aspects of their business to pay attention to what was happening in the workshops. The foremen, themselves working on piece rates, and eager to produce more for less, imposed typical sweatshop conditions—erratic pay scales, speedups in production, fines, and other petty persecutions.[62]

Early in December two strikers were killed. Charles Lazinskas, one of three strikers arguing with two young workers who were being escorted home, was shot by a private detective.[63] During a skirmish that broke out when strikebreakers tried to enter Kuppenheimer's, a policeman killed Frank Nagreckis and severely injured his companion.[64] In both cases, the crowds turned on the police and private detectives. Priests officiating at the funerals of the two Lithuanians asked for donations to the strike fund. Approximately 30,000 strikers and sympathizers, led by bands playing the Marseillaise, paraded through the West Side following Lazinskas' funeral. They had been refused permission to march past the clothing firms' central offices in the Loop. In defiance of another police stipulation banning red flags, marchers carried red and white banners inscribed with rousing slogans. The marchers ended up at West Side Ball Park, where they heard passionate oratory delivered in six languages. Charles Murphy, owner of the Chicago Cubs, donated coffee and sandwiches as well as the ball park.[65]

By the time of Lazinskas' funeral, Hart, Schaffner & Marx had presented their proposal to the City Council mediators, and the terms had been accepted by the Joint Conference Board. To the consternation of their leaders, the strikers rejected the compromise. After hearing funeral orations urging them to stick together until all the manufacturers conceded their rights, strikers went to their separate meeting halls. Workers who spoke in favor of the settlement were drowned out. Father Lawczyinski, of St. Mary's Independent Catholic Church, exhorted Polish workers to hold out for a closed shop and, holding up a crucifix, called on them to make a solemn promise not to accept the terms.[66]

At a meeting at Hod Carriers' Hall, emotions ran so high that John Fitzpatrick and Margaret Dreier Robins were unable to speak. Strikers at the meeting felt betrayed. Discussion was delayed until the agreement could be printed in nine languages and an educational campaign launched. After ten days the Joint Board acknowledged defeat.[67]

While reformers were pressing for an end to the walkout, a split occurred in the socialist ranks. Robert Dvorak, reporter for the *Chicago Daily Socialist*, was reprimanded by Raymond Robins (husband of Margaret Dreier Robins) and Emma Pischel, a socialist working with the WTUL, for writing about the strong rejection of the agreement. Robins argued that the strikers were in a desperate condition and that the funds "were not large enough to continue."

Pischel "upbraided him for sticking with the stupid strikers, who knew not what was best for them." A group of Socialists allied with the Chicago Federation of Labor were responsible for arranging Dvorak's dismissal.[68]

Disagreement about the strike among Socialists was reflected in another incident involving the *Chicago Daily Socialist*. The editors cut so as to alter an address by Eugene Debs in December, in which he had made an appeal on behalf of the garment workers. "If the workingmen of Chicago were not inert as clods, white-livered excuses for men, they would rise like a whirlwind in defense of these shivering, starving children at their doors" was edited to read: "Let the workingmen rise like a whirlwind in defense of these shivering, starving children at their doors." Another section, calling for industrial unions and condemning craft unionism, was completely eliminated. What did remain intact was the plea to men not to allow women and children to suffer. "Women and children by thousands, who spend their wretched lives making clothes for others are themselves naked, without shoes, their wan features distorted by the fangs and pangs of starvation."[69]

The violence accelerated. Just before Christmas John Donnelly was delivering a wagon filled with unfinished garments to home workers from a nonunion tailor shop. Three men shot the eighteen-year-old to death, then disappeared into the crowd. According to his mother, he had been threatened earlier and had intended to quit the next day.[70] Since people lived as well as worked in the neighborhoods in which such clashes were occurring, nonstrikers became unwitting victims. Ferdinand Weiss, walking in the vicinity of a group that was arguing with strikebreakers and private detectives, was killed by a gun fired by a private detective. Mourning garment workers attended his funeral en masse.[71] The fifth victim of the strike, Fred Reinhart, who was a guard at Hart, Schaffner & Marx, was apparently much hated by the strikers. On January 3 he was ambushed and killed by strikers while escorting two young strikebreakers home.[72]

At the beginning of January, two manufacturers who were members of the Chicago Wholesale Clothiers' Association agreed to sign contracts with the United Garment Workers, thus breaking the impasse. But the strike was far from over.

The settlement with Hart, Schaffner & Marx was accepted, finally, on January 14, 1911. It provided for the reemployment of all strikers and guaranteed that there would be no discrimination in favor of or against membership in the union. Although no prior settlement on wages and working conditions was made, the agreement called for the establishment of an Arbitration Committee to settle current and future grievances. No adjustment in wages or working conditions was to take place until after the workers returned to their jobs.[73]

On January 17, Hannah Shapiro, Bessie Abramovitz, and 2,000 of their fellow workers were greeted by their foremen as they returned to their jobs at the Hart, Schaffner & Marx workshops.[74]

The approximately 18,000 people still on strike against those Clothiers' Association members who had not settled, elected a committee to continue to strike. They denounced the agreement with Hart, Schaffner & Marx, the Chicago Federation of Labor, the Women's Trade Union League, and the United Garment Workers. Representatives of the radical Industrial Workers of the World appeared at these meetings, and tried, according to one organizer, "to revitalize the strike."[75] Several foreign language newspapers disclosed discontent among immigrant workers. A Bohemian newspaper charged unfair treatment by the leadership. Bohemian strikers conducted their own relief work through an independent group that had formed early in the strike, with Alberta Hnetynka as secretary. The halls rented by the Bohemian workers were the only ones open to the protesters. *La Paroladel Socialisti* complained that Italian garment makers residing in the Hull House district were refused meal tickets and no longer allowed to use Hull House for daily meetings because they rejected the proposed agreement with Hart, Schaffner & Marx.[76]

On the other side, most of the members of the Chicago Wholesale Clothiers' Association refused to budge, in spite of tremendous public pressure and negative publicity, including an investigation by the Illinois Senate. In the face of this intransigence, Thomas Rickert, president of the UGWA, took drastic action. On February 3, without consulting the Joint Strike Conference Board, let alone the strikers who were still attending meetings, he called off the strike. This time the leaders of the CFL and the WTUL, as well as the strikers, felt betrayed. Robins called Rickert's action a "hunger bargain."[77] As Sidney Hillman later recalled, the great majority of the workers

> were forced to return to their old miserable conditions, through the back door; and happy were those who were taken back. Many who had partici-pated in the 1910 strike were victimized for months afterward. They were

forced to look for other employment and to wait until their record in the strike was forgotten.[78]

After four and a half months the strike dissolved. At Hart, Schaffner & Marx, most of the workers returned to their jobs with only the promise that a Board of Arbitration would adjust their grievances. One of the board's first acts allowed UGWA representation. The board would prove successful in the resolution of differences over work rules and wages and in the prevention of future strikes. A few other firms signed union agreements, but the Wholesale Clothiers' Association steadfastly refused to arbitrate, cooperate with the union, or to accept other offers of mediation. The uprising had started in the shops of Hart, Schaffer & Marx but because grievances in most companies were similar, the walkout spread. Reformers had been mistaken in their belief that once the largest firm acquiesced, the others would cooperate. Not until 1919, after two more strikes, did the majority of Chicago's firms agree to deal with workers' representatives.

The Board of Arbitration that formed—with Carl Meyer representing Hart, Schaffner & Marx and Clarence Darrow representing the workers—proved effective. Whereas the Protocol of Peace hammered out in New York City had to deal with a multitude of companies, these arbitrators dealt with only one firm.

The men's garment workers in New York City experienced a strike two years later in which there was a similar encounter between immigrant laborers and the United Garment Workers. Thomas Rickert again concluded an unsatisfactory truce. At the 1914 UGWA convention held in Nashville, Tennessee, dissidents formed a new union, the Amalgamated Clothing Workers of America (ACWA). In 1915 the ACWA again tackled the Chicago market. Instead of taking shape as a "spontaneous rebellion," the 1915 strike was coordinated by the ACWA, which submitted demands to the Wholesale Clothiers' Assocation. A mass meeting endorsed a strike, but the people continued working until informed by shop chairmen that the negotiations had failed. Manufacturers requested police protection before the walkout. A few more companies accepted unionization— but on the whole, the strike failed. Not until another strike in 1919 did the Amalgamated Clothing Workers penetrate the holdout firms.

When the Chicago market finally was unionized, following the conflict in 1919, many manufacturers left the city in search of more tractable workers (in the 1920s that meant heading south), in order to remain competitive. Through pioneering industrial unionism, the garment unions helped to improve working conditions and to stabilize the needle trades. But the garment unions have never solved the basic problems arising from extreme competition. An important commodity that attracted the clothing trades to urban America in 1900 was disappearing from Chicago in the 1920s: abundant, flexible, cheap labor. Ironically, the improvement of wages and working conditions had the effect feared by so many manufacturers—it threatened their profits in a highly competitive industry.

The Chicago garment strikes played a major role in American labor history. The significant contribution made by the WTUL to the Chicago strike of 1910–1911 represented one of the league's greatest historic successes. As a delegate to the CFL and the Joint Committee operating the strike, Margaret Dreier Robins's role proved crucial. Women allies in the community were observed on the streets aiding pickets and collecting relief, and were recognized for their work behind the scenes. Working women also behaved in a fearless fashion, as they put down their shears and seized their picket signs. But very few union women transcended the image and function of "girl striker" to become leader, although women comprised half of the work force and half of the union membership. The older women failed to cultivate the leadership potential of their protégées, or to hand down a tradition of female leadership. Male union members, not surprisingly, showed no interest in promoting leadership among women.

The ACWA recognized the importance of the 1910–1911 strike for its development of leaders. In this connection, the name of Bessie Abramovitch was occasionally mentioned. Abramovitch served as a member of the Strike Committee, then on the Hart, Schaffner & Marx grievance committee and trade board formed after the strike.[79] She represented her Chicago UGWA vest makers' local at the Nashville convention and was one of the delegates (along with Frank Rosenblum and Anzuino Marempietri) fighting to seat the New York delegation. Only one other woman—Miss S. Goldblatt, of Rochester—was among the mavericks who formed the new union. Abramovitch also assumed an active role as a delegate from her vest makers' local at the New York convention, two months later, along with Miss Goldblatt, two women from Baltimore, and one hundred and thirty men.[80]

The May Day parade of 1916 became a wedding march, as Bessie Abramovitch and Sidney Hillman led a large assemblege two days before their marriage. Their honeymoon was spent in Rochester at the ACWA convention. Upon her marriage, Abramovitch resigned her post as business agent of the ACWA and as organizer of the WTUL.[81] Later she became a vice-president of ACWA where her presence reminded the men that more than half their members were women. During the strike, Clara Masolotti, an effective speaker before women's groups, also became a WTUL organizer. Between jobs, she went to New York and probably participated in the Lawrence strike. She remained active in the labor movement until 1925. After 1925 she moved to California, where she operated a flower shop and lived with her married younger sister. She spent her last years in England with another sibling.[82]

Hannah Shapiro was pleased to return to work at Hart, Schaffner & Marx, following settlement of the strike. Would the strike have taken place if Shapiro had not protested? The other women had been afraid to complain; the men, afraid of losing their jobs, laughed at her. Shapiro herself agonized over her boldness, feeling guilty because her financial position differed from that of the mass of strikers: her father was able to support her. During the strike she had gone regularly to union meetings and, encouraged by Agnes Nestor, she spoke before women's groups. But once the strike ended, Shapiro did not become involved with either the union or the WTUL. She was proud that her earnings helped her brother to attend college. Shapiro met her future husband at a party during the strike. He was also a Russian immigrant, but his superior knowledge of English enabled him to be a printer. Two years after their meeting, Shapiro quit her job to marry and raise a family.

Hannah Shapiro Glick did not make her experiences part of her family history. She never mentioned them to her daughter until some pictures of her appeared in a bicentennial exhibit, "Forgotten Contributors: Women in Illinois History." Then, at the prompting of her daughter, Glick contacted the director of the exhibit and thus enabled historians to include her forgotten contribution.[83] Most important, the old woman reminded them of the feelings of the young girls: "We had to be recognized as people."

NOTES

1. Mary O'Reilly, "After the Strike," from Women's Trade Union League of Chicago, "Official Report of the Strike Committee" (Chicago, 1911; repr. from *Life and Labor*), 40.

2. Nancy Schrom Dye, "Creating a Feminist Alliance," *Feminist Studies*, 2 (1975), 111–125. See also Alice Kessler-Harris, "Where Are the Organized Women Workers?" *Feminist Studies*, 3 (Fall 1975), 92–110.

3. WTUL, "Official Report," Committee," 3.

4. Matthew Josephson, *Sidney Hillman: Statesman of American Labor* (Garden City, N.Y.: Doubleday, 1952), 51 (quote), 58, 62, 69–70.

5. Charles P. Neill, *Men's Ready-Made Clothing*, 443–444, *Report on Conditions of Women and Child Wage Earners in the United States*, 61st Congress, 2d Session, Senate Document #645 (Washington, 1911), vol. 2.

6. Factory Inspectors of Illinois, Third Annual Report, Dec. 15, 1895 (Springfield: 1896), 56. Neill, *Men's Clothing*, 492–494, 443–480. Florence Kelley, "The Sweated Industry," in *Hull-House Maps & Papers* (Chicago: Thomas Y. Cromwell, 1895) 28: Harry A. Cobrin, *The Men's Clothing Industry* (New York: Fairchild, 1970), 75–76.

7. Hart, Schaffner & Marx, "Hart, Schaffner & Marx History" (Chicago, April 1977, mimeograph); Abraham Hart, "The 50 Years of Hart, Schaffner & Marx, (Chicago, April 4, 1937, reprint of speech); Sara L. Hart, *The Pleasure Is Mine* (Chicago: Valentine-Newman, 1947), 118–119; Factory Inspectors of Illinois, *Third Annual Report*, 8–9.

8. Robert James Myers, "The Economic Aspects of the Production of Men's Clothing," PhD diss., University of Chicago, 1937, 21, 24–25, 381–382.

9. United States Department of Commerce, Bureau of the Census, *Thirteenth Census of Manufacturers* (1910), IX, 296, 299.

10. *Immigrants in Industries*, vol. 11 of *Clothing Manufacturing*, 61st Congress, 2d Session, Senate Document # 66 (1911), XI, 433–434.

11. Neill, *Men's Clothing*, 33–34, 45–46, gives the following percentages for Chicago workers:

Ethnic Group	% Women	% Men	% Children
Polish	23	13	32
Bohemian	26	16	37
Italian	12	7	9
Jewish	12	44	6
Scandinavian	11	4	0
German	9	5	10
American-born	1.5	0.5	1.3

Women accounted for 53 percent of the Chicago total. The proportion of women as well as ethnic groups varied among the five cities studied—Chicago, New York, Rochester, Philadelphia, and Baltimore.

12. *Clothing Manufacturing*, 434.

13. Myers, "Economic Aspects," 40–41, 46.

14. Abraham M. Rogoff, "Formative Years of the Jewish Labor Movement in the United States (1890–1900)," PhD diss., Columbia University, 1945, 46–47; Charles Zaretz, *The Amalgamated Clothing Workers of America* (New York, 1934), 80–82, 88–89.

15. John B. Andrews and W. D. P. Bliss, *History of Women in Trade Unions*, vol. 10, *Report on Conditions of Women & Child Wage-earners in the United States*, 61st Congress, 2d Session, Senate Document #645, (Washington, 1911), 160, 168–170. The exceptions were Detroit and Boston where UGWA members were immigrants.

16. Melvyn Dubofsky, "Organized Labor and the Immigrant in New York City, 1900–1918" *Labor History*, 2 (Spring 1961), 188–189.

17. Andrews and Bliss, *Women in Trade Unions*, 164–167. Margaret Hoblitt, "A Labor Tragedy," *The Commons*, 10 (May 1905), 273–281. Ellen Lindstrom served on the WTUL board for a short time, then moved to Iowa to edit a Swedish newspaper.

18. Illinois General Assembly, "Special Senate Committee to Investigate the Garment Workers Strike," 47th General Assembly (1911), testimony of Thomas Rickert, Feb. 6, 1911.

19. "Committee to Investigate the Garment Workers Strike," testimony of Louis Kuppenheimer, Jan. 26, 1911; Martin J. Issacs, Jan. 20 and Feb. 2, 1911; Thomas Rickert, Feb. 6, 1911. Cobrin, *Men's Clothing Industry*, 82–89. The Labor Bureau was not disbanded until 1919.

20. Robert Dvorak, "The Chicago Garment Workers," *International Socialist Review*, 11 (Dec. 1910) no. 6, 353–355. According to Dvorak, the WCA also formed to gain strength against the most formidable competitor, Hart, Schaffner, & Marx.

21. Luke Grant, *Chicago Inter-Ocean (I-O)*, Apr. 23, 1905; and Hoblitt, "A Labor Tragedy," 278. See also *Chicago American*, Mar. 17, 1905, where strike breakers were described as "clad in dirty garments, with shawls for their only wrap, and their sleek, greasy black hair combed tight without covering."

22. "Committee to Investigate the Garment Workers Strike," testimony of Anna Shapiro, II, 242–272. Videotaped interview with Hannah Shapiro Glick, by Rebecca Sive-Tomeshivsky (Chicago: University of Illinois Chicago Circle, 1976). The names of the other young women have been lost. Mrs. Glick did not remember them, and did not think Bessie Abramovitch was among them. (However, Josephson, *Sidney Hillman*, 47, says she was among the "fourteen.") Shapiro was the only female worker interviewed by the Illinois Senate Commission.

23. *Chicago Daily Socialist (CDS)*, Sept. 30, 1910, 1.

24. Josephson, *Sidney Hillman*, 38, 47–48.

25. Interview with Jacob Potofsky from Elizabeth Balanoff, director, "Oral History Project in Labor and Immigration History" (Chicago: Roosevelt University, Aug. 4, 1970), 4–5.

26. *CDS*, Oct. 11, 1910, 1.

27. "Committee to Investigate the Garment Workers Strike," testimony of Harry Hart. *CDS*, Oct. 12, 13, 1910, 1; *Chicago Record-Herald (R-H)*, Oct. 15, 1910, 5; *Chicago Daily News (CDN)*, Oct. 15, 1910, Oct. 17, 1910, 1; 1 (quote).

28. "Committee to Investigate the Garment Workers Strike," testimony of Harry Wolf, superintendent at The House of Kuppenheimer; testimony of Kuppenheimer. *CDS*, Jan. 28, 1911, 1, reported that Wolf "cringed with the same fear which has filled hearts of women and girls who have stood before him: The 'bully of the sweatshop' pleaded for mercy."

29. "Bricks without Straw—Story of an Italian Girl among Striking Garment Workers in Chicago, taken down by Katharine Coman," *Survey*, 25 (Dec. 10, 1910), 424–428.

30. "Bricks without Straw," *CDS*, Nov. 21, 1910, 1; article written by Masilotti, "We Can't Make Our Living"; *Trib*, Mar. 3, 1912, pt. 7, 1.

31. "Committee to Investigate the Garment Workers Strike," testimony of Thomas Rickert. Amalgamated Clothing Workers of America, *The Clothing Workers of Chicago, 1910–1922* (Chicago, 1922), 27.

32. WTUL, "Official Report," 11–12.

33. Potofsky interview, 6. *I-O*, Nov. 6, 1910, 1, 4; *Trib*, Nov. 6, 1910, 1.

34. ACWA, "Clothing Workers," 34–35; WTUL, "Official Report," 13–17; Josephson, *Sidney Hillman*, 50–51. Zelie P. Emerson and Katharine Coman, "Co-operative Philanthropy, Administration of Relief during the Strike of the Chicago Garment Workers," *Survey*, 25 (Mar. 4, 1911), 942–948.

35. WTUL, "Official Report," 4–5.

36. Josephson, *Sidney Hillman*, 50. "Extracts from the minutes of the Chicago Federation of Labor," Nov. 6, 1910, John Fitzpatrick Papers, Chicago Historical Society.

37. WTUL, "Official Report," 12–13. "Extracts CFL," Nov. 6 and 20, 1910, Fitzpatrick Papers. There is little information about the "committee of 35."

38. ACWA, *Clothing Workers*, 27. The first *CDS* articles appeared Sept. 30 and Oct. 1, 1910. Also see Robert Dvorak, "The Garment Workers Strike Lost, Who Was to Blame?," *International Socialist Review*, 9 (March, 1911), 550–551. *CDS* Strike Editions, Nov. 21 and Dec. 18, 1910; *CDS*, Nov. 6, 1910, 1; employees also donated their time. See also Mary Jo Buhle, "Socialist Women and the 'Girl Strikers,' Chicago, 1910" *Signs*, 1 (Summer 1976), 1043–1046. Buhle interprets the special strike extra as a phenomenal success, and details its planning.

Despite the obvious bias, *Chicago Daily Socialist* articles provided the most complete daily chronical of the strike. The other papers skipped periods of relative quiet, describing "riots," although they were usually supportive of the needs of the strikers. Community group efforts to end the strike also were stressed in the daily press.

39. WTUL, "Official Report," 41.

40. Report of the subcommittee of the Citizens Committee, "Concerning the Garment Workers Strike," (Chicago, Nov. 5, 1910). WTUL, "Official

Report," 24–25. *Trib*, Oct. 30 and Nov. 3, 4, 5, 6, 1910; *CDN*, Nov. 10, 11, 1910; *R-H*, Oct. 31, 1910 (lists participants), Nov. 1, 2, 7, 1910.

41. *I-0*, Nov. 6, 1910; *Trib*, Nov. 5, 1910. Hart, *The Pleasure Is Mine*, Jane Addams to Darling Mary Rozet Smith, Nov. 16, 1910; Nov. 22, 1910; Nov. 24, 1910, Jane Addams Papers, Hull House, University of Illinois Chicago Circle.

42. WTUL, "Official Report," 17, 41–42. "Extracts CFL," Nov. 20, 1910, and Feb. 19, 1911, Fitzpatrick Papers.

43. Katharine Coman, "Chicago at the Front," *Life and Labor*, 1 (Jan. 1911), 11.

44. *I-0*, Nov. 2, 1910; *CDS*, Nov. 2, 1910; see also *CDS* Nov. 4, 21, 1910.

45. *I-0*, Dec. 12, 1910. See also Hannah Shapiro Glick interview.

46. Emerson and Coman, "Co-operative Philanthropy," 942–948.

47. Mary E. Dreier, *Margaret Dreier Robins* (New York: Island Press Cooperative, 1950), 74.

48. WTUL, "Official Report," 17.

49. WTUL, "Official Report," 20. *R-H*, Nov. 13, 26, 1910, 2; *Trib*, Nov. 28, 1910, 3; Jan. 6, 1911, 3, other newspapers for that date.

50. Howard Barton Myers, "The Policing of Labor Disputes in Chicago: A Case Study," PhD diss., University of Chicago, 1929, 646; for the 1910 strike, see 701–727. Myers classified the 1910 strike as second in violence only to the teamsters strike of 1905.

51. WTUL, "Official Report," 10–11. See ACWA, *Clothing Workers*, 30–31; the picket committee was "perhaps most important service rendered."

Rules for Pickets:

Don't walk in groups of more than two or three.

Don't stand in front of the shop; walk up and down the block.

Don't stop the person you want to talk to; walk alongside of him.

Don't get excited and shout when you are talking.

Don't put your hand on the person you are speaking to.

Don't touch his sleeve or button; this may be construed as a technical assault.

Don't call anyone "scab" or use abusive language of any kind.

Plead, persuade, appeal, but do not threaten.

If a policeman arrests you and you are sure you have committed no offense, take his number and give it to your Union officer.

52. WTUL, "Official Report," 10–11. ACWA, *Clothing Workers*, 29–32. *I-0*, Nov. 2, 3, 1910; *R-H*, Nov. 2, 3, 24, 25, 1910; *Trib*, Nov. 3, 5, 24, 25, 1910.

53. Myers, "Policing," 701–702.

54. *R-H*, Oct. 16, 1910. The article said that ten strikers and five policemen were hurt and identified the mob of 150 women and girls as wives, sweethearts,

and daughters of strikers. Later articles recognized that the women were strikers; see *CDN*, Oct. 16, 1910; *I-0*, Oct. 16, 1910. There are many other newspaper examples.

55. *CDN*, Nov. 2, 1910; *Trib*, Nov. 2, 3, 1910 (75 arrests, police forced by rioters); *R-H*, Nov. 3, 1910 (37 arrests, police forced); *I-0*, Nov. 3, 1910 (nearly 100 arrests); *CDS*, Nov. 3, 1910 (4 loads of people arrested, workers set upon by police).

56. Myers, "Policing," 707.

57. *CDS*, Nov. 26, 1910.

58. *I-0*, Nov. 18, 1910; *CDN*, Nov. 17, 1910.

59. *CDS*, Nov. 21, 28, 29, 1910; *CDN*, Nov. 22, 28, 1910; *I-0*, Nov. 26, 29, 1910; *R-H*, Nov. 26, 29, 1910; *Trib*, Dec. 13, 1910.

60. WTUL, "Official Report," 20–24. "Extracts CFL," Dec. 4, 1910, Fitzpatrick Papers, 4–5. *CDS*, Nov. 30, Dec. 3, 5, 1910; *CDN*, Nov. 29, 30, Dec. 1, 3, 1910; *I-0*, Nov. 29, 30, Dec. 2, 4, 5, 1910; *R-H*, Nov. 29, 30, Dec. 1, 4, 1910; *Trib*, Nov. 29 through Dec. 5, 1910. See also Dvorak, "The Chicago Garment Workers," 358, for the same attitude expressed by Socialists. "Committee to Investigate the Garment Workers Strike," testimony of Harry Hart, Emil Rose, president of National Wholesale Clothiers' Association, and Charles Pies, member of State Board of Arbitration. *CDS*, Jan. 11, 17, 1911; *Trib*, Jan. 9, 10, 1911; *R-H*, Jan. 10, 1911.

61. Frank P. Walsh, 64th Congress, Commission on Industrial Relations, *Final Report and Testimony*, Senate Document #415, 1916, I, 565.

62. Hart, *The Pleasure Is Mine*, 135–138. *Joseph Schaffner 1848–1919: Recollections and Impressions of His Associates* (Chicago: private printing, 1920), 85–87.

63. Myers, "Policing," 704. ACWA, *Clothing Workers*, 32–33. *CDS*, Dec. 5, 1910; *R-H*, Dec. 3, 1910; *Trib*, Dec. 3, 1910.

64. *CDS*, Dec. 16, 1910; *CDN*, Dec. 15, 1910; *R-H*, Dec. 16, 1910; *Trib*, Dec. 16, 1910; *I-0*, Dec. 16, 1910, confuses circumstances of the two deaths.

65. Myers, "Policing," 704. ACWA, *Clothing Workers*, 32–33. *CDS*, Dec. 8, 1910, reported a crowd of 50,000; *CDN*, Dec. 7, 1910; *Trib*, Dec. 8, 1910; *I-0*, Dec. 8, 1910, red and white banners with quotes: "A union shop means more bread & milk for our children"; "Give the fathers work and the children will go to school"; "Capitol is organized & labor must be organized"; "Child labor is child murder"; "We are organized & will stick to our union"; other signs in Hebrew, Polish, Bohemian.

66. *CDS*, Dec. 13, 1910; *I-0*, Dec. 14, 15, 1910, mentions the crucifix; *R-H*, Dec. 14, 1910; *Trib*, Dec. 14, 1910, mentions the crucifix. "Deadlock in the Chicago Strike," *Survey*, 25 (Dec. 24, 1910), 490–491, refers to frenzy of defiance by a misguided priest. The article finds it significant that killings took place near his church.

67. *CDS*, Dec. 7, 8, 15, 1910; *I-0*, Dec. 9, 13, 14, 1910; *R-H*, Dec. 7, 8, 14, 1910; *Trib*, Dec. 6 (meeting of 500 cutters accepted agreement) 7, 8, 15, 1910. On Dec. 15 both the *CDS* and *Trib* mentioned an elaborate plan for a secret ballot. WTUL, "Official Report," 23–24.

68. Dvorak, "Garment Workers Strike Lost," 551.

69. Eugene V. Debs, "Help! Help!! Help!!!" *International Socialist Review*, 11 (Jan. 1911), 394; and *CDS*, Dec. 12, 1910, 4.

70. *CDN*, Dec. 20, 1910; *CDS*, Dec. 22, 1910; *R-H*, Dec. 21, 27, 1910; *Trib*, Dec. 21, 24, 1910; *I-O*, Dec. 24, 1910 (quote from mother).

71. *Trib* Dec. 25, 31, 1910; *CDS*, Dec. 31, 1910, Jan. 3, 1911; *I-O*, *R-H*, Dec. 31, 1910.

72. *I-O*, *R-H*, *Trib*, Jan. 4, 1911; *CDS*, Jan. 5, 1911.

73. ACWA, *Clothing Workers*, 44. WTUL, "Official Report," 31–32. *CDS*, Jan. 12, 16, 17, 1911; *CDN*, Jan. 13, 14, 16, 1911; *I-O*, Jan. 12, 15, 1911; *R-H*, Jan. 11, 16, 1911; *Trib*, Jan. 11, 17, 1911.

74. *CDN*, Jan. 16, 1911; *I-O*, *Trib*, Jan. 17, 1911.

75. *I-O*, Jan. 15, 16, 1911; *Trib*, Jan. 14, 19, 1911 (claimed the secessionist movement disintegrated when W. E. Trautman suggested taking up a collection for a $1.50 bill); *CDS*, Jan. 16, 1911. Dvorak, "Garment Workers Strike Lost," 554, includes text of demands. Interview with Irvin Abrams in Balanoff, "Oral History Project," 2; Abrams came to Chicago toward the end of the strike.

76. Federal Writers Project translation of foreign language press: *La Paroladel Socialisti*, Jan. 28, 1911; *Denni Hlasatel*, Jan. 15, 1911. Dvorak "Garment Workers Strike Lost," 554.

77. WTUL, "Official Report," 34. ACWA, *Clothing Workers*, 46.

78. Josephson, *Sidney Hillman*, 57.

79. Potofsky interview, 9, 18, 20.

80. ACWA, *Documentary History of the Amalgamated Clothing Workers of America*, 1914–1916 (New York, 1920), 10–13, 46–48. See also Josephson, *Sidney Hillman*, 97–98, for Abramovitch's role at Nashville.

81. Josephson, *Sidney Hillman*, 152–153.

82. Correspondence with Clara's younger sister, Florence Masilotti Hurst, from Oct. 16, 1976, to Oct. 4, 1977.

83. Interview with Hannah Shapiro Glick, by Rebecca Sive-Tomeshivsky.

1. Sewing Room at A. T. Stewart's Department Store. **Source:** *Frank Leslie's Illustrated Newspaper*, April 24, 1875. Courtesy of New-York Historical Society.

2. Employees' Lunchroom at A. T. Stewart's. **Source**: *Frank Leslie's Illustrated Newspaper*, April 24, 1875. Courtesy of New-York Historical Society.

IN MEMORY OF
IDA BRAYMAN

17 YEARS OLD

**who was shot & killed by an Employer
Feb. 5th 1913 during the great struggle
of the Garment Workers of Rochester.**

 60

Copyrigted 1913 by U. G. W. Local 14 Rochester N. Y.

3. Postcard printed by the United Garment Workers in Rochester to
be sold to pay for Ida Brayman's funeral expenses. The mayor
refused the application to sell the cards, saying that they should
have read "met her death" rather than "killed by an Employer."
Source: *Rochester Herald*, February 16, 1913. Courtesy of E. A.
Rumball Papers, University of Rochester Library Archives,
University of Rochester, N.Y.

4. Dorothy Jacobs Bellanca. Work for women needleworkers gained her respect within the trade union movement. **Source:** Courtesy of Amalgamated Clothing Workers of America.

5. Parade by Chicago garment workers during their 1910 strike. **Source:** *Chicago Daily News.* Courtesy of Chicago Historical Society (ICHi 04938, gift of Field Enterprises).

6. Women at Farah's Gateway plant. **Source:** Courtesy of Emily Honig.

7. Women at Farah. **Source:** Courtesy of Emily Honig.

CHAPTER 5

The Great Uprising in Cleveland: When Sisterhood Failed

Lois Scharf

"I AM simply amazed," wrote Gertrude Barnum in September 1911, "to learn that the society women, club women and church societies sat passively through the Cleveland strike while the employers refused to arbitrate and insisted upon settling issues by the force of starvation and false arrests and intimidation by hired thugs and sluggers."[1] In the midst of one of the bitter clashes that wracked the garment industry during the early twentieth century, Barnum described the struggle and analyzed one possible reason for its collapse. But the story of failed sisterhood that she lamented represented only one level at which sex solidarity failed to materialize.

Solidarity among working-class women in the strike-locked Cleveland neighborhoods was equally lacking in the summer of 1911. Common grievances brought women into the streets of Cleveland, but they did not cut as deeply across class lines or even across internal class interests as they did in other cities. Cleveland provides a good example of just how fragile the common interests of women could be and how they could dissipate in the complex currents of a major strike.

The Cleveland strike of 1911 was only one of those mounted by an increasingly militant early twentieth-century work force, determined upon improving working conditions and gaining union representation. Bargaining and strikes did not bring total victory to workers; but gains were made, as the International Ladies Garment Workers Union (ILGWU) and the United Garment Workers (UGWA) became forces with which to be reckoned. First in New York, then in Chicago, a pattern emerged of immigrant, working-class commitment to unionization, and willingness and ability to endure the deprivation of long strikes. In addition, the strikes of 20,000 Jewish and Italian New York women and of hundreds of female workers in Chicago resulted in the forging of concrete ties with middle-class female reformers and suffragists, whose support played important roles in the outcome of the struggles. The same alliance among female garment workers in New York and Boston in 1913, although less familiar to labor history, was again responsible for economic gains and union recognition. The absence of comparable cross-class bonds in a strike that failed calls into relief the importance of these ties.[2]

In the Cleveland strike, the victorious ILGWU, encouraged by their success in the New York women's clothing industry, attempted to repeat that success elsewhere. The 60,000 New York workers had settled their dispute with the Protective Association of Manufacturers, with the outside assistance of Louis Brandeis and an ingenious instrument dubbed the Protocol of Peace. Strikers received a wage settlement and assurance that hiring would be on a preferential basis rather than the hoped-for closed shop arrangement. The conflict highlighted confrontation between German Jewish and upwardly mobile East European Jewish immigrant manufacturers and a largely immigrant Jewish labor force. Outside forces imposed settlement upon an industry publicly displaying its intraethnic, as well as economic, tensions. Whatever the motivation, however, the Protocol marked a compromised but positive victory for the principle of collective bargaining, as well as an invitation to standardize conditions in other manufacturing centers in an industry where markets were increasingly national in character.[3]

Organizing Cleveland represented more than just an effort by the ILGWU to equalize labor conditions; it also became a battle to protect New York manufacturers adhering to the terms of the Protocol from unfair competition. The markets for Cleveland's garments were considerably broader than those of Boston, Philadelphia, or Chicago. Although numerically a poor fourth in the manufacturing of women's clothing generally, Cleveland ranked directly behind New York in women's cloak and suit production. Between five and six thousand workers, about one-third of them women, worked in thirty-three shops of varying size, the biggest ones employing fifty to almost one thousand workers. Eight large firms belonged to a protective association adamantly opposed to organizing efforts; the others combined in an independent manufacturers association. The economic situation was complicated by outside contractors who made about one-quarter of cloaks and suits in the city, a factor that magnified the ethnic diversities and rivalries in the city. Most outside contractors were Bohemians who employed Bohemian women and girls, many of whom were suspicious and unfriendly toward the inside operatives, who were mostly Jewish and Italian immigrants.[4]

Determined activist workers in Cleveland were an important element in the ILGWU's decision to support a strike. The union's Cleveland president, Isadore Feit, who convinced the Bohemian contractors to join forces and publish joint complaints against the manufacturers, first announced intentions to press workers' complaints. The ILGWU in New York counseled patience. But resentful determination in the ranks had grown out of frustration in an earlier unsuccessful 1908 strike against one of the major firms, Prinz-Biederman. In addition, seasonal low-paying employment, periodic extensive overtime, and the example of the New York strike model motivated the workers to try for recognition and bargaining rights. The degree of union support and organization varied from shop to shop, and was especially weak in the largest firms. After a meeting of the General Executive Board of the International, however, leaders bowed to the wishes of the Cleveland locals and reluctantly called a general strike, rather than expose members in specific shops to the possibility of nonstriking coworkers in firms more capable of withstanding union demands. On June 3, a union letter asking for immediate negotiations and enclosing a list of eleven general demands, as well as demands from cutters, cloak operators, tailors, dressmakers and skirt makers, pressers, and outside contractors was sent to all cloak and suit manufacturers. Since even direct, negative response would constitute implicit union recognition, all communication was ignored by employers.[5]

On the morning of June 6, 1911, the *Cleveland Plain Dealer* headlines read, "Big Strike Looms in Garment Trade." The accompanying article described the demands sent by the union to the thirty-three firms, individually identified, and to the Out-side Contractors Association. Four thousand workers, principally Jews, Italians, and Bohemians, gathered at Grays Armory in downtown Cleveland to hear leaders describe employee demands and emphasize the importance of union recognition. General demands included the call for a fifty-hour week, with only a 7:30 A.M. to 12:30 P.M. schedule on Saturdays; no more than two hours of overtime during the regular five-day work week, and double pay on overtime; observance of legal holidays; elimination of shop agreements with individual employees and of inside contracting, as well as elimination of charges for machines, electricity, and thread.[6]

At the rally, leaders presented an impressive united front. John Dyche spoke on behalf of the International. Isadore Feit spoke as head of the local union, delivering his talk in English and in Yiddish. John Tomasek announced the support of the outside contractors in Bohemian. Charles Pagonni came from New York to represent the Italians and attend to their interests. Josephine Casey, organizer for the International, described the working conditions of women in the industry and pledged special attention to their concerns. What those concerns were was not clear, however. The specific demands of male cutters, tailors, shirtmakers, and pressers concentrated on wages and piecework rates, and on apprentice wage scales in the case of the cutters. Sex segregation in garment manufacturing was implicit only when skirt makers demanded that they "not be required to do finishing work, such as sewing on buttons, hooks and eyes, bottom basting, or tucking plaits." These were women's jobs, but how women were to be compensated was not mentioned in the demands of male strikers.[7]

Speakers at the rally stressed the importance of nonviolence. Lawyers Meyer London from the International Union, Louis Katz from the local, and Jay O. Dawley all agreed nonviolence was necessary for public support. Dawley was a well-known Cleveland counsel who had established his reputation as a union legal advisor for the Cleveland Employers Association, and although the appearance of this apostate on the side of the workers engendered some suspicion in labor circles, he was welcomed. Dawley was especially eloquent on the subject of a peaceful strike. "Womanhood, childhood, and virtue were involved in the strike," he said, and strikers were to observe the law and refrain from physical confrontations at all costs, remembering "they were fighting for homes, for an honest living, for family, for religion, for freedom, and for better conditions." Dawley told workers they would preserve the reputation of the trade union movement by proving that organized workers were not cutthroats and dynamiters, "but an orderly aggregation of workers asking a living wage and fair treatment."[8]

As Dawley recommended, the strike began in a festive mood, without a hint of disruption or physical conflict. Employees reported on June 7 to their workplaces, where red cards that said "The General Strike Declared" were distributed. "Sisters and Brothers" were ordered by the General Strike Committee to leave their shops promptly at 10 A.M., to take their tools with them, to argue with no one once outside the factory, and to march directly to a strike meeting at Utopian Hall at East 31st and Woodland Avenue, in the heart of an eastside, immigrant, worker neighborhood. Newspapers reported joyful parades proceeding to the meeting hall. Women workers who had young babies and were generally employed by outside contractors, joined the strikers at a westside hall, where Bohemians assembled. Workers who did not respond to the walkout were sent home by employers.

The extent of the walkout exceeded expectations. To accommodate the enthusiastic thousands who responded to the strike call, six separate halls were needed. Workers assembled according to shop, to nationality, or, in the case of striking girls and women, to sex. Women leaders from Local 29 (finishers) and Local 27 (shirtmakers) signed up their fellow strikers and proceeded to convince 200 others in small dressmaking and tailor shops to join their ranks. Josephine Casey assisted the women's organizing campaign. Workers received instructions on work benefits, picket activities, and future meeting sites.[9]

Three days later, on June 10, the Cloak Manufacturers Association ran full-page advertisements in Cleveland papers, decrying the strike. According to their statement, the strike was unwarranted, because optimal working conditions had always prevailed in Cleveland, because most workers did not approve the walkout, and because the purpose of the strike was to benefit the New York market. The eight large owners affirmed their willingness to meet with their employees individually or in groups from each factory department, "but not through outside representation."[10]

The first outbreaks of violence occurred about the same time the manufacturers issued their statement. Two separate incidents involving strikers and police took place, with resulting injuries and arrests. The following day, Josephine Casey, five young women, and two men were arrested for disorderly conduct on the picket line. Although Casey was soon released on bail, tensions rose, and union leaders suggested that strikers take their families to area parks. At the same time, leaders insisted that violence "had been provoked by the hirelings of the manufacturers and the unwarrantly action of the police." Newspapers quickly indicated how crucial the issue of violence was in influencing public perceptions and assessment of collective action by workers. The friendly *Cleveland Press* editorialized that during the early days, "It has been an orderly strike, and orderly strikes, when waged in a just cause, are almost certain to end in a victory for the wage earner." When sporadic confrontations began, however, the *Plain Dealer* held strikers entirely responsible for maintaining labor peace. Outbreaks of violence gave strike leaders the opportunity to demonstrate that there was no need for such actions to occur, the newspaper warned: "The people of Cleveland will be disappointed if this choice is ignored."[11]

Women now began to assume a greater role in the strike. Pauline Newman, a national union organizer for the International and a member of the Women's Trade Union League, joined Casey as organizer and as protector of the interests of the striking women. On June 14, the first of several parades of strikers and sympathizers filed through the streets, female Locals 27 and 29 leading the marchers along their route through the business section of the city and west through the factory district. About six thousand demonstrators took part; their pictures and stories were carried on front pages of Cleveland newspapers. Union leaders sang their praises: "There were women, grey-haired and bent with age and toil, marching beside girls garbed in white, who wore bright ribbons and gay flowers." But as strikers— men and women—took to the streets, the consequences were not always so colorful or peaceful. As employers used guards to protect their factories, hired nonstrikers locally, and imported others in attempts to maintain production, tempers flared. Female strikers on the picket line used bare fists and handbags in direct assaults on female scabs and on police as well. A long series of arrests of young women and men began in earnest. The women were arrested for throwing objects at automobiles transporting strikebreakers to work, for using their feet to trip workers entering plants, for "driving home arguments for unionism with [their] fists," for throwing eggs at taxis taking strikebreakers home.[12]

According to Ohio law, the mayor of the city or the probate judge of the county was to notify the Ohio State Arbitration Board when a strike was threatened. An early and unsuccessful visit by the board secretary had been unofficial because it preceded formal notice. Once notice had been given, the secretary, accompanied by the chairman of the Arbitration Board, returned to Cleveland. The manufacturers association remained adamant, however, restating its position that the "strike in Cleveland is not a question of wages or working conditions. It is an attempt to dictate to the Cleveland manufacturers that they shall run their business as it is carried on in New York." The board was powerless because one seat representing employers was vacant, due to a resignation. More important, the owners refused to meet with the representatives of the union or to submit the issues to arbitration. City officials and religious leaders, including the rabbis of the congregations to which the manufacturers belonged, urged conciliation and arbitration. The employers stood fast.[13]

Owner intransigence led to an escalation of strikebreaking, picketing, frustration, and confrontation. Strikers and union officials accused the police of collusion and the manufacturers of fomenting violence; the Chamber of Commerce accused the mayor of encouraging police laxity. Daily accounts of the industrial unrest became a litany of violence on the picket lines, arrests, importation of strikebreakers and armed guards, attempts by manufacturers to open shops in small nearby communities. By the third week of the struggle, a *Cleveland Leader* editorial demanded "Strike Violence Must Stop." Both sides were cautioned to obey the law; but the tone of the editorial carried a tacit condemnation of strikers, who were reminded that "the police would ensure order, and that behind them stood the national guard and even the regular army."[14]

The manufacturers had every intention of benefiting from the impact that violent confrontation had on community opinion. An unpublicized meeting between representatives of the Cleveland Garment Manufacturers Association and the Cleveland Chamber of Commerce Board indicated that the issue of violence could become a valuable tactic in the employers' union opposition arsenal. On June 27 representatives of the owners informed the board that they did not want a proindustry statement on the merits of the employers' position, but would, on the other hand, appreciate the adoption of strong resolutions calling for enforcement of order by city authorities. Counsel for the owners prepared the desired resolutions. The next day, calls for order were issued by Chamber of Commerce spokesmen.[15]

The owners did not passively wait for the frustrations and other emotional and physical responses to run their course. Harassment from police and guards and anger at the sight of imported strikebreakers could have accounted for the growing number of violent clashes. But to ensure that the onus of violence plagued the strikers, justified employer demands for peace and order, and brought credit to their antiunion position, the Cloak Manufacturers Association and Burns Detective Agency hired a nonunion cutter as spy and agent provocateur. Morris Lubin made his way to the core of the Picket Committee. Lubin's role in inciting and exacerbating such behavior was documented two years later in court, where he was convicted and sentenced. The *Ladies' Garment Worker* later concluded: "He inflamed the imaginations of these mere boys by revolutionary speeches" and convinced girls and young women that their tactics were "too ladylike, too peaceful."[16]

Despite provocateurs the ranks of the strikers held. The defection of the Bohemian subcontractors after only two weeks of united action was a blow to strike strategy, but the outside contractors explained that they worked solely for the large manufacturers and were deeply in debt to them. Remaining strikers received regular benefits: $4 per week for unmarried men and women; $6 for men with small families; $8 for those with large families. But suffering and hardship increased as days became weeks, and weeks turned into months of unresolved battles of wills, fists, and clubs. In the third month of the strike, 3,000 men and women voted to continue the strike with ballots printed in English and five additional languages. Only 117 votes were cast in favor of returning to work, although the maximum weekly benefit had been cut to $6. When the more than $200,000 raised from various segments of the national labor movement proved insufficient, local unions voted an assessment of 10 cents per member to augment the strike fund.

Strikers marched in a place of honor in the annual Labor Day parade, the Jewish High Holy Days passed uneventfully with a virtual truce tentatively called in the almost unceasing violence, and the

American Federation of Labor pledged its support and its intention to direct the struggle. In mid-October the socialist *Cleveland Citizen* suddenly announced that the strike had been called off for lack of financial support. Economic hardship took its toll. Well-financed and determined owners relentlessly stood their ground. The McNamara case (trial of union members for bombing of the Los Angeles *Times* building) diverted trade union attention. Violent confrontations undermined public approval at home. The Arbitration Board described the course and failure of the strike succinctly: "The strike began June 7, 1911, and ended October 15; number of weeks, twenty: number of employees engaged, six thousand. The strikers were forced to return to work without their demands being granted."[17]

Throughout the strike, women were highly visible, as they took to the streets as pickets, endured arrest and jail, and emerged as apotheosized figures in print. Pauline Newman and Josephine Casey devoted their efforts to enlisting girls and young women into union ranks, assisting local women organizers, and conducting special meetings for the female strikers in their neighborhoods. To mitigate family opposition to the unconventional behavior and activities demanded of young women during the strike, Casey and Newman called special meetings for strikers' mothers who were encouraged to advise their daughters to continue the struggle. An immigrant woman who addressed one group, reminded the mothers of their suffering in the old country and "that their daughters during the strike in Cleveland were bearing only a part of the burden of suffering which was the lot of women."[18]

Most of the accolades for young women, however, emphasized identification with class and devotion to the union, rather than identifying courage on the picket line and the battle for economic justice as elements of feminist struggle. The example of female strikers was used to arouse support for the cause of organized labor generally. Young women turned police stations into meeting halls, according to Newman, singing of their loyalty to the union and memorializing its battles in songs of their own composition. The heroism of women was celebrated as legion; their strength was recognized as stemming from admirable qualities of self-sacrifice; their expectations, their inevitable rewards were declared unlimited:

Mollie is one of those who does not look at the Trade Union Movement as an end, but as a means to an end! Mollie is an idealist, is yearning for a future where there will be no master and no slave, but all will enjoy the beauties of life! Admire Mollie because she is not only dreaming of a glorious future, as so many of her people do, but is giving her life to the movement that will some day bring about a realization of Mollie's dream. [19]

Rhetorical flourish was boundless. Becky Fisher, with a record of thirty-nine arrests in eleven weeks, was a model for all strikers, for she

has a horror of the police, the patrol wagon and the jail, but her union was as sacred to her as was Old Glory to Barbara Fritchie, and fear was an unknown quality to this little girl when she was fighting for her loved union and the cause it represented. [20]

Enduring the humiliation of police harassment, patrol wagons, and jail for the sake of the union may have epitomized courage and devotion to leaders of the labor movement, but to the Cleveland community generally, continuous public disorder created the impression of criminal irresponsibility. Escalating violence accomplished the goals of the intransigent employers, legitimizing their unyielding opposition to union recognition and worker demands. One factor could possibly have mitigated this development. Visible support from "respectable" middle-class and upper-class citizens, especially women, could have dramatized poor working conditions and brought increased pressure to bear on the manufacturers. Active participation by women reformers, demonstrating in concert with workers on the picket line and directly experiencing police brutality and indiscriminate arrest, could have further highlighted the inequities of the situation. This type of joint action had taken place in New York in 1909 and in Chicago in 1910, resulting in much positive publicity on behalf of strikers, and favorably influencing whatever terms resulted from strikes. As Gertrude Barnum said, cross-class cooperation was not replicated in Cleveland; Casey and Newman were first and foremost working-class, union organizers, and they could not lend the needed air of respectability to strikers in general, nor to women strikers in particular.

During the early days of the walkout, newspapers reported that suffrage leaders would protect the interests of young women if any were arrested while engaged in picket duty. That support never materialized. After her release from jail following her first arrest on disorderly conduct charges, Josephine Casey went directly to a meeting of the city's Women's Suffrage League. She requested that a resolution be drafted expressing sympathy for all women who were struggling to better their living conditions, support for the principle of equal pay for equal work and for any movement that would improve the lot of working women. Several of the women, including Elizabeth Hauser, former secretary of reform mayor Tom L. Johnson, wrote and signed a resolution but with an explicit note that signatures represented the support of individual women, and not of their organization.[21]

The position of the Suffrage League was underscored at a mass meeting of strikers and supporters held at the end of July. Casey again pleaded on behalf of "oppressed women," but Mrs. Myron Vorse, a suffrage leader who presided at the rally, reiterated the individual, not collective, support given by some suffragists. Resorting to the narrow focus of the league, Vorse defended the group's official neutrality. The suffrage group embraced a large membership of men and women whose sympathies and interests varied, according to Vorse. Under these circumstances the league could not be expected to endorse any measure not pertaining to women's suffrage. The handful of suffragists who did support the striking workers promised an investigation of working conditions and a formal report on the issues. Rose Moriarty, student and social worker, undertook the task of preparing the report. But however honorable the intentions, the undertaking failed to materialize; strikers could only express their disappointment and resentment.[22]

Timing and clashing interests worked against closer cooperation. Local women had just organized the city's suffrage group, and June 1 marked the beginning of their summer campaign. Hauser was busy visiting Cleveland's "first families," seeking recruits for the fledging League. Caution characterized the early stages of the campaign; organizational participation in a labor confrontation seemed like an invitation to self-destruction. Six months later, the group hesitantly adopted the "unladylike" procedure of soapbox oratory, and even invited a militant New York suffragist who had been arrested in a

Philadelphia garment workers strike to participate, but such bold action was unthinkable in the summer of 1911.[23]

Casey received a rebuff also from the Women's Christian Temperance Union during the early days of the strike. She appealed to the WCTU for aid, claiming that the larger manufacturers who retained some men in their factories were dispensing liquor to them. Picketing women, therefore, needed and deserved the protection of the women's organizations. The advocates of prohibition reportedly took no action on the plea for assistance.[24]

Even members of the Women's Trade Union League remained unsupportive. A local chapter of the WTUL had been formed in Cleveland in 1909 by Mrs. Frederick C. Howe, wife of the well-known Progressive reformer. In the Labor Day parade of 1910, a contingent of league members marched in the first division, but by the time of the strike, membership had dwindled. In mid-July, Margaret Dreier Robins, president of the national league, came to Cleveland at the invitation of Pauline Newman, in an attempt to drum up support. She was primarily responsible for calling the mass meeting at which she, Casey, and others pleaded for assistance. Newman dramatized the potential for an alliance when she described the circumstances that prompted the invitation to Robins to arrange the mass rally. "We all felt that the meeting ought not to be called under the auspices of the Union, because we wanted to get the public at large, and for fear that some might not come if it were held under the auspices of the Union, we thought the Women's Trade Union League was the proper organization to call the meeting." Robins could not locate a cadre of women committed to the cause, however, so she made whatever speeches she could to the Cleveland Federation of Labor and to the strikers, then left for Pennsylvania.[25]

Other women's groups were unable to transcend their own specialized interests to help strikers. The Cleveland branch of the YWCA was a well-established organization at the time of the strike, but genuine concern of board members and administrators for working-class women seldom extended to the workplace, and never to union organizing. Under the able industrial secretary, Marie Wing, the Cleveland Y did establish and run many recreational and educational programs for industrial workers—classes and social events scheduled to fill the leisure time of working women. Leaders visited factories at noon to enlist the girls into small groups, formed a "League of Industrial Clubs" to meet on Monday nights, and began activities with a ten-cent supper, followed by dancing, games, exercises, and a business meeting—all aimed at social uplift and infused with a heavy dose of evangelical morality. The tone was not likely to put Catholic and Jewish immigrants at ease at the Y.[26]

Another well-organized women's group, one apparently devoid of ethnic or religious conflict, still could not overcome economic class bias. The Cleveland Council of Jewish Women was fifteen years old at the time of the strike. In 1889 the organization, composed of the wives and daughters of settled German Jewish families, founded the Council Educational Alliance. The nonresident settlement house followed Cleveland's growing Jewish immigrant population from its original site to the heart of the eastside immigrant neighborhood in 1909. The full panoply of benevolent, acculturating classes and programs, especially those in English language and manual training, was available to the new arrivals from Eastern and Central Europe. The alliance was successful in attracting neighborhood adult residents to its fold, certainly more sensitive to its constituency than neighboring Hiram House, directed by the well-funded, patronizing George Bellamy. Among the services available at the Council Educational Alliance were sewing classes, including a cloak shop. The shop was fully equipped with "electric motors" donated by the council president and staffed by a part-time instructor whose $15-per-month salary was paid by the council. The women's organization boasted, "The cloak shop was a very beneficial feature of Council activity. Those who completed the course were placed in good positions." But a discordant note crept into the self-congratulation in which the council engaged on the occasion of its thirtieth anniversary, in 1924: "The unskilled immigrants were taught to make skirts. Owing to the garment strike of 1911, this shop was discontinued."[27]

Council minutes are missing from the strike period, and one can only infer the motivation behind the canceling of sewing classes. Council Educational Alliance, with its wide range of lectures and debates, gained a city-wide reputation for its liberal policies and tolerance toward controversial issues. But there were limits. In 1903 when a brochure of the Ladies Garment Workers Union appeared at the settlement, the board issued a resolution: "that we deem it inexpedient that meetings favoring unionism or antiunionism be held within the grounds or buildings of the alliance, but nothing herein shall be construed as restricting free discussion of social and economic problems."[28]

The leadership of the council and the board of trustees of its settlement house shared the background and class position of the garment manufacturers; occasionally they were relatives. The president of the council had married into the family of the city's most prominent men's garment firm, Joseph and Feiss. Her sister married the owner of a large woolen mill. One other board member was the wife of an owner of a struck shop, still another was married to an agent for a struck manufacturer. Furthermore, the council was affiliated with the Federation of Jewish Charities, the umbrella organization for a number of Jewish welfare agencies. Morris Black, owner of H. Black and spokesman for the Manufacturers Association, was a member of the charities board, along with Isaac Joseph and Julius Feiss.

The board had an opportunity to play a role in the strike. At a board meeting held at the time of the outbreak, prominent trustee and rabbi Moses Gries suggested that the federation board appoint a committee to try to bring about an early settlement, "thus adverting the certain trouble and suffering which must necessarily follow a continuation of the strike." After discussion, however, the board decided to refrain from action, merely suggesting that individuals act as mediators if they so wished. If individuals chose to do so, their activities have gone unrecorded. The weekly English language publications of the German Jewish community ignored the strike. The *Jewish Independent* printed reports of anti-Semitism and physical assaults on Jews all over the world, but detailed only the elaborate social activities of the German Jewish community at home. In the spring of 1911 the *Independent* printed an article deploring the use in printed form of Anglicized Yiddish accents and idioms as reflecting negatively on American Jews. Yet when the *Plain Dealer* printed a report of a neighborhood altercation in which a confrontation between wives of strikers and the spouse of a worker who had returned to work was described in that manner, no protest followed.[29] The settled, prosperous Jewish community, of which the manufacturers were part, refused to apply their sensitivity to the indignities suffered by Jews elsewhere to their own city.

Only once did the weeklies refer to the strike, and then in oblique fashion. In early September, social worker Emanuel Sternheim was hired as new director of the Council Educational Alliance. At the end of the month he officiated and delivered the sermons at the "People's Synagogue" services during the High Holy Days. How many neighborhood residents attended these services is difficult to determine, since the area was dotted with small orthodox congregations, usually organized according to immigrants' place of origin. Few practicing Jews had no affiliation, but adequate numbers of occasional observers undoubtedly justified religious services at the Alliance. Sternheim's long rambling discourses were delivered in English and reprinted in the weeklies. On Rosh Hashanna he insisted that religious observance and belief take precedence over economic concerns and actions:

> Does not God in His mercy bless the efforts of those who work with all their might? . . . Who is able to declare, this crust of bread is the first of my exertions, no stain of dishonesty clings to it, no robbery of the hireling of his wages, no grinding of the face of the poor, no sweating, no compulsion of workers to toil in unhealthy workshops. . . .
>
> You may say, this is for masters not for the men; but I say to you, true dear friends, but what of the men? Ah, my brethren, how many have thought of God, as well as of gold during the anxious weeks that have passed? How much of wrong has been done to both sides in the losing sight of God's ways, and the bitter fight for outward prosperity?[30]

Sternheim's appeal was even more direct on Yom Kippur: "Once more I appeal to you all, my brothers," he said, "whether right or wrong, in this great struggle, remember that our God, our religion, our nation, our Judaism, these are greater things than trade disputes, and bow yourselves down in shame before your God."[31] Probably more German Jewish readers than immigrant Jewish listeners noted references to the strike buried in the text of the sermons. They are significant only to the extent that they are brief exceptions to the reticence of Cleveland's German Jews on the question of the labor struggle. The strike illuminated the complexities of economic interests and intraethnic divisions. The women caught in the conflict displayed their loyalties to class over gender.

While women had difficulties in surmounting class barriers to alleviate suffering and deflect the onus of violence, dissention and confrontation in the workers' neighborhood added another element of discord. Five days after the walkout began, a nonstriker was assaulted at Woodland Avenue and East 40th Street, treated at the local hospital, escorted home, and guarded at company expense. Less than one week later, a melee (though hardly a riot, as confrontations were continuously labeled) occurred eight blocks east on Woodland Avenue—with screaming women and children involved, according to newspaper reports.[32]

Woodland Avenue was one of the major east-west arteries in the strikers' neighborhood, an area densely populated by unskilled, Eastern European Jewish immigrants who had rapidly replaced former residents (almost 100 percent turnover in the neighborhood bounded by 22nd and 37th streets, from 1896 to 1906). The eastern exodus that was to characterize Jewish residential patterns for the next seventy years had already begun, with increasing numbers of Italians moving into homes west of 37th Street, while growing numbers of Jews located as far east as 55th Street and even beyond. As with their Jewish neighbors, employment in the clothing industry was significant among Italians, and they were well represented among strikers. After the desertion of the Bohemian subcontractors and their workers, the neighborhood became synonymous with clothing worker unrest. Scovill, Orange, and Woodland avenues between East 22nd and East 55th identified strikers' residences, just as the West 6th Street clothing factories defined their work space.[33]

If tempers snapped on picket lines, the same could be said for the neighborhoods. One of the hottest summers in history exacerbated conditions. While reports of 100-degree temperatures in June and July were exaggerated, even 90-degree heat in crowded urban, non-air-conditioned areas was physically dangerous and emotionally trying. When supplies of ice ran short, the ensuing problems made newspaper headlines. In the strikers' neighborhood, where patience was obviously wearing thin, women staged an ice riot at the ice station at Orange Avenue and 27th Street. This expression of female working-class solidarity toward temporary shortcomings in local services was not duplicated in united support of economic protest.[34]

Wives of striking garment workers supported their husbands' demands with visible presence on the streets. A parade of more than 6,000 strikers, family members, and supporters marked the seventh week of the strike. Several days later, an even larger crowd ("mob" in the language of the *Cleveland Leader*) marched from Woodland and

55th Street to Cleveland's Public Square, where speakers denounced the police harassment and lack of official retaliation against association-hired "thugs." Widespread participation by Socialist Party members, local unions, and Jewish fraternal organizations swelled the ranks along with hundreds of women and girls. A parade one month later was less peaceful and was marked by several arrests, including an arrest of one woman. That march was led by strikers' wives with go-carts; but many dropped out because of the effect of the heat on their babies.[35]

There were wives of nonstrikers as well. Strikers' spouses formed a committee to try to persuade them to convince their husbands, in turn, to join the ranks of the protestors. Confrontations resulted. When a sixty-year-old peddler of tea and spices tried to sell her wares to the wife of a nonstriking cutter, she was attacked by a younger neighborhood woman who supported the walkout. Wives who visited the wife of one working tailor were sent scurrying before they had an opportunity to convince the woman of the righteousness of their cause: The wife greeted the delegation by dousing it with a pan of hot milk.[36]

Matters became even more violent when the son of a woman approached by a member of the wives' committee shot and wounded the spokesperson of the group. The incident incited brick throwing by neighbors—bricks wrapped in Yiddish newspapers according to the *Plain Dealer*. It was not clear who the bricks were meant to target, but to Pauline Newman, the attempt of one striker's wife to help another was just one more example of working-class, trade-union solidarity. "A woman who had never been in any fights before, a mother of children, risked her life to help another! In what other movement can you find these types? In what other movement can you see such sacrifice? . . . In no other but the Labor Movement." As described in newspapers, however, the shooting brought little credit to strikers, women, or immigrants generally.[37]

Danger was real, and one strikebreaker obviously believed potential conflict warranted sending his wife and children to their family in Indianapolis. For the husband, work meant living on the factory premises, with Sunday reprieves consisting of company-sponsored automobile rides for which he paid $1.25, but a worthwhile trip and "especially enjoyable after having been locked up all week." As an indication of neighborhood sentiment, this strikebreaker wrote his wife that regardless of the outcome, "I would sell the house at any price and would rent in an area where no strikers would be living." As for the wife's role in family decision making, "I am sure you will leave that up to me," he added. As the summer dragged on, he advised his wife to enroll the children in school in Indianapolis. Company guards and friends looked after their home until it was finally sold. When the strike collapsed, he rented an apartment north of the original neighborhood and wrote to his wife, informing her of these developments, instructing her on school transfers for the children and train tickets for the return trip to Cleveland. Dislocation and implicit passivity characterized this woman's strike-related experience. [38]

Female strikers and strikers' wives for a time worked together, but ultimately some of the women found themselves on opposite sides of the struggle as the strike entered its final weeks and economic pressures became increasingly difficult to endure. Twenty women attacked the home of one cutter who returned to work, throwing stones and hurling insults. At the same time, the mayor received a delegation of ten female workers and wives of ex-strikers who appealed for protection from their angry neighbors when they returned to work. [39]

Strike action of working-class women may have come as a surprise to participants, although precedents had already been set in New York and Chicago. Josephine Casey applauded the female strikers, indicating that their new-found activism was not unexpected as far as their working sisters elsewhere were concerned:

> Oh you girls of Cleveland! You who a short time ago wept instead of protesting when you were unjustly treated, will in the future fight instead of weeping. The Bosses did not think you could fight. The men who worked along side of you did not count on you. The only ones who knew you would make good were the women throughout the country, who had been on the fighting line some time themselves! You have justified their faith in you and it is because through the fight you have found out how fine and strong you are that the Garment Workers' Union is going to stay in Cleveland. [40]

The ILGWU did not stay in Cleveland, and while there is no evidence that women workers returned to weeping (a common rhetorical alternative), there is little evidence to indicate that their introduction to worker militancy had lasting impact on them. Between the end of the strike and a strike in July 1918, the union made no headway in Cleveland. The owners instituted benevolent, welfare capitalism on the one hand, and reorganized scientific management on the other. The latter resulted in increased division of manufacturing processes as well as a growing number of women in the industry. The "Cleveland Experiment" of 1918, a novel plan to recognize the union and jointly monitor work and incentive standards, along with guaranteed weeks of employment, was primarily the handiwork of federal referees and an "enlightened" Morris Black. Clothing manufacturers in a precarious industry were first to recognize the advantages of union recognition and mutually-enforced production standards.[41]

In the aftermath of the 1911 strike, however, these developments were unforeseen. Men and women returned to work; only strike leaders encountered blacklisting. Female strikers had demonstrated their willingness and ability to endure labor struggles, but events demonstrated to them the precariousness of their collective action. Working-class leaders were not enough to ensure favorable public reaction to their needs and demands. Middle-class social feminists and suffragists did not come to their aid, as they had done in struggles in other cities. Equally important, working-class solidarity also proved elusive. Interests diverged within the workers' neighborhood, pitting striker against nonstriker, with their female relatives taking sides accordingly. Neighborhood confrontations between women highlighted the complexities of women's experience. Even when appropriately modified by ethnicity and class, impediments to female unity remained all too evident in Cleveland in the summer and early fall of 1911.

NOTES

1. *Cleveland Press*, reprinted in the *Ladies' Garment Worker*, 2 (Dec. 1911), 4.

2. The definitive early history of the ILGWU is Louis Levine, the *Women's Garment Workers: A History of the International Ladies Garment Workers Union*, (New York: B. W. Huebsch, Inc.: 1924). The New York strikes are also described by Melvin Dubofsky, *When Workers Organize: New York City in the Progressive Era* (Amherst: University of Massachusetts Press, 1968). Chapter 4 of Gladys Boone, *The Women's Trade Union Leagues of Great Britain and the United States of America* (New York: Columbia University Press, 1942) describes WTUL efforts on behalf of New York and Chicago strikes. Philip S. Foner, *Women and Trade Unions to the*

First World War (New York: Free Press, 1979), and Barbara Wertheimer, *We Were There: The Story of Working Women in America* (New York: Pantheon Books, 1977), describe ferment in the garment industry before 1914. Foner's brief description of cross-class cooperation in Cleveland is questioned in this paper. On women worker-reformer conflicts, see Robin Miller Jacoby, "The Women's Trade Union League and American Feminism." *Feminist Studies*, 3 (Fall 1975), 126–40.

3. Levine, *Garment Workers*, chaps. 22 and 23. Small-scale manufacturers in New York were more likely to be Russian Jews than elsewhere. The classic tale of the thin line between worker and owner is described by Abraham Cahan in *The Rise of David Levinsky* (New York: Harper Bros., 1914).

4. "Lessons of the Cleveland Strike," *Ladies' Garment Worker*, 2 (Dec., 1911).

5. Ibid.; Ohio State Board of Arbitration, *Annual Report* 1911–1912, 20.

6. *Cleveland Plain Dealer*, June 7 and 8, 1911.

7. Ibid, June 8, 1911; Board of Arbitration, *Report*, 20–22.

8. *Cleveland Plain Dealer*, June 8, 1911; *Cleveland Leader*, June 9, 1911.

9. *Cleveland Plain Dealer*, June 8 and 9, 1911; *Cleveland Press*, June 8, 1911.

10. Board of Arbitration, *Report*, 22–23; *Cleveland Plain Dealer*, June 10, 1911.

11. *Cleveland Plain Dealer*, June 10, 11, 13, 1911; *Cleveland Press*, June 9, 1911.

12. Board of Arbitration, *Report*, 24–26; *Ladies' Garment Worker*, 2 (July 1911), 7; *Cleveland Plain Dealer*, June 15, 18, 20, 21, 1911; *Cleveland Press*, June 14, 1911.

13. Board of Arbitration, *Report*, 28–30; *Cleveland Plain Dealer*, June 20 and 21, 1911; *Cleveland Press*, June 20, 21, 22, 1911.

14. *Cleveland Press*, June 20, 1911; July 11, 1911; *Cleveland Leader*, June 27, 1911.

15. Cleveland Chamber of Commerce, Minutes, 1911–1912, in Greater Cleveland Growth Association Records, 1881–1969, container 15, Western Reserve Historical Society, Cleveland (hereafter WRHS); *Cleveland Plain Dealer*, June 28, 1911; *Cleveland Press*, June 28, 1911.

16. "Cleveland Cloak Manufacturers," "Mighty Mean Partner," exposed in the Lubin Case, *Ladies' Garment Worker*, 4 (Aug. 1913), 1–3.

17. *Cleveland Press*, June 19 and 23, 1911; *Cleveland Plain Dealer*, September 12, 1911; October 11, 1911; *Cleveland Citizen*, September 23, 1911; October 21 and 28, 1911; *Ladies' Garment Worker* 2 (Oct. 1911), 14; 2 (Nov. 1911), 15.

18. *Cleveland Plain Dealer*, July 26, 1911.

19. Pauline M. Newman, "From the Battlefield," *Life and Labor*, 1 (Oct. 1911), 297.

20. *Cleveland Citizen*, Oct. 14, 1911; *Ladies' Garment Worker*, 2 (Nov. 1911), 17.

21. *Cleveland Press*, June 9, 1911; *Cleveland Plain Dealer*, June 11, 1911.

22. *Cleveland Plain Dealer*, July 25, 1911; August 4 and 9, 1911.

23. Virginia Clark Abbott, *The History of Women Suffrage and the League of Women Voters in Cuyahoga County, 1911–1945* (n.p., 1949), 13–18. In 1912,

Rose Schneiderman of the ILGWU and the WTUL began factory talks on behalf of suffrage. H. Black Co., largest of the 1911 strike targets, was her first stop. Abbott, *History*, 23.

24. *Cleveland Plain Dealer*, June 21, 1911.

25. Newman, "From the Battlefield," 294; *Cleveland Plain Dealer*, July 21, 1911; Mary E. Dreier, *Margaret Dreier Robins, Her Life, Letters, and Work* (New York: Island Press Cooperative, 1950), 70, 82.

26. Marie Remington Wing, unpublished memoir, WRHS.

27. Cleveland Section, National Council of Jewish Women, MSS3620, container 2, folder 4; container 27, folder 2, WRHS.

28. Quoted in John Joseph Grabowski, "A Social Settlement in a Neighborhood in Transition, Hiram House, Cleveland, Ohio, 1869–1912," Ph.D. dissertation, Case Western Reserve University, 1977, 104.

29. Minutes of the Board, June 7, 1911, Jewish Community Federation Archives, Cleveland. Rabbi Gries represented the Council Educational Alliance on the Federation board, yet his concerns did not seem to be shared by women on the CEA board. The Federation board met on June 10 and failed to mention the strike. Jewish Community Center of Cleveland, MSS 3668, series 1, container 1, folder 7, WRHS; *Jewish Independent*, May 5, 1911; *Cleveland Plain Dealer*, July 3, 1911.

30. *Jewish Review and Observer*, Sept. 29, 1911.

31. *Jewish Review and Observer*, Oct. 6, 1911.

32. *Cleveland Plain Dealer*, June 18, 1911.

33. Grabowski, "A Social Settlement," chapter 4.

34. *Cleveland Press*, July 7, 1911. Throughout the summer, papers carried front-page stories of the record-breaking heat.

35. *Cleveland Press*, July 19, 1911; *Cleveland Plain Dealer*, July 20 and 23, 1911; August 17, 1911.

36. *Cleveland Plain Dealer*, July 3 and 20, 1911.

37. *Cleveland Plain Dealer*, August 6, 1911; Newman, "From the Battlefield," 297.

38. I am grateful to Judah Rubinstein of the Jewish Community Federation of Cleveland for his translations of these letters written by a Hungarian Jewish nonstriker, Ignatz Friedman. Written between July 20, 1911, and October 7, 1911, the letters present a unique perspective on one family's experience. Histories of strikes usually describe striking workers or employers. The nonstriker is lost in the mass of "scabs," who played a major role in strikes before World War II yet a minor role in the literature.

39. *Cleveland Plain Dealer*, Sept. 29, 1911.

40. *Ladies' Garment Worker*, 2 (Oct. 1911), 5.

41. Levine, *Garment Workers*, 328–361.

CHAPTER 6

The Uprising of the 20,000:
The Making of a Labor Legend

Ann Schofield

ON NOVEMBER 22, 1909, Clara Lemlich rose to address a meeting of garment workers in New York's Cooper Union building. Like Lemlich herself, the crowd were immigrant teenagers, mostly Jewish and Italian, who knew firsthand the low wages, squalid conditions, and sexual inequities of New York's sweatshops. Two hours of cautious speeches by male union leaders were ill suited to their volatile mood, but Lemlich, her slight body still showing the effects of a beating by company thugs, went straight to the heart of the matter. Speaking in Yiddish, she said: "I have listened to all the speakers, and I have no further patience for talk. I am one who feels and suffers from the things pictured. I move we go on strike." The crowd shouted their agreement while the chairman responded to the melee with a call for a vote and the solemn question: "Do you mean faith? Will you take the old Hebrew oath?" Three thousand hands rose and swore, "If I turn traitor to the cause I now pledge may this hand wither from the arm I now raise." The "first great strike of women" in America had begun.[1]

On some level, to tell history is to tell a tale, and as historical lore, the "Uprising of the 20,000" is richly satisfying. Few events in the history of the American working class contain the drama and romance of the strike of gallant shirtwaist makers. The swearing of the oath at Cooper Union, the battered strikers' appeal to society matrons at the Colony Club, and socialite Alva Belmont's motorcades through the

Lower East Side all ask us to believe in the unique character of the strike. The actors call attention to the female and political nature of the strike—Clara Lemlich, the fiery and impassioned worker; Anne Morgan, acting in defiance of robber baron J. P.; and Rose Schneiderman, the intense young Socialist. The temptation is great to revel in this tale of good and evil, heroism and turmoil, and to accept it as a labor legend and a feminist myth. We do so, however, at the risk of obscuring significant patterns in American labor and women's history. The events of the strike will be briefly sketched here, followed by a discussion of the historiography of this familiar story which will illuminate the historical changes that altered work, the structures of community, and the systems of power in the early twentieth century.

The strike and the popular response to it represented more than an accumulation of grievances. By 1909 the needle trades were struggling to bring order out of a particularly chaotic industry. New York, the garment capital of the world, offered a paradigm of the structure and problems in the manufacture of women's clothing. Two factors resulted in the rapid appearance and disappearance of garment shops—the low capital requirements for opening a shop and the sensitivity of the market to the vagaries of fashion. Despite this instability, by the turn of the century large shops employing several hundred workers began to dominate the New York trade. The subcontracting system distinguished the work in these large shops. Workers, always men, contracted with manufacturers for a certain amount of work and then distributed it to apprentices, usually women, for minimal wages.

Just as size of firm distinguished garment manufacturers, workers were sharply divided by skill, sex, and ethnicity. Men, who comprised 70 percent of the labor force, held the higher paying, more skilled jobs of cutters, pressers, and tailors. Women were finishers, operatives, and trimmers. By 1910 Russian Jews represented 55 percent of garment workers and dominated the International Ladies Garment Workers Union (ILGWU); the rest of the work force consisted of 35 percent Italians and 7 percent native-born Americans. These divisions, which employers frequently played upon by placing workers who spoke different languages next to each other in the shop, hardly augered well for solidarity in a strike situation.

Accounts of the initial week of the "first great strike of women" vibrate with the enthusiastic commitment of the strikers. Union halls were mobbed with workers, while the massive response to the strike call "stunned" even the union leaders and the Women's Trade Union League (WTUL). As numerous small manufacturers capitulated to the union's demand for higher wages, an end to harassment, and union recognition, the scent of victory filled the air. In four days, over ten thousand workers returned to work under union contracts.

By November the tide turned, however, and garment manufacturers started to fight back. They formed the Association of Waist and Dress Manufacturers and vowed to hold fast against the drive for the union shop. As New York entered a bitterly cold winter, the strikers geared up for what one historian has described as "siege warfare against larger firms." The manufacturers' arsenal consisted of unlimited financial resources, hired strikebreakers, imported goods, and, more important, the continued support of the courts. The brutality with which employers attacked workers, however, was publicized and won support for the strike. The image of fragile (albeit working-class) young girls being beaten by thugs moved reformers to rage and philanthropists to open their purses to support the strike. The spirit of the young women astonished observers; one of them commented: "There was never any thing like it. . . . An equal number of men would never hold together under what these girls are enduring." Not only were countless workers beaten and mauled by police and thugs, but by December 22, 707 strikers had been arrested for vagrancy and disturbing the peace, nineteen were sent to the work house on Blackwell's Island, and the rest were fined.

While the militance of the women formed the tenacious core of the strike, the activities of the WTUL, the ILGWU, and the Socialist Party were also essential elements in the struggle. The WTUL had actively organized in garments since its formation, and viewed the strike as an exceptional opportunity to recruit female workers for the labor movement, as well as to educate middle-class women about trade unionism. League support consisted of fund raising, aid on the picket line, and an attempt to throw the mantle of class protection over workers in the courts. League members did picket duty themselves, and they also recruited college students from Vassar, Barnard, and Wellesley to walk the line along with the working women. This strategy grew from the premise that the police would treat all pickets with more respect if there were middle-class women present and, if that tactic failed, these women would act as witnesses of police abuse.

In one telling incident the arresting officer commented when WTUL president Margaret Dreier was brought before a judge: "Why didn't you tell me you was a rich lady? I'd never have arrested you in the world." Additionally, the league issued a brochure written in Yiddish and English entitled "Rules for Pickets" which advised strikers of their legal rights and urged them to conduct themselves with "order and decorum." The league organized a march on City Hall in early December to protest specifically police treatment of strikers. Ten thousand marchers confronted Mayor McClellan, some carrying banners that proclaimed "Peaceful picketing is the right of every woman." This march was followed by a mass meeting at the Hippodrome on December 5, which netted $1500 for strikers, while a smaller, more elite group of socialites, meeting on December 15 at the Colony Club, contributed $1300. In all, the league collected $20,000 for the strike fund from various women's clubs and organizations.[2] The financial involvement of the league was critical not only to the continuation of the strike, but also to its beginnings. In 1909 the ILGWU, and in particular Local 25, had a virtually empty treasury.

Local 25, the Shirtwaist Makers Union, reflected the ethnic structure and sexual politics of the ILGWU itself. Founded in 1906, six years after the parent organization, its membership in 1909 fluctuated from one to eight hundred.[3] Men held all union offices and eight of fifteen executive board positions in this union representing a trade whose rank and file was 80 percent female. The ILGWU was a semi-industrial hybrid, organized by skill or job, yet striking by shop. Women in the trade consistently faced the lack of regard that male unionists had for female workers' ability as trade unionists, plus a social ideology that defined their social role as domestic rather than industrial. WTUL organizers and the experiences of walkouts and lockouts during the summer of 1909 altered that situation. Two thousand shirtwaist makers joined the ILGWU at that time, becoming enthusiastic promoters of the union cause.

The history of the ILGWU, particularly in its formative years, is inexorably linked to Jewish socialism. The "Uprising of the 20,000" well represents this fact. American Judaism became increasingly secularized during the early decades of the twentieth century. Ideals of social justice traditionally associated with Jewish life and thought became mediated through the trade union so Jewish labor leaders embraced the concern for human dignity that was a central element in this strike. A strong radical strain also animated the Jewish labor movement before and immediately following World War I. Fueled in part by Russian émigrés who participated in the revolutionary Bund movement, these young people came to view the labor movement as the best hope of effecting social reform for the working class in America. Idealistic and sometimes unrealistic, they were part of both the leadership and rank and file of the ILGWU.[4]

By early December, then, each of these groups—WTUL, ILGWU, and the Socialists—was solidly behind the strikers. Sympathetic and sensational press coverage, as well as the support of prominant clergymen, lined up public opinion for the union. Faced with such support as well as with steadily declining profits, the Manufacturers Association entered its first negotiating session with the union on December 10.

From December to February negotiations between the Manufacturers Association and the union pivoted around the issue of union recognition and the closed shop. Manufacturers felt especially pressed to settle after the Philadelphia shops, where they had been subcontracting work, went on strike on December 20. On December 23 the association and union reached a compromise settlement that met virtually every union demand on wages, hours, and conditions except the closed shop. Four days later, strikers, dismayed and disappointed by this settlement, voted "overwhelmingly" to reject it. In January, the union asked the New York State Bureau of Mediation and Arbitration to arbitrate disputes between the association and the ILGWU, but the manufacturers adamantly refused to discuss union recognition in the garment trades.

January proved to be the cruelest month of the strike. Although the community rallied to make another mass meeting at Carnegie Hall on January 2 a great success, discouragement and the winter began to take their toll. The WTUL opened a soup kitchen for strikers, and the United Hebrew Trades stepped up its fund-raising efforts, but certain socialites withdrew their support, offended by the radical—and, to their minds, unreasonable—position taken by the union. Women began to go back to work as the union signed individual agreements with a number of firms. By February 1 the trade was operating at almost full production, and on February 13, 1910, the ILGWU called the strike off.

Even though the strike ended far less explosively than it began, it affected the trade in several important areas. First, it demonstrated the structural strengths and weaknesses of the garment industry, and, in particular, the shirtwaist industry. Highly sensitive to fluctuations in style and fashion, waist manufacturers maintained small inventories and so were hard hit by a protracted strike. Banding together in a manufacturers association, however, gave them the ability to control both the commodity and the labor market in such a way as to hold out against union demands.

The strike also reflected the extent of support and cooperation that trade unions could anticipate from New York's reform community. Alliances forged during the uprising would continue through subsequent years of labor upheaval and reform activity until the New Deal. The waist makers laid the groundwork for the 1910 cloak makers' strike, which brought the Era of the Protocol to the needle trades. Finally, during days of picketing and arrest, meetings and speeches, workers experienced true labor solidarity that cut across ethnic and sometimes gender lines. They demonstrated, in a particularly dramatic way, that the "unorganizable"—youths and immigrants and women—not only could be organized but could be effectively mobilized in a labor conflict.

In the seventy-odd years since the strike galvanized New York's Lower East Side, historians have analyzed the event from numerous perspectives. Their interpretations roughly follow three themes: first, the changing nature and control of work and the character of the labor movement; second, feminist questions concerning the historical intersection of class and sex; third, the links among culture, community, and work. In part, the development of these various themes is connected to the way in which American labor history has evolved from the early economic and institutional orientation of the Commons-Perlman or Wisconsin school to the interdisciplinary and politically inspired research of the new social history. The strike also reflects concerns of contemporary American labor and of social and women's historians such as: Who will control industrial work—and the rhythms and organization of the workplace in the twentieth century? What shape will the American labor movement take? How and why do labor concerns become those of the city? Can feminism as a political movement of women transcend class to form cross-class alliances? What does the collective action of women indicate about their political awareness and sensibilities?

The early institutional histories of the ILGWU written between 1920 and 1950 rarely addressed these questions. For them the strike formed a building block in the construction of the union, an event of unchallenged benefit to the worker. This was progressive history at its most basic, and reflected the influence of the Commons-Perlman or Wisconsin school. That is, when Louis Levine, Joel Seidman, Lazare Teper, Benjamin Stolberg, and Hyman Berman[5] wrote of the strike, the union rather than the worker was center stage and the closed-shop demand was the dominant theme. Their work, despite its unanalytical quality, was applauded by labor historian David Brody who reminded us that they wrote in a time when labor historians "were contesting the primacy of classical economics in the academy and, in the outside world, and its pernicious message that collective action by workers constituted an inadmissible interference with the free play of the market."[6]

All that is true and should be remembered. Still, these authors' lack of concern for such issues as class, gender, and community mirrored the sexism and ethnocentrism of the ILGWU. Consider, for example, Benjamin Stolberg's dismissal of the uprising as part of the "emotional folklore of the union" and his labeling of female activists of Local 25 as "Chickens in a China Shop." He condemned these "rank-and-file Jeanne d'Arcs" who with their "chronic exaltation over the Class-Conscious Worker and the Toiling Masses" made "life miserable for nearly every leader in the union." Stolberg then reaffirmed the patriarchal mentality of union leaders with the statement: "To all this transcendentalism of the girls the bureaucrats reacted with bored difference [sic] and the heavy humorists among them offered cynical advice on how to get it out of their system."[7]

A new generation of historians emerged in the 1950s and 1960s, who turned the focus of labor history from the trade union toward the industry, the community, and the shop floor. In the "new labor history," workers moved downstage to take a more active role in their own past. Economics, of course, still played a critical part in explaining why and how workers organize and strike. Melvyn Dubofsky, for example, characterizes the uprisings as "an organizational strike" but also stresses that the active reform movement in New York, the values and institutions of the Jewish community, and the chaotic situation in garments created by subcontracting all created an environment condusive to the strike. The strike threatened a key industry in a city where one-sixth of all workers were employed in garments. For Dubofsky, the strike represents a clash between the fundamental interests of capital—"industrial discipline"—and the commitment of labor to industrial democracy. The interests of employers, in other words, demanded "efficiency, economy and elimination of waste in the workplace and the right to select the most productive workers to accomplish that end." Workers needed to limit the employer's absolute control of production through collective bargaining.

Dubofsky makes the important point that the trade union for Jewish immigrants became a cultural institution during this period. Specifically, the ILGWU with its affinity for socialism and moral reform came to represent a secular alternative both to religious orthodoxy and radical socialist politics for working class Jewish men. In urban America, the trade union became to the Jews what urban politics had long been for the Irish. The impetus for the strike, however, as Dubofsky correctly notes, came not from the union but from the workers themselves; the combined action of skilled and unskilled workers made the general strike an effective weapon "in the needle trades decades before its appearance and triumph elsewhere in the U.S."[8] James Green, like Dubofsky, interprets the uprising as a struggle for control of work and the workplace.[9] Philip Foner's account, while comprehensive, is far less analytical than either of these two historians.[10]

Two specialized studies, one by John Laslett, *Labor and the Left*,[11] and the other by Graham Adams entitled *Age of Industrial Violence, 1910–15*,[12] emphasize prominent features of the uprising. Laslett claims that the ILGWU was an institutional expression of Jewish socialism, "a unique combination of militancy and idealism, coupled with practical trade unionism." For Laslett, the uprising occurred at a critical moment in the ILGWU's history. By 1909, a number of political activists committed to the Bund had their hopes of a Russian Socialist state dashed by the failure of the 1905 Russian revolution. Turning their revolutionary vision from the old world to the new, they mastered their earlier impatience with the American labor movement and channeled their energies into building strong unions in the needle trades. True to a Jewish tradition of intellectual leaders, by

1900 most of the leaders of the ILGWU were radicals who themselves had worked in the garment industry. In contrast to the "pure and simple" unionism of most other American Federation of Labor (AFL) unions, the ILGWU saw at least at this time the trade union in politicized terms, with a mission of social reform. The ILGWU enjoyed the solid support of the AFL, however, because AFL leader Gompers feared incursions by the syndicalist Industrial Workers of the World into garments between 1905 and 1909. Laslett is careful to note that neither the 1909 shirtwaist strike nor the cloak-makers' strike the following year had a clearly Socialist impulse, the root causes being workers' grievances. Socialist leadership and moral and financial support were nevertheless vital elements in the strike.

Graham Adams explores another facet of the uprising in his study of industrial violence based on the reports of the United States Commission of Industrial Relations. Adams points out that employers hired prostitutes and thugs with criminal records to taunt and abuse picketing strikers. The violence was so extreme, however, that newspaper accounts such as the following gained publicity and community support for the strikers.

> Gangs of men used their fists against girl strikers. Two strikebreakers hurled a picket to the ground and then stamped on her. A group of thugs pounced on a strike committee chairman while he was collecting funds and injured him so badly that he had to remain in bed for three weeks. Another assailant jumped upon a 19 year old girl, smashed her side, and broke one of her ribs. He disabled her for life.[13]

Additionally the indifference and even participation of police in these violent activities, ostensibly in support of private property, brought to the fore the issue of "the place of the police in our modern industrial and social life."

Moses Rischin's rich descriptions of New York's Jewish community between 1870 and 1914 in his seminal monograph *The Promised City*[14] are incorporated into many of the works cited above. Rischin in particular captures the "contagious idealism" of the uprising and sets it in the context of a vibrant lower East Side Jewish culture. What was the garment workers' world like apart from the shop? Rischin tells us there were Yiddish theater and Yiddish and English vaudeville, there were dancing academies for the moderns, newspapers for the literate—close to 150 Yiddish journals were published between 1885 and 1914—and the Educational Alliance offered classes in Yiddish. Like Dubofsky, Rischin acknowledges that the manifestation of ideals of social justice through labor activity indicated the increasing secularization of Judaism in the New World.

Rischin's sensitivity to ethnic culture leads him to describe the way in which the uprising helped to both mend and accentuate the sharp ethnic fissures in the garment trade labor force which employers traditionally had used to divide workers. In one particularly striking example he captures the impact of the uprising on a young black worker as well as her mixed feelings toward the more activist Jewish workers:

> It's a good thing, this strike is, it makes you feel like a real grown-up person. . . . But I wish I'd feel about it like them Jew girls do. Why their eyes flash fire as soon as they commence to talk about the strike—and the lot of talk they can put up—at time they make a body feel like two cents.[15]

Essentially, Rischin shows us that the uprising was more than the sum of shop floor grievances and trade-union politics and that it also included the cultural environment of the immigrant workers. Rischin does not, however, explicitly identify the distinctively female dimension of the strike. It remained for feminist historians writing in the 1970s and 1980s to ask and answer pertinent questions about the connections between women and work, politics and culture.

Historians of women, in a sense, have expanded the parameters of the "new labor history" to include gender and its implications for the behavior, consciousness, and perception of the female worker. For these scholars the sexual division of labor in the garment trade—which relegated women to lower-paid, less-skilled jobs—as well as the cultural prescriptions for women—which assigned them to a subordinate social position—translated into a secondary role in the trade union. Their work has enlarged our knowledge of the WTUL, for the uprising presents a classic case study of a feminist attempt to bridge class distance between women in a united effort to improve women's social situation. Finally, women's historians interpret the strike in terms of its political importance for women. What does it mean when politically disfranchised women engage in collective action? Does it reflect a political consciousness? Does it structurally alter their position in a male-dominated workplace and labor movement?

Meredith Tax, a Marxist-feminist, addresses these questions in a chapter case study devoted to the "Uprising of the 30,000" (number is her estimate) in *The Rising of the Women: Feminist Solidarity and Class Conflict, 1880–1917*.[16] Tax's theme is that of the historically recurring "united front" of women who transcend class and social divisions in the struggle for feminist goals. In 1909, for example, the front consisted of trade unionists, Socialists, and feminists. The promise of the united front almost materialized in the uprising but was ultimately defeated by the contradictions of a male-dominated labor movement, a socialist movement that failed to acknowledge women's unique oppression under capitalism, and a feminism that did not recognize the significance of class differences among women.

Mary Jo Buhle further explores the questions of cross-class cooperation, ideology and collective action in her history of one politicized group of women. In *Women and American Socialism, 1880–1920*,[17] Buhle describes the ideas and personalities that led to Socialist participation in the uprising. By 1909, Socialists had come to recognize that female wage labor was a permanent feature of capitalism that defined the woman worker as a proletarian. Buhle points out, however, that in taking this stance the "special qualities of women's lives became insignificant because they were subsumed by their new proletarian identity." The strike, rather than addressing the demands of domesticity and workplace made upon women, offered the opportunity to test the double-barreled labor strategy of the Socialist Party, which consisted of an economic thrust through trade unions and political involvement in the party. While the strike involved socialist women through consumer boycotts, fund raising, moral uplift activities, and the formation of shop committees, often in close collaboration with the WTUL, it did not succeed in lining up large numbers of female workers under the Socialist banner. Strike activists such as Rose Schneiderman and Leonora O'Reilly joined in the Socialist Party following the strike and socialist women assumed more influential positions in both the ILGWU and the WTUL but, in general, the strike experience heightened the animosity between socialist women and what they viewed as the class collaborationists of the WTUL. A significant number of league members were Socialists; others such as Eva McDonald Valesh or Anne Morgan publicly expressed fears that Socialists would taint the league with radicalism.

The socialist-reform split is only one aspect of the history of the WTUL explored by Nancy Schrom Dye in her comprehensive history of the New York league, *As Sisters and As Equals*.[18] While Foner evaluates the functional value of the league and Dubofsky sneers at the condescending attitude of its socialite members, Dye views the strike from the perspective of both the strikers and their middle-class "allies." The uprising represented the culmination of five years of organizing in garments by the league. But, like any crisis, it brought long simmering factionalism to the surface. Socialist women felt that their contributions were slighted while prominent wealthy women were lauded. Such working-class activists as Pauline Newman and Rose Schneiderman chafed at the direction of middle-class "allies." Finally, by the strike's end, the league's relations with the ILGWU had deteriorated, as many league members found themselves disillusioned with the union's inherent paternalism. Through their fund raising, picketing, and legal aid they successfully educated large numbers of middle-class women about trade unionism and the plight of the working girl. Once the excitement and drama of the strike ebbed, however, they found that the average worker had learned little about union organizing and tactics. The continued male leadership of the union had, if anything, reinforced women's marginal position in the labor movement and, paradoxically, reinforced a sexual division of labor among workers in the garment industry.

The most significant facet of the strike for feminist historians is the interplay between cultural ideals for women and the reality of working women's lives under industrial capitalism. On the one hand, the dominant American culture dictated that female behavior be ladylike, demure, and circumspect (the advent of the "new woman" notwithstanding)—all qualities at odds with appropriate strike action. On the other hand, Jewish immigrant culture offered alternative standards that cast the shirtwaist makers in a positive, even heroic mold. As both Alice Kessler-Harris[19] and Charlotte Baum[20] point out, Jewish women, unlike other immigrants, frequently worked for wages in East Europe shtetls to support scholarly husbands. In the New World, as in the Old, Jewish women were expected to contribute to the family economy as daughters and as wives. This is not to say that Jewish culture encouraged careerism among women but rather that it did not censure women's work outside the home. Furthermore young Jewish women, just as Jewish men, were exposed to the crosscurrents of modern and Socialist thought that coursed through the Lower East Side. The Bund tradition included revolutionary heroines; Rischin writes of young female workers "drowning weariness and disillusionment with nostalgic choruses of 'O Dubinushka,' 'Tortured and Enslaved,' and other Russian folk and revolutionary airs."[21] A contemporary observer wrote of women's presence in the radical coffeehouses of the time. There, he said, "where the cigarette smoke is thickest and denunciation of the present forms of government loudest, there you find women! . . . These are the stalwarts of the radical movements, the Amazons." Paradoxically, he continued, they are "unromantic, perhaps, and yet we hear of them toiling, slaving, denying themselves until some man has won a degree and an entry into one of the professions."[22]

Finally, many young strikers in 1909 could remember mothers, aunts, and sisters who took to the streets in the violent 1902 Kosher meat riots and the 1907 rent strikes. While these events concerned consumption rather than production, they formed part of an activist community heritage for New York's Jewish women.[23]

In short, as described by Kessler-Harris and Hyman, women's public collective action met with cultural and community approval rather than censure. Buhle, in fact, makes the point that the working woman was a "central cultural figure" in Jewish community and popular literature. For inexperienced teenagers, the reference points of the Bund and the consumer riots guided their actions, while politicized women in their neighborhoods provided role models and leaders.

The historiography of the "Uprising of the 20,000" reflects the state of the art in labor history. Proceeding from the early institutional historians of the ILGWU to later attempts at workers' history, to specialized studies, and finally to feminist concerns, one gets a sense of an ever-enlarging stage featuring the strike as a social drama. The metahistorical questions of issues, focus, and perspective that structure the drama are keys to understanding the continued fascination that the uprising had for historians. Those such as Dubofsky who provide us with information regarding changing work and its impact on workers, the drive for workers' rights, and the context of urban politics point to the way in which labor becomes a significant factor in the equation of power in America. To explain how and why the "unorganizable" were organized, however, leads to the questions of women's historical position of inequity both at the workplace and in the labor movement. Feminist historians have placed this issue and its implications for the history of working women high on their research agenda and have found that despite activist experience, the paternalism, even patriarchy, of the trade union reinforced women's secondary social status. By 1909 the working-class woman could work and engage in union and political activities, but only during a limited period of her life. Those union careerists who departed from this pattern, such as Rose Schneiderman, Rose Pesotta, and Fannia Cohen, according to Alice Kessler-Harris, found personal fulfillment at the price of loneliness and social censure.[24]

Historical events such as the "Uprising of the 20,000" that captured the attention of numerous historians demonstrate how ongoing revision enriches and informs historical narrative, the tale that history tells. The concerns of feminist or labor history, for example, expose the limitations of the conventional narrative that accepts a shared set of assumptions by historian and audience. Traditionally, this sets women in the disadvantaged position of being absent from or unimportant in the continuing historical process. Historical reinterpretation then alters the shape of the narrative as well as adding to the information we have of an event.

The "Uprising of the 20,000" is a spirited and heroic chapter in the history of America's working women. But its underlying historical messages are somber ones. Women are foot soldiers rather than generals in labor's armies and, as Meredith Tax reminds us, "Only certain kinds of wars can be won by such an army, and a war for women's liberation is not among them."[25]

NOTES

1. Contemporary accounts of the strike include: William Mailly, "The Working Girls' Strike," *Independent*, 67 (Dec. 23, 1909), 1416–1420. Woods Hutchinson, "The Hygienic Aspects of the Shirtwaist Strike," *Survey*, 23 (Jan. 22, 1910), 541–550; Miriam F. Scott, "The Spirit of the Girl Strikers," *Outlook*, 94 (Feb. 19, 1910), 394–395; Sue Ainsley Clark and Edith Wyatt, "The

Shirtwaist Makers and Their Strike," *McClure's Magazine*, 36 (Nov. 1910), 70–86; New York *World*, Nov. 23, 1909; *New York Call*, Nov. 23, 1909.

2. Nancy Schrom Dye, *As Sisters and As Equals: Feminism, Unionism and the Women's Trade Union League of New York* (Columbia: University of Missouri Press, 1980).

3. Louis Levine, *The Women's Garment Workers* (New York: B. W. Huebsch, 1924), 149.

4. Melvyn Dubofsky, *When Workers Organize: New York City in the Progressive Era* (Amherst: University of Massachusetts Press, 1968); Melech Epstein, *Jewish Labor in the U. S. A.* (New York: Trade Union Sponsoring Committee, 1950–1953); Philip S. Foner, *Women and the American Labor Movement: From the First Trade Unions to the Present* (New York: Free Press, 1979).

5. Hyman Berman, "The Era of the Protocol: A Chapter in the History of the ILGWU, 1910–1916," PhD diss., Columbia University, 1955. Louis Levine, *Garment Workers*. Joel Seidman, *The Needle Trades* (New York: Farrar and Rinehart, 1942). Benjamin Stolberg, *Tailor's Progress* (Garden City, N.Y.: Doubleday, Doran, 1944). Lazare Teper, *The Women's Garment Industry* (New York: ILGWU, 1937).

6. David Brody, "The Old Labor History and the New: In Search of an American Working Class," *Labor History*, 20, no. 1 (Winter 1979), 112.

7. Stolberg, *Tailor's Progress*.

8. Dubofsky, *When Workers Organize*.

9. James R. Green, *The World of the Worker: Labor in the Twentieth Century* (New York: Hill and Wang, 1980).

10. Foner, *Women*.

11. John Laslett, *Labor and the Left: A Study of Socialist and Radical Influences in the American Labor Movement, 1881–1924* (New York: Basic Books, 1970).

12. Graham Adams, *Age of Industrial Violence, 1910–15: The Activities and Findings of the U. S. Commission of Industrial Relations* (New York, 1966).

13. Ibid., 106–107.

14. Moses Rischin, *The Promised City: New York's Jews, 1870–1914* (Cambridge: Harvard University Press, 1962).

15. Ibid.

16. Meredith Tax, *The Rising of the Women: Feminist Solidarity and Class Conflict, 1880–1917* (New York: Monthly Review Press, 1980).

17. Mary Joe Buhle, *Women and American Social Socialism, 1870–1920* (Urbana: University of Illinois Press, 1980).

18. Dye, *As Sisters*, esp. chap. 4, "Revolution in the Garment Trades, 1909–1913."

19. Alice Kessler-Harris, "Organizing the Unorganizable: Three Jewish Women and Their Union," *Labor History*, 17 (Winter 1976), 5–23.

20. Charlotte Baum, et al., *The Jewish Woman in America* (New York: Dial Press, 1976).

21. Rischin, *Promised City*, 70.

22. Charles S. Bernheimer, ed., *The Russian Jew in the United States* (Philadelphia: The John C. Winston Co., 1905), 225.

23. Paula Hyman, "Immigrant Women and Consumer Protest: The New York City Kosher Meat Boycott of 1902," *American Jewish History*, 70 (1980), 91–105.

24. Kessler-Harris, "Organizing."

25. Tax, *Rising of the Women*, 240.

PART III

INSIDE
AND OUTSIDE
THE UNIONS:
1920–1980

INSIDE AND OUTSIDE THE UNIONS: 1920–1980

Joan M. Jensen

ONCE women had entered unions in large numbers, their battles had to be fought on two fronts: inside and outside the unions. The unionization movement continued, with organizers fanning out across the United States to follow runaway shops as they fled organizing in the Northeast. Here organizers, mostly from old industrial centers, encountered new workers with different cultural traditions and languages. Hispanic, Asian, and native-born southern white women all provided new challenges to organizers in their attempts to expand union influence. At the same time, women within the two remaining major clothing unions encountered male opposition to their leadership. Male officials continued to maintain that women were difficult to organize at the same time that they denied union women a major voice in determining policies on the recruitment of the predominantly female clothing workers and their assimilation into the union.

Organizers devoted long careers to recruiting and supporting women within the unions and yet never achieved a major voice in those unions. These unions promised working women support for controlling their working conditions. Yet once inside the promised land of unionization, women had to face having no control over their organizational hierarchy. The tensions of these two contradictory conditions dominated the history of clothing workers after 1910.

The careers of women leaders in unions clearly indicated the difficulty of organizing and the lack of union support for rank-and-file leadership that might have been drawn from the masses of the new women workers in the runaway shops of the West. Some female union activists did become a species of honorary officials as vice presidents upon marriage to ACWA leaders: Bessie Abramovitz, for example, who married Sidney Hillman, and Dorothy Jacobs, who married Albert Bellanca. While the work of these women was important, as Nina Asher explains in her article on Dorothy Jacobs Bellanca, they

185

did not challenge the male leadership, but supported it. In neither the ILGWU nor the ACWA were women able to go beyond a well-defined place to reflect the predominantly female constituency of their unions. They could encourage women to organize, but they could not expand the role of these women in the unions. It must have seemed to the rank and file that only marriage with union leaders, even if that marriage was a partnership, could bring leadership roles for women. Women had to subordinate their interests as women to class issues—class issues as defined by the eastern male union leadership.

While Dorothy Jacobs Bellanca worked within the ACWA, other women organizers continued the battle within the ILGWU. The ILGWU emerged from World War I shorn of its cross-class allies in the Women's Trade Union League and torn by domestic political conflict.

In the aftermath of the Red scare of 1919 most militant left organizations disintegrated or went underground. But many militant individuals remained in mainstream labor organizations and the Communists emerged in the early 1920s as the main organizers of the left. In the years between 1924 and 1926 clothing unions bristled with conflict over control. Centrists attempted to keep the more radical leftists from being elected by rank-and-file members. In New York, the centrists failed in their attempt, and in July 1926, Communist members led the ILWGU into a massive and costly six-month strike involving 35,000 clothing workers. During this strike, the employers found public opinion and the police on their side; seventy-five hundred strikers were arrested. Conflict over the strike split locals clear across the country to Los Angeles, where factions battled over whether or not to send strike funds to New York.[1] Following the strike, centrists again gained control; and in 1928 the internal conflict was finally settled through reorganization. The ILGWU expelled its Communist members (actually it dissolved all dissident locals and required members to reregister), and the Communists began a policy of dual unionism, that is, organizing independent rival unions rather than working for influence within AFL unions. Thus, yet another union emerged, the Industrial Union of Needle Trade Workers (IUNTW) to contend for the leadership of the women sewers.[2]

The period of dual unionism ushered in a bitterness among contending union factions which has lasted to the present. All accounts of union politics are colored by these factional disputes, making it difficult to reconstruct an unbiased account of events. The struggle over control of the rank and file gave employers the opportunity to play one group off against the other. ILGWU accounts accuse the IUNTW of offering "scab" labor to employers and allowing the trade to be overrun with "scab shoplets." Defensiveness led the ILGWU away from its progressive politics into a highly structured, centralized organization unable to allow freedom to locals in organizing the militant Hispanic women who had become the new reserve army of labor, the women whose labor had to be organized if the runaway shops were to be halted in their march to the Southwest. To the more militant rank and file, ILGWU leadership seemed committed to avoiding conflict that could endanger its leadership. Only in the context of this domestic quarrel among the male leadership of the clothing workers can the failure of women organizers of the 1930s, such as Rose Pesotta, be understood.[3]

Rose Pesotta's career in some ways is the most significant for understanding the ultimate failure of the Jewish women who organized for the women's clothing unions after World War I. Such earlier organizers as Pauline Newman and Fannia Cohen, who organized primarily among Jewish and Italian women, have been judged passive but successful by Alice Kessler-Harris in both their personal and professional lives. While always battling intolerance of male unionists, both Newman and Cohen established warm supportive relations with both working-class and middle-class women.[4]

Rose Pesotta began full-time organizing in 1933, at a time when women were being accepted as part of the permanent work force, but she was not recruited to organize among women of her own culture. Instead she went west to Los Angeles, San Francisco, Seattle, Portland, and then to Puerto Rico. In these places she had to work with Asian and Hispanic women and yet be responsible to an increasingly conservative male union hierarchy. The difficulties of such a task finally caused her to abandon organizing and return to the shop. Her account of organizing in *Bread upon the Waters* carefully defends the ILGWU leadership, but even her own account indicates that the ILGWU could not provide the leadership needed by Hispanic and Asian women.[5]

Pesotta's experience in Los Angeles is an excellent example of this conflict. When the Los Angeles clothing industry expanded during the 1920s, unions followed the eastern pattern, with Jewish and Italian workers forming the core of the locals. Beginning in 1920, the ILGWU sent out organizers to work with the Spanish-speaking women workers, but throughout the 1920s these attempts were sporadic and unsuccessful. Part of the difficulty was due to the employers not being interested in stabilizing the industry in a geographic area that could not specialize in the high-fashion skilled operations common to New York. Communist influence in Los Angeles was also stronger than in New York, and the centrists were not able to regain control as quickly. By the time Pesotta arrived in 1933, Communists had formed their own union, but they remained a formidable threat. The ILGWU was never able to provide a united front against the employers. Pesotta was conscious that the Communists presented a serious threat to the ILGWU because they challenged its tactics and its leadership.[6]

Chinatown sweatshops in San Francisco were even more difficult and complex to organize than the Hispanic sweatshops of Los Angeles. Chinese males sewed most of the clothing in the first late-nineteenth-century sweatshops, but women began operating sewing machines in the early twentieth century. By the 1920s Chinese women were a majority; by the 1930s women were organizing. Jenny Matyas helped organize the first ILGWU local in Chinatown. In the thirteen-week strike that followed, however, the National Dollar Store closed rather than agree to unionization. When Pesotta arrived, she found she could give the Chinese women little help. Women desperately needed the work to support their families, the Chinese community was ghettoized without cross-class or cross-ethnic support, the community did not have the resources to sustain extended strike activity, and the companies did not have enough capital investment in their businesses to make paying higher wages worthwhile. The women remained unorganized.[7]

In the Northeast, meanwhile, the male-dominated unions managed to strike a balance that allowed them to survive a discouraging decade for labor. Unions emerged in a declining but controlled place in the clothing industry. Sex segregation and low wages were the price women paid for unionization. Women continued to dominate the industry numerically as low-paid stitchers, and the movement of employers out of New York City continued to draw women into the garment industry and to leave them there, at the bottom. As this movement has had such a long history and continues to the present day, we need to examine it in some detail, studying the overall conditions of the industry, the ingredients of the compromise, and its effect on women workers.[8]

In 1981 sewing remained one of the most sex segregated of all United States occupations: 96.7 percent of all stitchers are women, exceeded in percentages only by secretaries and dental assistants (99.3 and 97.9 percent respectively). Median wages were also the third lowest, after waiters and retail sales clerks.[9] At the same time, clothing was a highly unionized industry compared to other industries in which women predominated. Thus, its unique position requires explanation.

The clothing industry as a whole experienced a decline in sales in the 1920s, which especially affected New York and the women's clothing sector. While this period saw a great increase in pattern sales, the primary reason for the decline in ready-made clothing sales, particularly women's clothing, appears to have been a shift in household spending patterns. With the appearance of new consumer durables—especially cars and appliances—families chose to spend more of their income on these items rather than on clothes. A family's status now seemed to be linked to these purchases. While the trend first affected upper middle-class families, it had reached the working classes by the 1950s. Clothing continued to be "democratized" during this period, but mainly because new material items were available which could more easily set off one class from another. As one commentator remarked in the 1950s: "Not only do Americans of all classes look much the same when they dress up, they are indistinguishable when they are not dressed up, and that is a larger and larger part of the time." The new leisure wear began a trend that culminated in blue jeans. Only vestiges of the former function of clothes as a status definer remained.[10]

As a result, there was an actual increase in home-made women's clothing in the 1920s and the 1930s, a trend that may have given both the scantier and less-form-fitting clothing an additional attraction. Most women could now make their own clothing if they wished to, and dressmaking gradually disappeared as an occupation for poorer middle-class women. Millinery also disappeared as an occupation in the 1930s, as women ceased to create their own headwear or to order it specially made. A store-bought hat frequently topped a home-made outfit. After World War II, the higher percentage of married women and higher fertility rates also diverted income from clothes. Women over fifty were not yet expected to keep up with styles; thus, as the female population aged, so did their clothing.[11]

As competition for markets again increased, women's sewing wages were pushed still lower compared to the wages in male-dominated occupations. The struggle of employers usually took the form of flight west to upstate New York or to the coal mining areas of Pennsylvania, where there was little work available for women, and to the Southwest, where Hispanic women had little available paid labor except agriculture and domestic work. The flight continued overseas in the 1970s, as multinationals reached out to the even lower-paid women of Asia and Latin America.

The great compromise between union leaders and employers in the sewing industry—solidified in legislation, union contracts, racketeering, and union ideology—was to maintain New York as a center for cutting and marketing of high fashion women's clothing, especially dresses and suits. Meanwhile, the sewing of less changeable clothing, especially blouses and other casual wear, moved West out of New York City. While many New York employers had abandoned the protocols signed in 1914 and 1915, those who decided to move to the new place in the market remained committed to collective bargaining. By the 1920s and 1930s, clothing unions were beginning to resemble more and more the old Knights of Labor in their opposition to strikes. Strikes, according to the new industrial relations experts, were regrettable outbreaks of class warfare, to be avoided at all costs.

In the context of this emerging compromise between employers and union leaders to stabilize the New York segment of the volatile clothing industry, the militant strike of 1926 seemed like madness. Once centrists had regained control, unions opposed strikes in union shops, organized the nonunion markets, made concessions on wage rates, and cooperated with management to cut costs. Total employment and the proportion of workers unionized dropped, but union-dominated shops retained a large share of the market.[12]

Like the earlier Knights of Labor, the ILGWU had difficulty in avoiding strikes and still attracting women workers, for whom strikes seemed to remain the speediest form of education to the benefits of unionization and politicization. Strikes did continue in the 1930s, and the number of women involved in them reached a new high in

1934. At the same time, the percentage of union workers involved in the clothing strikes of the mid-1930s declined as the totals of workers increased. The mass uprisings of 1933 to 1935 (almost 315,000 workers struck in 1933) brought greater emphasis on collective bargaining and government support for mediation. The largest of these strikes occurred in New York state and Pennsylvania, indicating that the workers employed in runaway shops had taken the initiative in using the strike as a weapon.[13]

In this context, then, the unions became a more and more conservative force, hoping to organize women, but unwilling to give them a larger place in the unions or to encourage the militant sewers to strike. Usually, union organizers moved in to settle strikes and to enforce control. The Farah strike of 1972 in El Paso, which lasted two years and became a national symbol of organized women workers, may seem an exception to this generalization. In fact, it was part of the pattern.

The El Paso garment industry was already almost seventy years old when the Farah strike began in 1972. From a small overall factory at the turn of the century, the industry grew slowly, finally burgeoning in the 1930s, when companies flourished in Los Angeles, San Antonio, Dallas, Laredo, and El Paso. As in Los Angeles, eastern union men never committed enough money to make the sporadic organizing drives of the 1930s successful. While clothing workers were "union-minded," as one historian has emphasized, and the Hispanic workers militant, union leaders did not trust local Hispanic female leadership. When the trade in New York increased during World War II, the ILGWU lost interest in even its sporadic organizing attempts in Texas, and after the state passed its right-to-work law in 1947, it became difficult for women to organize.[14]

It was, as the authors of "Women at Farah" explain, the rapid expansion of Farah in the 1960s that led to the militant Chicana workers' engaging in a protracted strike with the support of the Amalgamated Clothing Workers. The successful organization of a national boycott of Farah pants, the support of a Catholic church politicized by the civil rights movement, and a militant rank-and-file group within Farah calling for reforms, caused the company to sign a contract recognizing the union. But the victory faded as workers faced the prospect of new production techniques, company financial difficulties, and the union officials' ensuing concern with keeping its new members at work. Instead of pressing for innovative ways to control runaways and increase wages of foreign women workers, unions once again chose to control women's wages. The result has been the continued flight of sewing to Third World countries and the return of subcontracting, especially in New York and Los Angeles.[15]

In "A Stitch in Our Time," Elizabeth Weiner and Hardy Green explain the conditions in the New York clothing district that have led to a resurgence of the sweatshops that the unions and their middle-class allies fought so hard to eliminate in the great uprisings of the 1910s. Similar conditions exist in clothing districts of Los Angeles. Streets there are lined with sweatshops where both legal and un-documented workers from Latin America and Asia sew under conditions little better than those that so outraged early twentieth-century reformers. Neither unions nor reformers any longer make any attempt to curtail these activities. Even the left seems stumped. Although equal pay for comparable work has made it possible to argue for increased wages for skilled and managerial women, sewing is simply not comparable.[16] The number of women waiting to work for even sweated wages has created a Third World at home, a garment ghetto allowed to grow relatively unhampered.

So too have the Third World sewing ghettoes flourished abroad. Linked by multinationals that arrange for cutting in the United States and for sewing where women will work for low pay, the new clothing industry can ignore any pressure to raise wages at home or abroad. In Puerto Rico, the federal government gives companies tax incentives. Governments elsewhere do the same. With unions still dominated by male leadership, women have remained as they were—underpaid and overworked in homes and factories.

The history of sewing women is still being written. The women stitch on. The only possible solution to the continued degradation of their work is a unified demand by working-class and middle-class feminist allies for legislation that will enable the raising of women's wages at home and abroad. Control of their unions is a first, long overdue step. Leadership must be assumed by union women, who are the most politically conscious of sewing women.[17] Until that time, the sewing women of the world will remain united only by the stitches they take in the never-ending pieces of cloth that come to their worktables. They remain enslaved to the machines that could have liberated them to share in the benefits of their society.

NOTES

1. Irving Bernstein, *The Lean Years: A History of the American Worker, 1920–1933* (Boston: Houghton Mifflin, 1960), 136–141, sees conflict as between conservatives and Communists. For Communists in Los Angeles, I have relied on an unpublished paper by Dian Degnan, "The International Ladies' Garment Workers' Union in Los Angeles: 1919–1930."

2. For a selection of the articles by moderate ILGWA supporters see Leon Stein, ed., *Out of the Sweatshop: The Struggle for Industrial Democracy* (New York: Quadrangle, 1977), 202–221.

3. Dwight Edwards Robinson, *Collective Bargaining and Market Control in the New York Coat and Suit Industry* (New York: Columbia University Press, 1949), 55–57, gives a brief, somewhat dispassionate union view.

4. Kessler-Harris, "Organizing the Unorganizable: Three Jewish Women and Their Union," *Labor History*, 17 (Winter 1976), 14–20.

5. Ibid., 20–22; Rose Pesotta, *Bread upon the Waters* (New York: Dodd, Mead, 1945).

6. Degnan, "International Ladies' Garment Workers' Union," gives the Los Angeles background. For similar difficulties see 7.

7. Dean Lan, "The Chinatown Sweatshops: Oppression and an Alternative," *Amerasia Journal*, 1 (Nov. 1971), 43–45. In the 1938 pecan shellers strike in San Antonio, the union replaced a Hispanic woman leader who was Communist with a moderate Anglo male. Similar struggles seem to have gone on within the clothing unions. See Richard Croxdale, "The 1938 San Antonio Pecan Shellers' Strike," in Richard Croxdale and Melissa Hield, *Women in the Texas Workforce: Yesterday and Today* (Austin: People's History in Texas, 1979).

8. Helen I. Safa, "Runaway Shops and Female Employment: The Search for Cheap Labor," *Signs*, 7 (1981), 418–433.

9. "Sex Segregation Doesn't Pay: Can Comparable Worth Close the Wage Gap," *Dollars & Sense*, 76 (April 1982), 16–17.

10. The best discussion of New York's clothing industry from the 1920s to the 1950s is in Max Hall, ed., *Made in New York: Case Studies in Metropolitan Manufacturing* (Cambridge: Harvard University Press, 1959), esp. 98–122; the quote is from 122. See also Paul H. Nystrom, *Economics of Fashion* (New York: Ronald, 1928), 436–441.

11. Hall, *Made in New York*, 121–122.

12. Bernstein, *Lean Years*, 100–101; and Jesse Thomas Carpenter, *Competition and Collective Bargaining in the Needle Trades, 1910–1967* (Ithaca: New York State School of Industrial and Labor Relations, Cornell University, 1972).

13. Florence Peterson, *Strikes in the United States, 1880–1936* (Washington: Government Printing Office, 1938), 50–51, 138, 161.

14. For El Paso see Mario T. Garcia, "The Chicana in American History: The Mexican Women of El Paso, 1880–1920—A Case Study," *Pacific Historical Review*, 49 (1980), 315–338, and Melissa Hield, "Union-Minded: Women in the Texas ILGWA, 1933–50," in Croxdale and Hield, *Texas Workforce*, 1–23.

15. Safa, "Runaway Shops," 418–433; Elizabeth Weiner and Hardy Green,

"Bringing It All Back Home," *In These Times* (March 11–18, 1981), and Barbara Ehrenreich and Annette Fuentes, "Life on the Global Assembly Line," *Ms.*, 9 (Jan. 1981), 53–59, 71.

16. "Sex Segregation Doesn't Pay," 17; Mario F. Vazquez, "The Election Day Immigration Raid at Lilli Diamond Originals and the Response of the ILGWA," and Lisa Schlein, "Los Angeles Garment District Sews a Cloak of Shame," in Magdalena Mora and Adelaida R. Del Castillo, eds., *Mexican Women in the United States* (Los Angeles: Chicano Studies Research Center Publications, University of California, Occasional Paper No. 2, 1980).

17. Edna E. Raphael, "From Sewing Machines to Politics: The Woman Union Member in the Community," unpublished paper that compares three samples of women: one unionized, one not, and one not in the paid labor force.

CHAPTER 7

Dorothy Jacobs Bellanca: Women Clothing Workers And the Runaway Shops

Nina Asher

> The Board of Trade and the Chamber of Commerce of Scranton [Pennsylvania] boost their thriving city as a "cheap labor" town. They extend alluring invitations to eastern manufacturers to come to Scranton and enjoy the benefits and profits to be derived there. They guarantee protection from labor agitation and they proclaim their American belief in the "open shop."[1]

IN 1920 Ansorge Brothers, a New York clothing manufacturing firm, moved to Scranton to escape union agitation. The firm and other clothing manufacturers had prospered during World War I and consequently had agreed to the Amalgamated Clothing Workers of America's (ACWA) standards of wages, hours, and conditions rather than risk wartime profits in industrial conflict. By 1920, as demand for clothing declined, manufacturers resorted to cutting labor costs. As unionized workers struggled to retain improvements achieved during the war, such firms as Ansorge Brothers began to seek "open shop" communities such as Scranton, with many unemployed women and children.

This chapter will focus on the particular problems of organizing women in the men's clothing trades of the Northeast. The Amalgamated Clothing Workers of America and Dorothy Jacobs Bellanca are central to such a study. Half of the membership represented by the ACWA was female, while Dorothy Jacobs Bellanca, a committed

trade unionist, devoted her life to unionizing women garment workers. Dorothy Jacobs Bellanca's career as an organizer and vice-
president of the ACWA exemplifies the challenges and contradictions
faced by women organizers, and sheds light on the union's impact on
women workers. The runaway shop was of particular concern to
Dorothy Bellanca and to the ACWA, inasmuch as women composed
the primary work force.

The phenomenon known as the "runaway shop" was peculiar to
the labor-intensive clothing and garment industries, where capital
costs were relatively low, and employers could easily move their
plants to escape the unions. Moreover, because clothing work was
seasonal, the employer could wait until orders arrived to commence
production and hire workers. Since most small-scale clothing manufacturers operated on a low profit margin, they were anxious to secure
cheap labor. This labor was available in abundance in the economically depressed communities penetrated by the runaway or "outside"
shops. Manufacturers customarily represented their arrival as a boon
to such communities, because the employment they offered enabled
women and children to contribute to family incomes.

Mining and farming communities drew runaway shops like mag-
nets. During the 1920s, the male breadwinner in these communities
often did not earn enough to support his family. The perils of coal
mining also often killed or crippled adult males. Thus, although
many wives believed that work outside the home was inappropriate,
they were willing to labor fourteen hours a day inside their homes on
work sent to them by the garment manufacturers.[2]

Ansorge Brothers' move to Scranton was typical of runaway shops.
Scranton's location in the anthracite-coal-mining region of eastern
Pennsylvania made it a good target for fleeing manufacturers.
Ansorge employed the children of immigrant miners as well as "an
abnormally large percentage of widows of miners," all with large
families of young, dependent children to support on salaries ranging
from $9.20 to $15.20 a week.[3]

These people needed a strong union to help them, but the drive to
reach workers in such small, isolated shops required enormous energy. Eventually, the ACWA brought unionism and better conditions to workers in Scranton and in other, similar communities.
Employers throughout the ACWA's history, however, continued to

run away and to resist. Unionizing the runaway shops required the tireless efforts of just such an organizer as a Baltimore buttonhole sewer named Dorothy Jacobs Bellanca.

Born in Latvia in 1894, Dorothy Jacobs was the youngest of four daughters of Bernice and Harry Jacobs.[4] In 1900 Dorothy and her family immigrated to the United States. They settled in Baltimore, where the father found work as a tailor and Dorothy attended the Baltimore public schools. Bernice Jacobs died a few years after their arrival.

Dorothy was thirteen years old when she took her first job, as a hand buttonhole sewer on men's coats. After a four-week training period, during which she received no wages, she earned $3 a week for a ten-hour day. Her wages were never steady, because her index fingers often became infected, causing her to lose a week's work without compensation.[5] From her vantage point, it seemed logical to join a union, and she tried to organize the other workers. Her employer, who regarded Dorothy as no more than a child, responded to her activities in a cavalier fashion, often firing and then rehiring her with only a warning against further union agitation. In 1909, when she was fifteen years old, she succeeded in organizing the Baltimore buttonhole makers into Local 170 of the United Garment Workers of America.

In December of the same year, two thousand clothing workers from three large shops in Baltimore walked out on strike, to protest the discharge of a union member. The central point of contention was the attempt by the Clothiers' Board of Trade to blacklist all union members. The Clothiers' Board of Trade had been organized in 1870 by several of the large companies in Baltimore to resist unionization of their shops, for the skilled cutters had recently joined together to win some control of the workplace; the board responded by firing all involved workers.[6] Although the board had smashed the workers' attempt at unionizing by 1873, it remained on guard against further union agitation. The 1909 Baltimore strike was yet another effort by the workers to gain union recognition from their antiunion employers. It was also part of a larger unionizing drive. In the same year in New York City, over 20,000 women's garment workers had walked out of their shops to protest wages and working conditions.

The news of these New York strikers reached Baltimore, encouraging young clothing workers, such as Dorothy Jacobs, to form trade-union locals and to strike.

What sort of people were these Baltimore clothing workers? Why did they respond as they did? The Baltimore clothing workers' community was not as large or as radical as its counterpart in the Jewish ghettoes of New York City. In some ways, however, the communities had developed along similar lines, and union activity in New York City had parallels in Baltimore. As in New York City, Baltimore's Jewish immigrants had flocked to clothing shops to secure employment. The early or "old" wave of immigration introduced German Jews to Baltimore clothing production. A group of these early arrivals (in the 1840s) achieved some mobility, and purchased small clothing shops in time to greet the "new" wave of immigrants arriving between 1880 and 1920. Although Italians, Poles, Lithuanians, and other South and East Europeans entered Baltimore's clothing center at this time, the overwhelming majority of workers were Russian Jews. They also predominated in other key clothing centers, such as New York City and Chicago. The more skilled and fortunate among them secured work in the large "inside" shops, or factories, while others were left to work on the "outside," in sweatshops. Baltimore, however, had fewer of the latter and more of the former than New York City.

The Eastern European Jews had characteristics that distinguished them from other newcomers to America. First, the Jews fled persecution in Czarist Russia and did not plan to return; they had to succeed in the new milieu. Second, Jews had acquired easily marketable skills, since in Europe they were forbidden to own land. Third, Judaism forbade Saturday work, fostering a dependence on other Jews for employment. Fourth, the Eastern European Jews placed a high value on education; as a consequence, they were more literate than many other new immigrants. Finally, some Jewish immigrants were already Socialists, with previous experience in trade-union activities.

Jews, compared to other immigrants, were well prepared for the clothing trade that awaited them. Over one-third of the Jewish men entering the United States between 1909 and 1910, for example, claimed they were tailors while over one-tenth of the Jewish women said they were seamstresses.[7] It has been estimated that 70 percent of the Jews in Baltimore lived directly from the clothing industry. This fostered a sense of ethnic solidarity within the industry.

By 1900 competition among the numerous small-scale clothing manufacturers was intense. Their ability to survive under the conditions described above—low-profit margins and seasonal trade—depended on reducing costs, primarily in wages. In the large factories, where all phases of clothing production were performed, wages and working conditions were fairly tolerable. The large factories, however, found themselves under attack by outside shops, whose contractors imposed a minute division of labor. These contractors employed family groups in a sweatshop or homework setting. The group divided the work, and labored prolonged hours to perform its task.[8]

The revival of the contract system added new recruits to the work force. Married women and small children labored in tenements for a pittance. Single women preferred factory work if it was available. Although they too, labored long hours under deplorable conditions, work in a factory offered a means of moving beyond the traditional home setting and into a changing society. In the factory, young women sometimes learned the lessons of socialism and trade unionism. Although most women workers expected to marry and escape from factory toil, some were radicalized by their experience. These women would form the core of the trade-union groups, often led by young Jewish radicals.

Jews had proved to be good strikers but not strong trade unionists.[9] Although they had participated in numerous strikes before 1905, the seasonal nature of the trade produced seasonal unions. Hence Jewish workers had established a pattern by 1900 which was described as follows:

> In July there is a strike. In August it is settled. . . . A walking delegate is chosen to collect dues. In October it becomes known that there are more unsettled shops than union shops. In November wage rates were reduced. Then they begin to scold the bosses for breaking the agreements. In December it becomes apparent that the agreements are not worth a whiff of tobacco. In January dues are no longer paid. In February the walking delegate is tossed out of the shop. In March mass meetings are called to revive the union. In April the union ceases to exist . . . and in June they decide to strike. And strike they do.[10]

Despite their anarchist character, these strikes broadened the social experience of many garment workers and altered their consciousness. As Moses Rischin noted, "Few immigrants would forget the exhilaration of the first shop strike, vivid testimony to the grandeur of American freedom."[11]

It remained, however, for the Jewish immigrants who fled Russia after the abortive 1905 Revolution to provide leadership in constructing more permanent labor organizations. This new group of immigrants had participated in Russia and Poland in economic and political action as members of the *Bund*, and they brought a socialist-radical consciousness to the American shores. The Bund, a trade-union-like organization, attempted to organize Jews for secular political action. It emphasized "the unity of politicial and economic efforts, operating simultaneously for material betterment and political reform," and it attracted many male and female Russian Jewish revolutionaries.[12]

These more radical Russian Jews, like their other immigrant *Landsleit* (people from the same town or region, who share ethnic and cultural ties), accepted employment in the clothing trades and were welcomed into the local Jewish community. Their pleas for a more humane world fell on receptive ears. The radical but practical ideology that the Bundists provided served as the catalyst necessary for strengthening the Jewish trade-union movement.

In 1910 the population of Baltimore was 558,485, of which approximately 50,000 were Jewish.[13] By 1914 this number climbed to roughly 65,000.[14] The growing Baltimore Jewish community, closely tied to the clothing industry, had a radical heritage that was reinforced continually by the new Russian Jewish arrivals. They often challenged the wage rates and working conditions awaiting them, but found it difficult to build a durable trade union. The clothing manufacturers in Baltimore had organized to combat unionization, and the union with jurisdiction in the clothing industry, the UGWA, evinced a lack of interest in immigrant workers. The UGWA had scored a few early victories in organizing the industry. During the 1893–1897 depression, however, the UGWA suffered setbacks. The moderate leadership then chose to place greater emphasis on selling union-label work clothing (overalls and workshirts) not produced on the East Coast, than on striking for union recognition and increased wages. In every issue of the weekly union paper an advertisement appeared picturing the union label and proclaiming, "Insist on this label when buying clothing. Discriminate against unclean inferior sweat-shop goods. Union label used by leading manufacturers."[15] There were instances of manufacturers unionizing their own plants in order to tap the market for union-label clothing.[16] The union willingly sold its label, since it was the union's greatest source of income and power.

The UGWA leadership showed scant interest in organizing the mass of semiskilled immigrant garment workers, many of whom were female. In fact, the union president, Thomas Rickert, sought to protect his skilled workers by favoring immigration restriction, in line with AFL policies. Rickert and the other AFL officials also believed that women belonged in the home, not in the labor movement. These divisive tactics deeply antagonized the more radical Jewish tailors, who had hoped to organize the entire industry. Upon numerous occasions between 1894 and 1904 the more radical rank and file confronted the leadership and found it lacking. Joseph Schlossberg, one of the founding officers of the ACWA, characterized those years as follows:

During all those years there was no point of friendly contact between the International officers of the clothing workers' union and the [immigrant] rank and file; no sympathetic understanding on the part of the former for the latter, and no desire for such understanding. The two belonged to different worlds . . . where the officers are unable to understand the member's cooperation is out of the question.[17]

Therefore 1909 was a significant year. The ILGWU, the women's clothing union, grew substantially through the addition of immigrant women to its ranks. The immigrant men's clothing workers hoped that they, too, could organize and receive UGWA recognition. The Baltimore clothing workers succeeded in having the discharged union member reinstated, and thus protected their right to join a union, but the clothing firms refused to recognize the union as the bargaining agent for the workers.

Then in 1910 all eyes turned to the long and bitter struggle of the clothing workers in Chicago (see Chapter 4 above). There, on September 22, 1910, a small group of women led a spontaneous protest over the arbitrary drop in the piece rate for seaming pants, from 4 cents to 3 3/4 cents. Within a month, 18,000 Chicago clothing workers had joined the walkout for decent wages and union recognition. Finally, on October 27, 1910, between 35,000 and 40,000 men's clothing workers began a city-wide general strike.

The Chicago strike illustrated the mounting hostility between the UGWA leadership and the garment workers. Most of the strikers were new immigrants who were not members of the union. The UGWA's leadership could have seized this opportunity to increase its membership, since the semiskilled strikers turned to it for assistance. But Rickert feared the "greenhorns" who, he contended, could not be organized. Rickert attempted to negotiate a settlement with Hart, Schaffner & Marx which was rejected by the majority of strikers because it did not grant union recognition to the semiskilled workers. Rickert obviously doubted whether he wanted these workers in his union and whether they could be good trade unionists.

In this five-month strike the foreign-born clothing workers recognized their need for a more responsive union. The long and bitter Chicago struggle proved to be decisive in the relationship between UGWA leaders and the rank and file:

> The outlook, philosophy and tactics of the two became irreconcilable. The workers demanded a fighting organization which would improve their conditions; the officers considered the union a store for the sale of labels, the returns from which were to be used not for organization work but to maintain union office payrolls. [18]

Dorothy Jacobs and other Baltimore clothing workers were asked to donate clothing to help the Chicago strikers. Jacobs contended that it was "the irony of asking a family of [clothing] workers for clothing for other workers who made clothes" that started the sixteen-year-old Dorothy thinking that something was very wrong. [19] The Jacobs family, after all, lived in a tenement in the poor Jewish section of Baltimore. That they, and their neighbors, shared what little they had with the strikers convinced Dorothy Jacobs that collective action was possible and necessary. She credited the clothing donation incident with directing her toward a career as a trade-union activist.

In 1914 the immigrant men's clothing workers, tired of President Rickert's discriminatory practices, sought more responsive leaders. At the UGWA's October 1914 convention in Nashville, Tennessee, one hundred and thirty men and women delegates, representing 75 percent of the union's membership, were denied seats in the main hall. They held a rump session at which they elected the Jewish Socialist Sidney Hillman their president. These immigrant trade unionists had taken the first step toward forming a new, more powerful union in the men's clothing industry—the Amalgamated Clothing Workers of America.

Dorothy Jacobs' participation in the 1909 Baltimore strike and a subsequent 1913 organizing drive provided valuable trade-union schooling for the young woman. By 1914 she had emerged as one of the leaders of the ACWA in a crucial struggle with the UGWA in Baltimore.

The conflict in Baltimore began in early October 1914, at the beginning of the slack season. The large inside shop of Henry Sonneborn and Company planned to modernize its machinery, discharge many workers, and renew production with a smaller, lower-paid work force, once the busy season began. Its 3,000 garment workers, some of whom had been organized into the UGWA, walked out between October 1 and 3, 1914, when they discovered the company plan.[20] Under normal circumstances, a strike of primarily unorganized workers is difficult for a union to coordinate. The workers at Sonneborn, however, were faced with not one organization, but two union factions, both unprepared to lead a strike.[21] The strike progressed with the two rival factions in conflict, one representing the skilled cutters (about 10 percent of the work force), and the other representing the semiskilled tailors and operators.

Dorothy Jacobs, who had led her buttonhole-makers local into the secessionist camp, served as one of the four leaders of the strike. She worked alongside Hyman Blumberg and the Bellanca brothers, Frank and August, both of whom went to Baltimore to help in the campaign against Sonneborn.

For Dorothy Jacobs and the other immigrant clothing workers, joining the insurgents made sense. Jacobs remembered the reports of the Chicago 1910 strike, and the treatment the nonunion semiskilled workers received from the UGWA. In contrast, the insurgents had fought for the semiskilled and immigrant workers, and thus offered hope to the majority of Baltimore's clothing workers. If some semiskilled workers had short memories, or chose to ignore Jacobs' warnings, the tactics of the UGWA's leadership provided a reminder. The UGWA dispensed substantial strike benefit checks to the loyal cutters, but refused to offer any aid to the tailors or operators. The insurgents tried to muster financial aid to the semiskilled strikers, but they lacked the resources of an established AFL union. Then, in November, the strikers learned that, just as in Chicago, the UGWA had negotiated a secret settlement for the cutters. Sonneborn agreed to reinstate all the cutters with pay increases, if the UGWA allowed the semiskilled strikers to return to work without union recognition.

This attempt at a settlement by the UGWA hierarchy hardened the insurgents' desire to hold out for recognition of their union. Sidney Hillman, president of the insurgents, initially had hoped to compromise with Sonneborn, but encountered rank-and-file resistance after the tailors learned of the UGWA's actions. In this instance, the militancy of the rank and file prevailed. The cutters attempted to resume work, but without the tailors and machine operators, the UGWA agreement settled nothing. Finally, because the company was anxious to resume production, Sonneborn negotiated a settlement with Sidney Hillman. The agreement granted union recognition to almost 3000 new ACWA members.

Dorothy Jacobs was in large part responsible for the success of the 1914 Baltimore strike. The local of women's hand buttonhole sewers she organized in 1909 had continued to grow in membership. Jacobs might very well have stopped her organizing there. After all, as she observed, "no matter how little work there was, buttonholes had to be made. The coats could not be held together by means of pins."[22] She realized, however, that the machine buttonhole makers must also be organized. Women and girls performed the hand buttonhole sewing, but oftentimes men were machine buttonhole makers. Jacobs had been extremely effective in organizing women workers, but now, at age twenty, she embarked on a new, more challenging campaign.

Dorothy Jacobs and a few other women formed groups and visited the homes of the unorganized men. They worked quietly since "talking union" was grounds for dismissal. Jacobs described their campaign this way:

> Night after night was given up to the cause by energetic committees, who met with little success at the beginning, but who never lost hope. We found the men were quite ignorant of organization and very much afraid of what their fellow-workers would do and say. Some of them also objected to organization, because the work had been commenced by women. Our work

was kept up, however, despite all difficulties. While visiting the men's homes, we would appeal to their wives, or any member of their families who were open to argument and conviction.[23]

In this case, Jacobs had to educate and organize the men. Other times she stressed committing union money and effort toward educating women workers. In either case, her practice consisted in months of hard work teaching women and men the benefits of unionization and collective action.

During this campaign, Jacobs succeeded in organizing the buttonhole makers from the inside shops or factories. They then demanded and won pay increases. Dorothy Jacobs learned the need for solidarity between male and female workers during her early organizing work in Baltimore, and taught collective action to many clothing workers. Her words became more sophisticated with time, but her ultimate goals remained unchanged.

Jacobs had emerged as a popular leader among immigrant clothing workers by the time of the 1914 Nashville convention. She then faithfully served on the picket line at the Sonneborn factory during the thirteen-week strike. She addressed numerous strike meetings, and won the respect of the Baltimore tailors and operators. Philip DeLuca has described the strikers' reaction to Dorothy Jacobs when she addressed the first meeting of the Sonneborn workers:

> The chairman gave the floor to a young, slender and attractive girl, a buttonhole maker and secretary of the council. She rose, waving a telegram in her hand and smiling. It was a contagious smile, and her voice was like a bell, sweet and most effective. A murmur of approval went over the hall. The next instant it became so quiet that one could hear a pin drop.[24]

Jacobs read a telegram from Sidney Hillman in which he encouraged the strikers and promised his support. The workers burst into cheers. Then Jacobs again began to speak: "A new era is beginning for the people of the clothing industry. As we fight, so shall we make history. Our example will be followed by our brothers and sisters in other cities."[25] Moved by Jacobs' bearing and her invocation of history, the crowd responded by cheering and applauding. The audience also affectionately called out, "Our Dorothy!"

Her enthusiasm, confidence, and energy, coupled with her warm

personality and "vibrant and magnetic speaking voice," aided
Dorothy Jacobs in assuming the role of a female leader in a male-
dominated trade-union structure.[26] Working consciously at times to
prove her worthiness, she accepted the conditions thrust upon her by
union leadership. She attempted to balance the dictates of a trade
union with women's needs as both workers and organizers. She was
successful, and rose rapidly within the Amalgated Clothing Workers
of America.

At the founding convention of the ACWA in December 1914, at
New York's Webster Hall, Dorothy Jacobs was thrilled to be one of
two delegates sent by the buttonhole makers' Local 170. Only five
women, however, sat among the 175 delegates to the convention.[27]
Jacobs prepared and proposed a resolution calling attention to the
need for a woman organizer. Resolution Number 20 read as follows:

> Whereas, there are 19,784 workers engaged in the garment industry in
> the city of Baltimore, 10,183 of whom are women, and of whom only 800
> are organized and
> Whereas, with this preponderous majority of unorganized women in the
> trade the struggle for the maintenance of unions by the small organized
> minority is wrought with tremendous difficulties, and
> Whereas, experience has shown that with such a majority of unorganized
> women in the trade, strikes have few chances of being won, unions are
> always in danger of their existence, and wages consequently low, hours
> long, and conditions of work generally very unsatisfactory,
> Be it therefore resolved:
> That we the Button Hole Workers Union, Local 170, call upon you to
> provide the City of Baltimore with at least one woman organizer.
>
> > Yours in the struggle for organization
> > of the working class.[28]

The resolution employed language appropriate to the day. Jacobs
appealed to the vast majority of male unionists not as a feminist, but
as an advocate of a stronger trade-union movement. The 1914 convention passed the resolution; but the General Executive Board was not to
appoint a full-time woman's organizer until 1917, when Dorothy
Jacobs accepted the position.

Dorothy Jacobs Bellanca served the ACWA in various positions
between 1914 and her death in 1946 at 52. She served as Local 170's

representative to the Baltimore Joint Board (the ACWA's central body in Baltimore), and on October 21, 1915, became its secretary. In this capacity, she established the Educational Department, participated in all Baltimore strikes, traveled to assist in organizing campaigns and strikes in other cities, helped settle disputes in organized shops, and occasionally negotiated contracts with employers. Her primary interest, however, remained the organization of women, as well as addressing their specific needs within the trade-union framework. She used her post on the Baltimore Joint Board to monitor the treatment of female trade unionists, winning the support of her male colleagues.[29]

Jacobs was selected as a delegate to the ACWA's Second Biennial Convention in Rochester, New York, in 1916. There she continued to champion the cause of trade-union women by appealing to the delegates to establish a Women's Department within the union.[30] Her efforts on behalf of women clothing workers, as well as her tireless service to the ACWA, did not go unrecognized. The May 1916 ACWA Convention accepted Jacobs' name as one of the nineteen nominated for the Union's seven-member General Executive Board. In July 1916, before her twenty-second birthday, Dorothy Jacobs was elected to the General Executive Board (GEB). She was then the only woman vice-president of a major trade union.

The year 1916 was a critical and decisive one for the ACWA in Baltimore. It was still battling the rival UGWA, and was simultaneously under attack by the Industrial Workers of the World (IWW, also known as "Wobblies"). Union and antiunion violence permeated Baltimore, where AFL and IWW loyalists physically attacked Hyman Blumberg and August Bellanca. The ACWA had hoped to organize the inside shop workers of Baltimore, the nation's fifth largest men's clothing center. After concluding an agreement with one of the three big companies in Baltimore, the ACWA learned that John Ferguson, the president of the Baltimore Federation of Labor, had negotiated a substitute contract that recognized the UGWA cutters and permitted the far more radical IWW to organize the semi-skilled immigrant workers. Ferguson and the UGWA leaders felt that the ACWA was their real threat in the Baltimore markets, and therefore willingly entered into an "unholy" alliance with their ideological enemy, the Wobblies, to destroy the ACWA in Baltimore.[31]

The ACWA's leaders appealed to the IWW and to the Baltimore Central Committee of the Socialist Party for solidarity. The ACWA pointed out that the IWW workers were crossing union picket lines, and were demonstrating a lack of sensitivity to the plight of the majority of men's clothing workers (who were ACWA members). Ultimately, the Socialist party ruled in favor of the ACWA, and persuaded the Wobblies' rank and file to honor the ACWA protest. In this instance, and in other challenges by the UGWA throughout 1916, the ACWA emerged victorious. In these cases it demonstrated its unique ability to work with capitalists while simultaneously retaining its "radical-progressive" credentials and appealing to the majority of semiskilled and immigrant workers.

In her capacity as secretary of the Baltimore Joint Board and also as a GEB member, Jacobs was at the center of the 1916 maelstrom. A careful reading of her correspondence to General Secretary Joseph Schlossberg at ACWA headquarters demonstrates Jacobs' devotion to the ACWA struggles, the hard work she performed, and her reminders to the leadership of the ongoing participation of women in the ACWA-UGWA-IWW conflicts. Jacobs apologized to Schlossberg for not writing more frequently, but added, "We have been very busy and most all of my time was taken up in the [Joint Board] office and at Strouse's."[32] Her activities included addressing many meetings at Strouse and Sonneborn, in which she reported "a wonderful spirit prevailing, especially among the girls."[33] At one meeting organized by Jacobs for the women workers at Sonneborn and Strouse, she spoke on the topic "The Present Labor Troubles in the United States." That meeting, which two hundred and fifty women attended on August 16, 1916, was only one of many to which she attracted women workers. In fact, the women present requested that she hold similar meetings "at least twice a month."[34] Recognizing the importance of Jacobs' efforts, the women workers encouraged and supported her as best they could.

Jacobs was not called upon to serve only women workers, however. She confided to Schlossberg that during the 1916 struggle: "[I] took charge of settling disputes between our members and the manufacturers. To my surprise, the manufacturers received me with courtesy and it was not hard for me to straighten out every case."[35] She understood the value of such work, and was not above pointing it out to ACWA officials.

Yet on various occasions Jacobs asserted that the fighting among the rival unions in Baltimore, although important, was interfering with the real work of unionizing the women: "I am anxious for this affair to be over, so that I can start work among the women."[36] Jacobs realized that these crisis activities made small contribution to creating real trade unionists among the women workers. She reported: "These past few weeks I have been meeting with continual riots of the I.W.W. and the A.F. of L., and in order to keep up the courage of our girls, I have spent a good part of my time in the Strouse building."[37]

She continued to emphasize to Schlossberg, whenever possible, the spirit and accomplishment of the women:

> Most of my time now is spent in keeping in touch and encouraging the Strouse girls and as far as they are concerned, I can guarantee you that these girls will continue to meet the situation. This affair has brought more spirit into the girls than I expected. It seems as though nothing [not even the threat of violence] can frighten them out of the building.[38]

> I am proud to say . . . that in this fight, the girls . . . have not only contributed morally and financially, but were also the first in line.[39]

> I feel that a wonderful spirit can be brought out in our girls and I intend to call these [shop meetings for women workers]. . . . I only hope to have the cooperation of the organization at large.[40]

Jacobs' membership on the GEB also provided her with access to the more influential members of the union. She continued her crusade to organize women, and warned the male GEB members that the "men in the industry must take an interest in the organization of their women fellow workers, or some day be punished for their neglect."[41] When the board finally established the post of women's full-time organizer in 1917, Jacobs accepted appointment to the position.

In an interview published in the ACWA's official newspaper, the *Advance*, Jacobs discussed her new assignment and the problems to be confronted in organizing women:

> The terrible plight of the unorganized women workers has been ignored by the men. Organization of women has been neglected, although they are as important to the industry as the men workers. I am greatly pleased with the decision of the general executive board to extend organization work among the women. Of course it will be harder to organize the women now

than it would have been when they were beginning to enter the industry in large numbers. But I am sure the campaign will be successful, and know that when the women are once organized, and have been shown the worth of the organization in bettering conditions of work for them, they will remain loyal members.

I have found women slower to organize than the men, because they have so little experience in the labor movement. But when they are organized and educated I have found them the best workers for the organization there are.[42]

Jacobs said that she remained hopeful that the union men would embrace the female members and allow women to emerge as equals within the ACWA. She went on to observe, however:

A great deal of fault lies with the men for the lack of organization among women workers. It is time for the men to realize that women is [sic] their competitor in all industries. The men are not doing anything to keep away the menace of the cheaper job brought about by the introduction of women. The men always have looked upon the women workers as jokes. They believe they are waiting to get married and soon will leave the industry. For those who do leave the industry there are hundreds waiting to come in. The women are in the industry to stay. Unorganized they are a menace to the men. They must be organized to protect every labor organization in this country.[43]

In these concluding words, Jacob's dilemma as a female trade unionist is painfully apparent. Although obviously angry with the men for their neglect of women workers, she was unable to condemn them, since she desperately needed their cooperation to further her union campaign among women. She therefore began by indicting men for their behavior, and then proceeded to debunk the traditional myths regarding women's future as workers. Yet she concluded by stressing what would benefit the male workers. Jacobs thus chose to aid women workers primarily by emphasizing the theme of class rather than the issue of gender.

Still, Jacobs encouraged women to organize separately. In her capacity as the women's organizer in 1917 she participated in the ACWA's organizing campaigns in New York City, Philadelphia, and Baltimore, and as she traveled the northeast corridor, articulating the problems of women workers, she encouraged them to form separate women's branches. These organizations were needed, Jacobs argued, to unite women in a campaign to investigate their own needs and to improve their specific conditions.[44] She was quick to emphasize, however, that women should not withdraw from their respective mixed-sex locals. She saw the separate branches as necessary to help the women achieve "a better understanding of the labor movement."[45] In order to benefit from trade unionism, women had to become active members. Jacobs believed that special women's meetings would attract the less receptive women, thus spreading the trade-union message among a wider female audience.

In 1917 Dorothy Jacobs brought the union message to the female military-uniform factory workers. During 1913 and 1914, the United States economy experienced a recession. Clothing workers, along with others, struggled merely to keep wages from falling. But soon Europe's misfortune brought relief to the American worker. Industry after industry saw prosperity return, as the United States supplied a war-torn Europe. The wages paid by military-uniform factories, however, were half those paid by unionized firms. Jacobs and the ACWA launched an organizing drive to help these workers share in the wartime prosperity. More than half of the military-uniform workers were female, and that percentage rose as more men left for military service.

Jacobs spoke "daily at strike meetings and mass meetings arranged by the Organization [ACWA] to bring the uniform workers into the movement for better working conditions."[46] She directed her efforts toward the women workers who, by her estimate, had never before been exposed to trade unionism. These women were toiling more than sixty hours a week instead of the forty-eight hours established by the ACWA. Furthermore, they were earning only $4 to $6 a week for their efforts.[47] Jacobs challenged the employers' patriotic rhetoric, whereby female volunteers were "enlisted" into sweatshops and were criticized if they organized for higher wages, while American soldiers died on the battlefields. In the *Advance*, Jacobs stressed the opportunity and the need to organize the women workers: "There is sentiment for organization among the women in the clothing industry. All that they need is someone to show them the light, to show them what organization has done for their sisters in the organized factories. The women workers of America are becoming more class conscious every day."[48]

Jacobs argued that women must fight to better their working

conditions during the war. What better time than the present, she asked, to stand up for democracy, in the country and on the job? With men away fighting and dying, more and more women would be expected to fill their places in the work force. She warned women that they would not be able to escape the factory through marriage during wartime—and perhaps not after the war, either. With the deaths of so many young men on the battlefields, she noted, fewer women would be able to marry. Thus, more women would remain in the clothing industry. They should therefore work to improve conditions while they could.[49] This last argument was also directed at male clothing workers. By emphasizing women's permanent role in the clothing industry, Jacobs hoped to move male trade unionists to a commitment to organizing their female coworkers. Indeed, Jacobs rarely missed an opportunity to point out the benefits of working-class cooperation between men and women. Jacobs and the ACWA achieved success in their wartime organizing campaign. Overall, workers on the United States home front experienced prosperity, and trade union membership soared. Labor was scarce, and employers who had shunned union representatives in the past were frequently willing to negotiate rather than lose precious production time. Trade union bargaining therefore brought improved contracts to the rank and file.

By 1918 Jacobs was working simultaneously on preparations for the Amalgamated Clothing Workers of America convention and on vigorous organizing campaigns in Baltimore. She taxed her frail body beyond its capacity. Thus, although she was reelected to the GEB in 1918, she was forced to withdraw from union responsibilities. In her resignation letter dated August 20, 1918, she wrote: "Owing to my state of health I was unable to attend the meeting of the GEB in Rochester at the beginning of this month. . . . For the same reason I am unable to continue longer in my capacity as member of the GEB and as General Organizer."[50] That same month, however, Jacobs married August Bellanca, with whom she had worked during the early Baltimore struggles. He, too, was an organizer and a GEB member. There is little reason to suppose that Jacobs' resignation from the GEB was prompted by her marriage with a fellow board member, for far from decreasing her union activities at that time, Dorothy Jacobs Bellanca expanded them. The couple had no children (though this was probably not their choice) and devoted their lives to the ACWA.[51] Although for many women, marriage was the time to sever all union ties, in the case of Dorothy Jacobs Bellanca (hereafter Bellanca), marriage further intensified an almost total devotion to the cause of working-class women. Alice Kessler-Harris has suggested that women who married outside their ethnic or religious group, as Jacobs did, remained involved in trade-union activities more frequently than women who followed more conventional paths.[52] Certainly Dorothy's marriage to August did not force her into a traditional role; in fact her rebellious spirit probably was responsible for both her marriage to an Italian American and her lifelong commitment to the cause of women workers. She remained particularly concerned with the role and treatment of immigrant women workers in the men's garment industry and in the ACWA itself.

Throughout her life, Bellanca struggled with the conflict between her sensitivity to sex discrimination and her devotion to working-class and union solidarity. She posed the dilemma particularly in the following two quotations:

> Women have been organized but with all restrictions of sex prejudices, being considered as dues payers and competitors and never as organization units with all the rights of initiative, cooperation, leadership and struggle enjoyed by men,[53] [and]

> Women came into the trade and into the organization on grounds that were already established and fought out. One cannot expect equal consideration from men members . . . where such conditions exist without being patient and waiting for proper opportunities.[54]

What were the proper opportunities? How were women best organized? Bellanca counseled women to exploit the ACWA milieu to build strong, durable locals and become committed trade unionists. In that way, she reasoned, women would earn the respect of male unionists. Female trade-union leaders constantly made compromises to secure better treatment for working women within the male-dominated trade-union structure. Amalgamated women were not unconcerned with their own advancement; rather, the union was the best vehicle available to them. Although working-class men resisted female initiatives, the ACWA compelled men to work with women unionists.

These women had to be encouraged to join in trade-union activities, since they believed that union work was "man's sphere." Bellanca knew that women needed this special encouragement, and she understood that while they hoped to better their condition through the union, they were influenced by the dominant cultural norms, as well as by ethnic traditions, which dictated that women were to serve primarily as wives and mothers—and that, in fact, most working girls were destined for a domestic future. She was aware, as few male organizers were, of the sexual exploitation of women at home and on the job and understood women's double burden of industrial work and family responsibility. She did not, however, face male unionists with these issues; rather, she relied on class solidarity in her quest for recognition of women as valuable trade unionists.

Bellanca also attempted to break down the barriers between female and male workers. For example, while women felt it "unlady-like" to enter a union hall where they would encounter cigar smoke and beer, they were willing to attend union gatherings at which they were welcomed with food and entertainment. Bellanca changed the character of ACWA meetings by her own presence as a speaker at thousands of union gatherings, and by encouraging or providing an atmosphere acceptable to women. At the Third Biennial Convention of the ACWA in Baltimore in 1918, Dorothy Jacobs offered the women delegates an alternative to the "smoker" for men: she took the women delegates to the theater.[55] Recognizing that the union message could be brought to many "unorganizable" women simply by changing the social environment, she promoted union gatherings that could be experienced as friendly and pleasant occasions by women and men alike.

The ideas and techniques Bellanca developed in the early Baltimore struggles were tested in the organizing crusades of the 1920s. Her popularity among the women ACWA members increased as she chased the runaway shops and helped to organize the Women's Bureau of the union. She became the most requested ACWA organizer and speaker and gave of herself unselfishly wherever she was needed. Mamie Santora, a personal friend who had been Bellanca's coworker in Baltimore and her successor on the GEB, frequently consulted her on matters pertaining to organizing women. The 1920s, a prosperous time for sectors of American society, were generally disastrous for organized labor. During World War I, the government policies stimulated by wartime needs assisted workers to unionize more successfully than at any time before, but employers resented the workers' newly gained power. Employers used the postwar Red scare to smash many unions and launched a campaign to "inform" their workers that trade unions and the closed shop were "un-American." Large manufacturers in the rubber, electric, and steel industries substituted company unions and various benefits for trade unions. Many manufacturers in the clothing industry, however, could not afford to participate in the welfare capitalism of the 1920s. Instead they packed up their shops and moved away from the unionized regions. Whether companies avoided trade unions by running away or through establishing company unions, organized labor suffered.

The ACWA's leaders fought the paternalism and welfare capitalism of employers. They argued that what the boss gave he could also take away: Workers could retain what they achieved only through their collective strength. For the ACWA, the 1920s were not a period of retreat, as for other unions. Instead, the ACWA emerged as a progressive trade union, one of the most notable practitioners of the so-called new unionism. The ACWA pioneered cooperative housing, unemployment insurance, and one of the first successful labor banks; and, to some extent, it encouraged greater participation by its female members. Women represented 50 percent of the ACWA's membership; and during the 1920s, 25 percent of the organizers hired were female.[56] Although not representative of their relative numbers in the clothing industry, the presence of so many women organizers indicated a recognition of trade-union women absent from other major unions.

Women organizers were essential in the drive to unionize the runaway shops. The unionization of these shops presented a special problem for the ACWA. The workers, primarily women, were scattered in small shops throughout New York, New Jersey, Pennsylvania, and Connecticut. They had no trade-union experience, moreover. The ACWA established the Out-of-Town Organization Committee in 1920 to coordinate the campaign. Dorothy and August Bellanca helped to lead it.

Bellanca immersed herself fully in the runaway shop drive, which perfectly complemented her goal of organizing women. In the runaway campaigns during the 1920s and 1930s, she addressed thousands of meetings in an effort to bring women into the ACWA. Wherever an organizing drive or strike was in progress, Bellanca

defended the rights of workers and encouraged the women to participate. These campaigns brought into clear and dramatic relief her
unique philosophy and approach to the organization of the female
worker, as she argued the importance of involving the women employed in the runaway shops in the union's mission:

> Women in the Amalgamated should be grateful that they have a union.
> Never before was it needed as much as now. . . . A great duty develops on
> the women to assume responsibility in their union, to help educate the girls
> who came to us, to enlighten those who have no previous knowledge of the
> history of labor, its problems, hopes, and aspirations. Most of these girls
> entered the industry with the expectation that it will only be temporary,
> and thus not in a frame of mind to take seriously the problems of the
> industry. It is the duty of the unions to bring the workers close to the
> problems of the industry and to bring out the latent power of the girls for
> united union activity and the advancement of the ultimate aims of the
> movement.[57]

When Bellanca could not personally lead a local drive, she sent
suggestions such as these to the organizers:

> It is advisable that you throw yourself into the organization campaign and
> form a committee of the active girls, . . . to help you in shop meetings,
> visiting homes and so on. The committee should be made part of the
> organization campaign and make it appear as though the responsibility for
> the local situation depends on their help and on them directly.[58]

Bellanca was particularly successful in bringing the trade-union
message to otherwise uninformed women clothing workers in the
runaway shops. These new female recruits, previously judged as
inferior union material, responded favorably to a woman organizer.
Bellanca hoped to prove that women, if approached correctly, could
be excellent trade unionists. Women clothing workers met women
ACWA members at various concerts, picnics, dances, and other social
activities.[59] There, these women discussed social and trade union
issues in a more relaxed setting than the conventional union meeting.
These informal networks helped to introduce women to the ACWA in
their respective cities.

Long an advocate for a separate Women's Department within the
union, Dorothy Bellanca envisioned a department that would develop

more effective means of organizing women and creating "a closer relationship between our women members and the organization."[60] She believed that the Women's Department would benefit the ACWA by attracting more women into its ranks and encouraging their active union participation. As the department addressed women's specific needs, she reasoned, female workers increasingly would recognize the value of trade-union activity. In 1924 the Women's Department was established, with Bellanca as its first director.

Between July 1924 and the end of 1925, Bellanca made numerous trips to clothing-center cities and towns to address meetings and lead strategy sessions. She went out of her way on various occasions to address women's gatherings, but she also spoke to mixed meetings, discussing other ACWA campaigns, and appealing to all members to recognize and support the efforts of the Women's Department.[61] Bellanca continued to "sell" the Women's Department as a way of serving the entire trade-union movement.[62] She always stressed the permanence of women in industry. The woman worker, she asserted, was "lending a willing ear to the principles of organized labor in order to protect her job and in spite of tricks played by employers, women are organizing in great numbers and developing to be good fighters in the cause of labor rights."[63] By recognizing and stressing the need of twentieth-century women to operate within their own trade-union network, Bellanca exposed women who otherwise might have shunned trade union meetings to working-class ideology in a painless, "socially approved" manner. In this way, Bellanca's Women's Department helped further the cause of women clothing workers.

Such dual unionism was resented by some trade-union men. The men objected to the different treatment, private meetings, and entertainment that women trade unionists sponsored.[64] Ironically, for many years men held private trade-union meetings without considering women's feelings. Now these union men feared women's power as an autonomous group within the ACWA. They claimed the Women's Department divided the working class. So Bellanca abandoned it. A feminist as far as understanding the specific needs of working women and believing that they deserved special attention, whenever conflict arose between male and female organizers, Bellanca suggested compromise. Yes, women's issues were important, she argued, but, "very often one has to do things against one's self for the benefit of the organization. What I see always is the organization first and the individual second."[65] Bellanca had hoped her Women's Department would have educated both women and men, but since it did not, she was willing to sacrifice it rather than divide the mass of organized men's clothing workers in the ACWA. She continued to advocate separate women's activities for organizing women, and she continued to speak at women's functions, but without the fanfare associated with the Women's Department.

The defeats suffered by trade unionists during the 1920s followed by the onset of the Great Depression caused increasing sexual divisions, as employers forced workers to view each other as competitors for the few available jobs. Clothing manufacturers turned to hiring primarily women and children (by 1930, 37 percent of all working women were under twenty-five years of age), in preference to unionized male workers.[66] The clothing employers set up production in small towns where the ACWA had not yet penetrated, and exploited the population, most of whom were American born. The new recruits, lacking other options, were willing to accept substantially less than union wages. Thus, the runaway shop problem which emerged in the 1920s continued to flourish in the depression era. In Pennsylvania, for example, 200,000 women and children labored under illegal and deplorable conditions for wages below $4 for a work week of between fifty and ninety hours.[67]

The ACWA leaders, aware of such abuses, embarked upon a huge campaign to organize shirtworkers and men's clothing workers in the depths of the depression. The union followed the runaways to small towns in Pennsylvania, New Jersey, New York, and Connecticut. The drive began in January 1933 and continued throughout the decade, the ACWA sending its "seasoned fighters," many of them women, to aid in the shirtworkers' organizing drive.[68]

Bellanca threw herself into the shirtworkers' drive with her usual enthusiasm. Convinced that her efforts would improve the lot and "conditions of the workers," she derived genuine satisfaction from her difficult task. Yet Bellanca admitted that the work of a union officer was "not a bed of roses." In her travels throughout the northeastern states, she endured extreme physical exertion and stress.[69] Despite the personal costs, however, Bellanca continued to address groups of women workers to inform them of the benefits of organizing.

The New Deal legislation favoring trade unions had meanwhile granted workers the right to organize, and provided a catalyst for new unionization campaigns led by the Congress of Industrial Organizations (CIO). The CIO offered new hope for workers in mass-production industries and, because the CIO emphasized organizing workers of an entire industry, it encouraged men and women to work together. This differed dramatically from the divisive policies of the craft-based AFL. The ACWA, which had always advocated industrial unionism, participated actively in CIO organizing. Although the male trade unionists in such industrial unions as the ACWA and other CIO affiliates were bound by the same traditions as the AFL men, the CIO's goal of organizing all workers had important mitigating effects. The motivating philosophy of an industrial union was solidarity. A cornerstone of this philosophy was that skilled workers should help the less skilled, for the benefit of all. If the union did not intend to quibble over jurisdiction for specific workers, why should women be neglected?

Women probably benefited from the philosophy of industrial unionism by default. The CIO men generally had no wish to change societal roles; they did not doubt that women, ultimately, belonged in the home. Yet they needed solidarity, and strength in numbers. Thus they accepted women into their organization as junior partners. Carole Turbin has suggested that since workingmen's fears of women's competition was strong, they could only cooperate in trade unions if one or more of the following conditions existed: The men did not perceive the women as threats to their jobs; the women had demonstrated that they, too, had power; and, most important, the men and women both benefited from the collective action.[70] Many working women understood these conditions, and acted accordingly. Demonstrating their strength, they won the respect of their fellow workers in the CIO by first organizing as workers, and only later seeking gender-specific recognition within the trade union. In the 1930s, Bellanca traversed the nation spreading the CIO message to women. Pleased that the New Deal had sanctioned unions, she nonetheless warned workers to secure their rights through organization, not the state, because changes in the government could eradicate the New Deal reforms.

Bellanca helped the CIO staff in the Textile Workers Organizing Committee (TWOC) in the South. She was well prepared for this campaign because like the other shops she campaigned to organize in the 1920s, many of these shops had been moved south by the textile firms to escape the union. Bellanca was well received by the southern textile workers, most of whom were female, and had no trouble convincing them of her sincerity. The textile workers had only to observe her hands, gesturing as she spoke. Her crooked index fingers demonstrated that she had worked in the clothing industry, validating her plea for improved conditions so others would not suffer as she had.[71]

Bellanca recounted the history of the ACWA and of organized labor in general when she addressed meetings of working women. She stressed the need for their involvement in the union, although she cautioned:

> In the Amalgamated, as everywhere else, there exists some jealousy sometimes between men and women. But as the union has been the protector of both, so both serve it loyally, each giving first thought to the welfare of the union as a whole. In this way, women have been really the equals of men in the Amalgamated. They have received no favors for being women; they have won their places in the union on their record as union members. This is as it should be. A voice in leadership is the reward of active service in the cause.[72]

Once again, Bellanca tried to reconcile the contradictions faced by female trade unionists. Aware of the ever-present tension between male and female workers, she chose to stress the ideal: Male workers would learn the value of cooperation and reward the active women unionist with leadership positions.

Those positions went to only a few of the more outspoken women, however, those who either did not marry or did not have children. Those women who had family obligations, who worked a long day and then served time doing "women's work" at home, had to remain silent partners—paying dues, performing clerical functions for the union, and participating in strikes without receiving recognition. Fifty years later, unions had still not solved this problem.

The Amalgamated Clothing Workers of America even responded condescendingly to the class loyalty and exceptional leadership of Bellanca herself. For example, at the Twelfth Biennial ACWA Convention in 1938, Alex Hoffman announced: "We have on the GEB of the Amalgamated one woman and in appreciation of what women have done in the labor movement generally, and members of the

Amalgamated particularly, we choose at this time to present that member of the GEB, Sister Dorothy Bellanca, with a bouquet of flowers."[73] The bouquet of flowers and words bore weak testimony to the role Bellanca and other women had played in organizing women within the union, and to its many female rank-and-file members. While Bellanca was in the struggle for more than ACWA recognition, one wonders how she kept such petty annoyances at bay and retained her optimism. At the same 1938 meeting, Sidney Hillman, president of the ACWA, admitted the important position of women in the union:

> First of all, this is a man's world. It appears even in an organization that represents so many women, and in pointing out the leadership that has taken charge of the activities, I failed to mention that the staff of women organizers grows larger and larger, and that is why we are making so much progress in fields where we have not been successful before. On behalf of the National Office, we have had Dorothy Bellanca participate in all the activities.[74]

ACWA rhetoric encouraged women to expect better treatment from their union comrades, yet the contributions of women organizers and members were frequently ignored.

A more subtle indication of union attitudes toward women appeared in a cartoon in the ACWA newspaper *Advance*. The man in the cartoon inquires of the woman, "Are you coming to the dance tonight?" She replies, "I'd love to, but I'm working late." The man then exclaims, "Good lord: haven't you joined a trade union yet?"[75] The assumption that women would value trade unions if they shortened the work day to provide time for social activities is implicit in the unionist's statement.

Such patronizing messages made it difficult to convince women that male members sincerely wanted them in the union. Women members often appealed to the union leadership for better representation of the needs of the female rank and file. For example, they demanded additional official female leaders. In a November 1935 letter to the *Advance*, two women suggested that the General Executive Board be enlarged to include more women. Complimenting the current GEB and singling out Bellanca for specific praise, the letter nevertheless stressed that the special concerns of female workers required special attention.[76] In other letters addressed to Bellanca and the *Advance*, women voiced concern over the discrimination they experienced as female trade unionists.[77] Appreciative of the need for class solidarity, these women nevertheless sought to improve the position of women within the union. If they, and Bellanca, and other women organizers tolerated the patronizing stance of the male-dominated ACWA, it was not because they failed to understand its implications, but because they realized that the ACWA accorded women relatively better treatment than that offered by most other unions.

The ACWA hierarchy did appear to make a greater effort to treat women as partners than did such traditional unions as the AFL. In 1934, for example, while most United States workers were suffering the effects of the Great Depression, the Tenth ACWA Convention rejected a resolution calling for the hiring of men and self-supporting women in preference to married women.[78] This action was in clear contrast to positions of other trade unions which, in company with employers, forced married women to bear the brunt of depression layoffs. In the midst of the suffering caused by the depression, the ACWA did not accept restrictions on the employment of married women as a sound approach to economic recovery. Rather, it held to the principle that the working class must stand together.

Bellanca took further and still more positive action on behalf of women. She appealed to the Federal Emergency Relief Administration in Washington

> on behalf of the unattached women who are and have been unemployed for years. Due to the fact that they are unattached, it is hard for them to obtain relief, preference being given to people with families. . . . I therefore urge you to do everything possible in order to set aside a substantial amount to be used for providing work for the unattached women of the country.[79]

It was Bellanca's belief that aid to single women was to the benefit of the entire working class.

Throughout her career, Dorothy Jacobs Bellanca gave foremost importance to a strong, united working class, while consistently striving to improve the lives of working-class women. Her vehicle for both objectives was the industrial union. Successful within the trade union movement, she was able to rise in the union hierarchy. She was reelected to the ACWA's GEB in 1934, and remained on it until her death in 1946.

Despite her belief that unions offered the best alternative for working women, Bellanca worked with reformers outside the union. In the 1930s, she served on state and federal advisory committees, was an active member of the Consumers League and the Women's Trade Union League, and helped found the American Labor Party. Although an unsuccessful candidate for Congress, she was twice elected state vice-chairman of the American Labor Party. Nonetheless, most of her considerable energies were devoted to building the ACWA into a powerful union and to making a place for women within it.

In some respects, Dorothy Jacobs Bellanca was typical of the female union organizers of her day. She understood the American capitalist system and operated within it. She was able to deliver some of the benefits of the system to women workers, and they appreciated her services to them. Her example provided women workers with a model, encouraging in them the hope that through their own efforts, they could live decent, self-respecting lives. Female members of the ACWA filled the *Advance* with letters and articles describing Bellanca's visits and requesting return engagements. Yet, the distance between Bellanca and the rank and file was considerable. She was one of only a few female organizers who achieved real prominence in the Amalgamated Clothing Workers of America. Although she worked to improve the conditions of women within the male-dominated union, her achievements were limited. That Bellanca herself was not more successful in achieving her goals for working women points to the limits of both the ACWA and the society in which it operated.

Bellanca left a good deal of unfinished work for the generation of women trade unionists that followed her. Today's female trade unionists also must pursue the runaway industries as they flee south, southwest, and overseas. The inducements that drew Ansorge Brothers to Scranton in 1920—a willing Chamber of Commerce and other civic business groups, a large, exploitable, young and female work force, and community antagonism to trade unions—still attract the 1980s-style runaways. And although the feminism of the 1980s is increasingly applied by working-class women to their own lives, and affects working-class men to some extent as well, problems of class and gender remain endemic to labor union struggles. The experience and career of Dorothy Jacobs Bellanca, her triumphs and her failures, are pertinent and worthy of study by today's women organizers.

NOTES

1. Ann Washington Craton, "Ansorge Bros. Goes to Scranton," *Advance*, 4, no. 28 (Sept. 10, 1920), 6.

2. *Documentary History of the Amalgamated Clothing Workers of America, 1922–1924*, Sixth Biennial Convention, May 1924 (New York: The Amalgamated Clothing Workers of America, 1924), 45–49.

3. Craton, "Ansorge Bros.," 6.

4. A detailed biographical sketch of Dorothy Jacobs Bellanca can be found by Herbert Gutman in *Notable American Women*, 1607–1950, ed. Edward James (Cambridge, Mass.: Harvard University Press, 1971), 124–126, and by Melvyn Dubofsky in *Dictionary of American Biography*, Supplement 4, 1946–1950, eds. John A. Garraty and Edward T. James (New York: Scribner's, 1974), 69–70.

5. Interview with Dorothy Jacobs Bellanca in *Woman's World*, Jan. 1941.

6. Sherry H. Olson, *Baltimore* (Baltimore: Johns Hopkins University Press, 1980), 176.

7. Samuel Joseph, *Jewish Immigration to the United States, 1881 to 1910* (New York, 1914), table 59.

8. Moses Rischin, *The Promised City* (Cambridge: Harvard University Press, 1962), 64–65, and John Laslett, *Labor and the Left* (New York: Basic Books, 1970), 101.

9. Melvyn Dubofsky, *When Workers Organize* (Amherst: University of Massachusetts Press, 1968), 46.

10. Rischin, *Promised City*, 181.

11. Ibid, 183.

12. Dubofsky, *When Workers Organize*, 17.

13. *United States Bureau of the Census*, no. 43, 1920, 50: Olson, *Baltimore*, 280.

14. Olson, *Baltimore*, 279.

15. *The Garment Worker*; the advertisement appeared in numerous issues in 1902 and 1903, for example.

16. Joel Seidman, *The Needle Trades* (New York: Farrar and Rinehart, 1942), 89.

17. *Documentary History of the Amalgamated Clothing Workers of America, 1920*, xvi–xvii.

18. Jack Hardy, *The Clothing Workers* (New York: International Publishers, 1935), 82.

19. *Advance*, 30, no. 8 (June 1, 1944), 19.

20. Matthew Josephson, *Sidney Hillman: Statesman of American Labor* (Garden City, N.Y.: Doubleday, 1952), 111–115.

21. At about this time the radical immigrants at the UGWA Convention in Nashville had withdrawn to their own meeting. They represented a vast majority of the unionized Baltimore tailors and had plans to organize further.

22. *Advance*, 1, no. 18 (July 6, 1917), 6.

23. Ibid.

24. *Advance*, 32, no. 18 (Sept. 15, 1946), 7.

25. Ibid.

26. *Documentary History of the Amalgamated Clothing Workers of America, 1946–1948*, Sixteenth Biennial Convention, May 1948 (New York: The Amalgamated Clothing Workers of America, 1948), xx–xxii.

27. Barbara Wertheimer, *We Were There: The Story of Working Women in America* (New York: Pantheon, 1977), 330.

28. "Resolution for a Woman Organizer," *Proceedings*, Founding Convention of the Amalgamated Clothing Workers of America, Dec. 1914.

29. Hyman Blumberg to C. W., 1961, in ACWA files, Labor-Management Documentation Center, Martin P. Catherwood Library, New York State School of Industrial and Labor Relations, Cornell University, Ithaca, New York. Hereafter cited as ACWA Files.

30. *Documentary History of ACWA, 1914–1916*, 195.

31. Ibid, 168.

32. Dorothy Jacobs to Joseph Schlossberg, July 20, 1916, ACWA Files.

33. Ibid.

34. Dorothy Jacobs to Joseph Schlossberg, Aug. 20, 1916, ACWA Files.

35. Dorothy Jacobs to Joseph Schlossberg, July 20, 1916, ACWA Files.

36. Dorothy Jacobs to Joseph Schlossberg, July 27, 1916, ACWA Files.

37. Dorothy Jacobs to Joseph Schlossberg, Aug. 13, 1916, ACWA Files.

38. Dorothy Jacobs to Joseph Schlossberg, July 20, 1916, ACWA Files.

39. Dorothy Jacobs to Joseph Schlossberg, Aug. 13, 1916, ACWA Files.

40. Dorothy Jacobs to Joseph Schlossberg, Sept. 17, 1916, ACWA Files.

41. *Advance*, 1, no. 25 (Aug. 24, 1917), 1.

42. Ibid., 6.

43. Ibid.

44. *Advance*, 1, no. 36 (Nov. 9, 1917), 6.

45. Dorothy Jacobs to Joseph Schlossberg, Dec. 10, 1916, ACWA Files.

46. *Advance*, 1, no. 29 (Sept. 21, 1917), 6.

47. Ibid.

48. *Advance*, 1, no. 28 (Sept. 14, 1917), 6.

49. Ibid.

50. Dorothy Jacobs to Joseph Schlossberg, Aug. 20, 1918, ACWA Files.

51. Personal interview, June 7, 1980.

52. Alice Kessler-Harris, "Organizing the Unorganizable: Three Jewish Women and Their Union," *Labor History*, 17 (Winter 1976), 5–23.

53. *Proceedings*, Third Biennial Convention of the Amalgamated Clothing Workers of America, May 1918.

54. Dorothy Jacobs Bellanca to Bessie Malac, Sept. 2, 1925, ACWA Files.

55. *Proceedings*, ACWA, May 1918, 206.

56. Wertheimer, *We Were There*, 334.

57. *Advance*, 19, no. 10 (Oct. 1933), 13.

58. Dorothy Jacobs Bellanca to Hortense Powdermaker, Feb. 3, 1925, ACWA Files.

59. *Advance*, 8, no. 35 (Nov. 7, 1924), 2.

60. Dorothy Jacobs Bellanca to Mary Anderson, Feb. 3, 1925, ACWA Files.

61. For an example, see Dorothy Jacobs Bellanca to Hilda Shapiro, June 1, 1925, ACWA Files.

62. *Advance*, 8, no. 37 (Dec. 5, 1924), 1.

63. *Advance*, 9, no. 12 (June 19, 1924), 2.

64. Mamie Santora to Dorothy Jacobs Bellanca, Sept. 2, 1924, ACWA Files.

65. Dorothy Jacobs Bellanca to Mamie Santora, Aug. 5, 1925, ACWA Files.

66. *Advance*, 21, no. 1 (Jan. 1935), 19.

67. Irving Bernstein, *The Lean Years: A History of the American Worker, 1920–1933* (Boston: Houghton Mifflin, 1960), 329.

68. ACWA General Executive Board Report, 1930–1934, 51–62.

69. *Advance*, 16, no. 43 (Oct. 24, 1930), 6.

70. Carole Turbin, "And We Are Nothing but Women," in Carol Ruth Berkin and Mary Beth Norton, eds., *Women of America* (Boston: Houghton Mifflin, 1979), 216.

71. Interview with Dorothy Jacobs Bellanca in *Woman's World*, Jan. 1941.

72. *Advance*, 22, no. 5 (May 1936), 5.

73. *Proceedings*, ACWA, May 13, 1938.

74. *Proceedings*, ACWA, May 16, 1938.

75. *Advance*, 22, no. 3 (March 1936), 8.

76. *Advance*, 20, no. 12 (Nov. 1935), 19.

77. See for example, *Advance*, 12, no. 14 (Apr. 8, 1927), and ibid., no. 5 (Feb. 4, 1927).

78. *Proceedings*, ACWA, May 17, 1934.

79. Dorothy Jacobs Bellanca to Helen Woodward, May 2, 1935, ACWA Files.

CHAPTER 8

Women at Farah:
An Unfinished Story

Laurie Coyle, Gail Hershatter, and Emily Honig

INTRODUCTION

WHEN FOUR thousand garment workers at Farah Manufacturing Company in El Paso, Texas, went out on strike for the right to be represented by a union, many observers characterized the conflict as "a classic organizing battle."[1] The two-year strike, which began in May 1972 and was settled in March 1974, was similar in many ways to earlier, bloodier labor wars.

There was a virulently antiunion employer, Willie Farah, who swore in the time-honored manner that he would rather be dead than union. There was a company that paid low wages, pressured its employees to work faster and faster, consistently ignored health and safety conditions, and swiftly fired all those who complained. There was a local power structure that harassed the strikers with police dogs and antipicket ordinances, denied them public aid whenever possible, and smothered their strike and boycott activities with press silence for

Reprinted from *Mexican Women in the United States: Struggles Past and Present* (Los Angeles: University of California, Chicano Studies Research Center, 1980), with permission of the authors; © by the authors.

The authors wish to thank the real authors of this oral history—the women workers at Farah who generously shared their lives and opinions with three outsiders. Many of them asked to remain anonymous because they still live and work in El Paso, Texas.

as long as it could. There were strikebreakers, and sporadic violence was directed at the striking workers. On the side of the strikers there was a union, the Amalgamated Clothing Workers of America, which mustered national support for the strikers and organized a boycott of Farah pants. There was support from organized workers and sympathizers throughout the United States. Finally, there was a victory— an end to the strike and a union contract.

However, any account of the Farah strike that focuses exclusively on its "classic" characteristics misses most of the issues that make it an important and unfinished story. The Farah strikers were virtually all Chicanas. They were on strike in a town whose economy is profoundly affected by proximity to the Mexican border, in a period when border tensions were on the rise. They were workers in an industry plagued by instability and runaway shops. They were represented by a national union committed to "organizing the unorganized," but which often resorted to tactics that undermined efforts to build a strong, democratic local union at Farah.

Perhaps most important, 85 percent of the strikers were women. Their experiences during and since the strike changed the way they looked at themselves—as Chicanas, as wives, and as workers—and the way they looked at their fellow workers, their supervisors, their families, and their community.

The following account does not focus on Willie Farah's flamboyant antiunion activities. Instead, it attempts to explore the effect of the strike on the women who initiated and sustained it. In extensive interviews (approximately seventy hours) conducted during the summer of 1977, the women described their working conditions, events leading to the strike, the strike itself, the development of the union, and their lives as Mexican-American women in the Southwest. In an effort to accurately place the Farah strike in perspective, this chapter also deals with the social and economic context in which the strike took place. The account appears here primarily as it was told by the Farah strikers themselves—eloquently, sometimes angrily, and always with humor.

BEFORE THE STRIKE

The history of the Farah Manufacturing Company exemplifies the myth and reality of the American success story. Unlike many other southwest garment plants that ran away from the unionized Northeast, Farah got its start in El Paso. During the depression, Mansour Farah, a Lebanese immigrant, arrived in El Paso and set up a tiny shop on the South Side. Farah, together with his wife and two sons, James and Willie, and a half-dozen Mexican seamstresses, began to turn out the chambray shirts and denim pants that were the uniform of the working West.

When Mansour died in 1937, James was twenty-one and Willie only eighteen, but they were well on the way to becoming kingpins of the needle trade. Winning government contracts for military pants during the war mobilization effort enabled the company to expand, and it emerged from World War II in the top ranks of the garment industry. In the postwar period, the rapid expansion of the garment industry transformed the South into the largest apparel-producing region of the United States. The Farah brothers shifted production to meet the growing demands of the consumer trade, and sold their product to the major chain stores, J. C. Penney, Sears, and Montgomery Ward, for retail under the store names. In 1950 the Farah brothers began marketing pants under their own name, and built a loyal and growing clientele in men's casual and dress slacks. The company expanded until it employed 9,500 workers in Texas and New Mexico.[2] Before the strike, it was the second largest employer in El Paso.

Farah's major role in developing El Paso's industry and expanding the employment ranks made the family prominent in town. At least among some sectors of the population, Farah had the reputation of being a generous boss who lavished bonuses on his workers, gave them turkey at Thanksgiving, bankrolled an elaborate party each Christmas, and provided health care and refreshments on the job. The company's hourly wages, however low they were, seemed generous in comparison to the piece rates that were standard in the garment world. Farah was the only garment plant in El Paso which would hire the inexperienced. In a town where the overwhelming number of unskilled Chicanas had to find work in retail or as domestic servants, many women considered themselves fortunate to work at Farah.

After the sudden death of James Farah in 1964, Willie undertook a major expansion of the company, constructing or acquiring a plant in Belgium, one in Hong Kong, and five in El Paso—the Gateway, Paisano, Northwest, Clark Street and Third Street plants. Within ten years, from 1960 to 1970, Farah's share of the market for men's casual and dress slacks rose from 3.3 percent to 11 percent.[3] In 1967, the company went public and qualified for the New York Stock Exchange. The booming growth, new capital investment, and increased planning and control of marketing resulted in major changes within the plant, including increased pressure on workers to produce more and make higher quotas, and greater impersonality on the job.

WORKING CONDITIONS

Many workers felt that the expansion ruined what had been warm relations between management and employees. One woman remarked on the changes: "In 1960, there were only two plants. They had time for you. But it started growing and they didn't give a damn about you, your health, or anything. They just kept pushing."

While some workers saw these changes as significant departures from happier days, many felt that the public image of Farah as one big happy family had never accorded with the reality on the shop floor. Willie ran his business like a classic *patron*, conducting unannounced plant inspections and instructing women in how best to do their jobs. The most minute aspects of production, down to a seamstress's technique for turning corners, were matters of near fanatical personal concern for Farah. His overbearing presence led many workers to feel that he assumed responsibility for work problems.

In fact, he would shower the workers with promises of liberal pay raises which never materialized. One woman who began working in 1953 recollected:

> I used to tell my kids, work hard and your boss will love you and treat you well. So years and years passed, and though I was one of the fastest seamstresses, nothing was repaid, neither to me nor to the other workers. One day before the organizing drive began, I met Willie Farah and I asked him why he worked us so hard and never gave us a raise. He told me to come along to the office, and when we got there he said, "Listen, I don't know a thing about what happens to the workers on the floor. If it will make you happy, I will go myself to your supervisor and check to see if you are getting your due." Well, great, I thought, being sure of the quality of my work. Time went on and nothing happened. Seven months passed and no Willie. I asked, what happened, Willie doesn't want to give me my due?

For many, wages were never raised above the legal minimum, and workers were often misled to believe that legislated increases in the minimum wage were raises granted by management. Wages remained low under the quota system; since pay increases were based upon higher and higher production rates, workers' wages continually lagged behind spiraling quotas. Women were pitted against one another in the scramble to meet management demands and protect their jobs. As one woman observed:

> They would threaten to fire you if you didn't make a quota. They would go to a worker and say, "This girl is making very high quotas. It's easy, and I don't know why you can't do it. And if you can't do it, we'll have to fire you." So this girl would work really fast and if she got it up higher, they'd go to the other people and say, "She's making more. You'll get a ten cent raise if you make a higher quota than she." They would make people compete against each other. No one would gain a thing—the girl with the highest quota would make a dime, but a month later the minimum wage would come up. I knew a girl who'd been there for sixteen years, and they fired her, and another who was there for sixteen years and still making the minimum.

In the garment industry, where labor comprises a major portion of a firm's expenditures, southwestern companies like Farah keep their competitive edge over unionized plants in the Northeast by these cutthroat pay practices.

Many women who were pretty and willing to date their supervisors received preferential treatment. One seamstress, who had worked on a particular job operation for twenty years, received less than the attractive young woman who had begun the operation only a year before. The less favored women were subjected to constant harassment:

> Every day they would come around to your machine to see how much you'd make. If you didn't make your [quota of] 300, they would hurl things at us, yell at us like, "You don't do nothing, you don't do your job, I'm gonna fire you." Embarrass me in front of all those guys pressing seams next to me. I was so embarrassed, but I said nothing. I got to the point where I dreaded going to work.

Rather than hire Chicanos who had worked on the shop floor, it was standard practice for the company to hire Anglo males as supervisors. Their treatment of Chicana workers was frequently hostile and racist. Women were humiliated for speaking Spanish. When they could not understand a supervisor's orders, he would snap his fingers, hurl insults, bang the machines, and push them. One worker remembered:

> In my department, the cafeteria, there was a supervisor. . . . This man didn't like Latinos—he had a very brusque manner when talking to us. He wasn't a supervisor; he was an interrogator! He would talk to me in English, which I can't speak, and insist upon it, even though he knew I didn't understand. The others would tell me what he said—things that offended, hurt me. But I couldn't defend myself.

Workers who challenged arbitrary decisions were dismissed on the spot. "When I was just learning to sew," a striker remembered, "I made a mistake on three pieces and the supervisor threw them in my face."

> I couldn't say anything, being new there. But an old man who worked with the seamstresses defended me, saying that I wasn't trained yet and there was no reason to throw them at me because everyone made mistakes at the start. They fired him for that, because he wasn't supposed to meddle in those things. He'd been there for fifteen years.

All of these racist and abusive practices played a role in helping to control the work force.

Health problems in the plant were numerous. Some workers contracted bronchitis from working directly under huge air conditioners, while others suffered from a lack of ventilation. The pressure to produce was so great that women were reluctant to take time to go to the bathroom or get drinks of water. As a result, many workers developed serious kidney and bladder infections after several years of work. Equipment was faulty and safety devices were inadequate. Needles often snapped off machines and pierced the fingers and eyes of the seamstresses. Company negligence resulted in many accidents; such negligence was reflected in the care received by workers at the plant clinic:

> One time I felt sick. I knew I wasn't pregnant. He [the doctor] gave me a checkup, checked my blood and said I was pregnant. I *knew* I wasn't pregnant. "Yes, you are." Two weeks later I got really sick. You know what

it was? It was my appendix, about to erupt. I went to [the] emergency
[room].

Once, a needle broke on my little finger. The nurse said there was nothing
wrong with it. I said it hurt, but she just put a tape on it. The next day it
was *that* big. The nurse was very mean—didn't know how to get along with
people. I went to the clinic downstairs. I said, "Look, I cut my finger
yesterday. I feel something in it." They took some X-rays. I had the needle
point stuck in my bone. They should have taken X-rays or told the
supervisor to go check the needle to see if it was complete.

Several workers were fired after having been injured on the job.
Others had their injuries and illnesses misdiagnosed and were sent
back to work without proper treatment, sometimes with serious
consequences:

I saw several times people fainting. There was this time the doctor told this
guy there was nothing wrong with him and kept giving him pain killers. In
the afternoon, he was the guy who did cleanup and sweeping, he just bent
over—he couldn't stand the pain anymore. They took him to the hospital
and at the hospital he went into a coma. He was in a coma and they couldn't
operate on him. I think it was his gall bladder.

The doctors were not only incompetent, but they were also
unsympathetic and insensitive to workers' feelings. Many workers felt
that the company doctors and nurses were there primarily to keep
them at their machines, rather than to provide them with health care:

The plant doctor gave the same medicine to everyone in the factory and sent
you back to work. I remember I'd been working there for three years and had
heard a lot of stories about what was going on. I never went there. I took my
own aspirins to work.
    One day I was really sick and wanted to go home. I could hardly walk. I
was almost fainting and had chills. But I walked to the clinic, and the first
thing the nurse told me (she got my chart—it wasn't mine, it belonged to
somebody else and had my *name*. She didn't see my badge), and said to the
other nurse, "I think somebody just doesn't want to work." It kind of made
me feel bad because I'd never stepped into the office before. So I told her it
wasn't my chart, that I'd never been in before, and she said, "Oh, I don't
know." When I went in to see the doctor he didn't even tell me what was
wrong with me, he was already writing the prescription. So I said, "Doctor,

I want to go home." And he answered, "Why didn't you tell me that in the first place?" as if I were wasting his time.

When I walked out of their clinic I was sicker than when I walked in, because I thought they thought I was a pretender. After three years of not being sick.

If people had to go outside for additional medical care, the company would not assume financial responsibility.

In addition to "free medical care," company benefits included bus transportation to and from work and Christmas presents and bonuses. Since company expenditures for these "extras" were paid for in part by the interest on workers' savings in a company-controlled account, the "benefits" were more illusory than real. Real benefits such as maternity and sick leave, seniority, and a pension plan were absent from the company package. Women who took maternity leaves without compensation returned to the factory to find that they had been switched to new operations and that their wages had been cut. Pregnant women underwent substantial hardships in order to avoid the consequences of these practices. One woman recalled:

> When I was pregnant with my youngest, I was working there and my husband was also working there. But what he was making wasn't enough. I worked up to the eighth month. And let me tell you, it was pretty bad because they take no consideration; even if you're pregnant you still have to do the same thing, the same quota. They don't even take you down [from the machine] to rest your legs. If you're standing up you have to stand all day. Then after the baby is born you just take a month off, and that's it. You have to go back to work. If you didn't go back to work *exactly* a month after, you would just lose your whole seniority. That was another reason we decided we needed a union and we should organize.

The denial of maternity benefits caused a great deal of anger among the workers, the majority of whom were women.

Few Farah workers ever retired from the company. Usually workers were shoved out just before retirement age, so that Farah was not obliged to pay their pensions. Older workers were frequently the lowest paid and the least likely to be promoted despite their extensive work experience. Instead, they were expected to work long hours at the most demanding operations. Their health ruined by this ordeal, many workers quit prematurely. Farah absorbed new employees continually, and had little consideration for the needs of aging workers. Many women were bitter about the treatment of the older workers, and realized that their "benefits" were only guaranteed by their own wits, resilience, and ability to make the grade:

> They could keep their turkey. We didn't need their cake. We needed better conditions, better safety. Only the favorite people there could talk. Especially the older people were the people they tried to get rid of so they wouldn't reach retirement. They had a retirement plan, but only two people have reached it—the nurse and one other. At the Coliseum, there were twenty people who were going to retire [after twenty years of work]. They never did retire. They [the company] changed their quota and got them out.

The factory conditions described by women workers were by no means unique to Farah. Exploitation, low wages, no security, and minimal employer liability were the lot of working people whether they grew up in El Paso's *barrios* or across the Rio Grande in El Paso's sister-city, Juarez.

FAMILY BACKGROUND: MEXICO AND EL PASO

The border economy affected the lives of women at Farah even before they entered the work force, shaping their family backgrounds and presenting them with enormous obstacles when they tried to act on their own behalf.

Since the Spanish Conquest, El Paso has served as a major passageway for commerce and migration between north and south. The 1848 United States acquisition of the entire Mexican territory north of the Rio Grande River established an artificial division of a land that was one, geographically, economically, and culturally. This allowed for the increased penetration of both sides of the new border by United States capital. In the early twentieth century, the railroad drew large numbers of campesinos to the El Paso region from the interior of Mexico to lay the basis for agribusiness and industrial expansion in the area.

The boundaries policed by the border patrol scarcely disguise the historic integration and interdependency of the Mexico-Texas region. The border itself is marked by the Rio Grande River, which is a mere thirty feet wide and four feet deep on the outskirts of El Paso and

Juarez. Today, more than ever, the United States economy depends on cheap labor from the Mexican side of the river to harvest its seasonal crops, replenish its industrial workforce, and maintain profits in its labor-intensive industries.

The close cooperation of authorities on both sides of the border, as well as the special privileges granted to twin plants, allows for the optimum flow of labor and goods between El Paso and Juarez. The state of Texas has protected these privileges by establishing the right-to-work law. This law stipulates that no worker in a plant be required to join a union, and furthermore that *all* workers, whether they are union members or not, are entitled to the benefits provided by a union contract. Collective bargaining efforts have frequently been undermined by this law, and El Paso remains a largely nonunion town.

The availability of unorganized workers on the El Paso side, many of whom are Mexican nationals without rights of permanent residence, and many others who are unskilled Chicanos, has created an ideal situation for companies investing in labor-intensive operations such as electronics and garments. El Paso has become the last frontier of United States industry on the move south and out of the United States. "Runaways?" asked one Farah worker incredulously. "Industries in El Paso don't need to move. They have the advantage that they can get people from Juarez to work for less."

The United States government participates actively in depressing wages by manipulating the migrant work force to meet the needs of industry. The issuance of green cards, which are temporary permits for Mexicans to work in the United States, guarantees business an abundant supply of labor which can be curtailed or expanded when necessary. In addition, the H-2 program of the United States Department of Labor allows an individual employer to bring in a specified number of workers from Mexico if he can prove that a labor shortage exists. This program has been used to strikebreak in the cotton industry in the South, and more recently, against onion pickers in Texas. The Immigration and Naturalization Service (INS) also plays a role in regulating the presence of Mexican workers without documents. It allows them to enter during critical harvest periods or when there are labor disputes, and at the same time deports those undocumented workers who have joined strikes. "The INS knows that there are illegals," one Farah worker complained, "because when they need them, they send them in by the hundreds to the U.S. When they need them they look the other way. But when they don't need them, they get them out of there *fast*. They *know* they're there."

Even in normal times, and particularly in the last eight years with unemployment on the rise, there is intense competition for jobs in the El Paso area. The complexity of the El Paso labor market has the built-in potential for conflicts among United States-born Mexicans and Mexican nationals with or without documents. Employers in El Paso use the competition for jobs to create and exacerbate conflict among these groups whenever labor troubles arise.

Many Farah strikers maintained close ties with friends and family in Juarez. Women who had extensive personal contact with life in Mexico, either because their parents had crossed the Rio Grande or because they themselves had grown up there and come to the United States as adults, tended to see the Mexicans and Chicanos as one people. When they looked at the undocumented workers of today, they saw the experiences of their own parents. "I was born over there and raised here," one striker recalled.

> I was seven when we came here. I remember, when we were living in Juarez my father had to come back and forth every fifteen days. He used to live on a farm in the U.S. I don't have any grudges against wetbacks. I do support the Texas Farmworkers. If they want to sign up the whole border I don't mind. I understand how it is over there. I understand what it is to have a father as a wetback. I understand what people are trying to do with the border situation.

Many workers at Farah, as children, took part in the pilgrimage north to find work. Some of their families crossed the border illegally. "My father was a laborer," one woman recollected. "There was no work in Mexico. My parents were having a picnic one day, and zoom—they came across." Families contracted to work seasonally, harvesting cotton and pecans. Some never intended to make the United States their home, but they became permanent residents when they found that the money they earned during temporary work visits to the United States could not sustain them when they returned to the increasingly constricted economy of rural Mexico.

Other women at Farah came north as adults to seek work. Even when they succeeded in finding a stable job, the relocation entailed severe hardship and demanded major readjustments. Most of the women had grown up in the poverty-striken rural areas of northern Mexico. They had almost no formal education, and many married very early in life. While the daily struggle to survive prepared them for the grinding labor of the factory, nothing in their backgrounds had prepared them to assume roles traditionally restricted to male heads-of-household: to leave the home, enter the industrial work-force, and, for some, become the major breadwinner of the family. That the move was a radical departure from their upbringing can best be understood from the childhood recollections of the women who experienced these changes. "My childhood?" a striker reminisced:

> I was born in a village where they mine silver, Cusihuiriachi. My father worked there, as did his father and his grandfather. It was a company town. The company was American and there was a union. My family helped build the union. My father wanted to have schools, to have benefits. My father spoke to me often about how the company was very rich and that we were all making the company rich and it was just that the company give us a part for our children. My father talked a lot about this, and sometimes they would throw him out of the mine. After great fights, my father would be back in the mine.
>
> He was a product of his times. He thought that only men should go to school, that we women should only learn to write. Men are the ones who support the family, and so the women don't need anything more.
>
> My father named me after his mother, and even though I had two brothers and three sisters, I was my father's favorite. I was the only child until age four, when my brother arrived. Everything was for me. They took me to work, to the mines, to visit my father. He had a little office where they kept records of people injured on the job, etc. And they took me to the paymaster. In those days they paid cash. I went everywhere with my father and uncles, to union meetings where everyone didn't stop talking and shouting and discussing their problems. A child learns when it is born. When a child begins to breathe a child begins to learn.
>
> Thus I spent all my time with my father and uncles, but when I'd learned to read and write at nine years, I was not sent to school any more. "No, Papa," I began to cry and shout. When he saw me sitting with a long face and asked me why, I said, "Why can't I go to school anymore?" So he said to go ahead. So they cut my hair and I went. I finished elementary.
>
> Afterwards, I would look up at the mountains, so high. The mines were in the mountains. What more is there? I was dying to know. What's beyond the mountains? What are the people like? Of course my father wouldn't

consider my leaving home. He wanted me to get married and have children. One day my cousin went to the city of Chihuahua. When he returned, I asked him, "What is it like there?" "Oh, the buildings are tall, very tall, and the streets—some of them are paved." Here they were made of dirt. "Imagine! The streets are wide—wide as from here to the next village." The more he said, the more I wanted to know.

I thought and thought and one day I asked my father, "Don't we have any relatives in Chihuahua?" He answered that my godfather was there. I told him, "Father, I want to meet him. Maybe I can write." "Go ahead, write him," he agreed. I wrote the letter and asked my father, "Papa, isn't it true that the mail is sacred? You can't open a sealed envelope? Right?" "Yes," he answered. So I said, "Here's the letter for my godfather," and sealed it. He could do nothing but send it. In the letter I told my godfather that I wanted to come and meet him and his wife. He wrote back saying that he'd love to have me come and visit for a while. "My wife is expecting a baby and it would be fine." I wrote again asking him to ask my father for his permission to come if possible. He arrived. "How long it has been since we've seen each other, how great, couldn't she go with me for a while. My wife is having a baby, and it would be great if your daughter would accompany her." Since he was my godfather, my father accepted.

This woman came to the city, finished her studies, and became a teacher. She married, had a family, and decided once again to leave her home—this time for the United States. Hardship in Mexico pushed her, and promises of a better future for herself and her children drew her. Upon arriving in El Paso, she had to give up her teaching and enter Farah's factory. This was an immense shock to her hopes; the hardships continued. In making all of these decisions she made a radical departure from her upbringing and grew stronger as a woman. Part of this strength was her intense attachment to her origins.

Of course I still go back to Mexico frequently to see my parents in Cuahtemoc. My father can no longer get papers to come here, but when he comes to Juarez, to visit my brother, I go to see him. My children go all the time. They love the ambiente there. I believe that this is a good country, but I don't want them to become Americanized so that they don't want to see their own people. Our roots are there. I became an American citizen by my own choice. This was my decision, but I don't want to negate my roots, or say that I don't want to be there [Mexico]. I love this country as much as I love my own [Mexico]. For that reason I live here. But my children should love both equally: the land is one and the same.

Many other women experienced profound physical and emotional changes; yet their ties to Mexico remained powerful.

A major change for those who came from Mexico involved no longer being a "native" but being stigmatized as an "alien." This identification was applied to all Mexican people regardless of citizenship, and included a population indigenous to the region and more "native" than the later white settlement.

The pride of many Farah workers in their Mexican heritage—a pride often fostered by their parents—protected them somewhat from this hostility and enabled them to stand up to it. "For not having much of an education my father was a pretty smart man," one striker remembered.

> I wish I was like him. He kept up in his history. He used to say, "Americanos? We are the Americanos, we're the Indians, we were the first ones here." He was an Indian. He always argued about people calling an Anglo "Americano" and a Mexican "Mexicano." That really got him mad. He'd say, "*We* are Americanos; *they* are Anglos." That was one thing he always argued about.

Like their sisters in Mexico, Chicanas growing up in El Paso were expected to share responsibility for *la familia* at an early age. They were raised in poverty, received little formal education, began working when they were still children, married young, and spent their working lives in low status, low paying jobs.

Most of the Chicana workers at Farah had grown up in the *barrio* in south El Paso's Second Ward. Squeezed between the downtown area and the border, residents of "El Segundo" faced street violence, police indifference, or brutality, rip-offs from slumlords, and racism from uptown whites.

The violence in the streets was inescapable. "When I grew up," one woman recalled,

> Life was a lot different at that time. Everything was harder. At that time there were no youth centers. There was nothing to do for the kids, no recreation or things like that. So they would hang around on the corners, they would have gangs and fight against each other. You know it became a *barrio* where policemen were there all the time. That kind of reputation. I guess that's one reason why the police didn't care what happened to them

because they had that reputation. So they [the police] would beat them up and a lot of times they would just be sitting there with a quart of beer and the [police] would break it and kick them and take them to jail for nothing.

The unrelieved poverty operated as brutally on residents as attacks by the police. Many a childhood ended prematurely as young girls quit school to help support their families.

I grew up in the Second Ward. It was a poor neighborhood. We used to live in the projects. Some Mexican Americans try to help each other; others are selfish. My mother used to have three jobs: at Newark Hospital, at night, and at Levi's. After school I worked at Newberry's, babysitting, and as a maid when I was nine. With three young children and myself, I had to help my mother. It was a hard childhood. I didn't have a father. My mother had to work day and night. I told her to let me work for her at the Newark Hospital—so I cleaned the beds and floors.

While many quit school because of economic necessity, even more were driven out by systematic discrimination. They were penalized for being brown-skinned and Spanish-speaking. Like the Anglo supervisors at Farah, Anglo teachers in El Paso schools instilled deep-seated feelings of inadequacy, humiliation, and disaffection in their Chicano students. Chicanos were discouraged from finishing high school, and the strict tracking system prohibited college and career aspirations. "To me it was hard in school," one woman recalled.

People making fun of you, especially the way you talked. Your English or your understanding [of English]. I believe my older brothers and sisters had the most difficulty getting adjusted here because they couldn't speak any English. Neither could I, but I was put in kindergarten so it didn't matter to me. People in that small village [outside of El Paso] didn't know how to speak English so we talked Spanish, but it was very difficult for them because they were put in the fourth or fifth grade and they were fourteen. People were making fun of them. I just went to eighth grade, then I quit and got married. I was sixteen and I'm still married to the same man. I was sixteen and I was still in eighth grade. I used to get very disappointed that most of my friends were fourteen or thirteen in the same grade. I was supposed to be in tenth grade at the age of sixteen. That used to bother me a lot. Because of the language problem I had when I came across the border [sic].

Whether at home, in the streets, at school, or on the job, there was no refuge from personal hostility or institutionalized discrimination. Mature women workers are still nursing their childhood wounds, looking back on childhood dreams that were crushed and scorned whichever way they turned. Yet growing up Chicana in El Paso also provided these women with sources of strength, pride, and courage. They drew strength from El Segundo's sense of community, which was formed in response to confrontations with the Anglo power structure of El Paso. Their families transmitted to them pride in Mexican culture, as well as countless individual examples of courage in difficult circumstances.

Whether they were raised in the United States or Mexico, these women by no means suffered passively. To survive they had to struggle. They responsed with anger to the racism, deprivation, and systematic oppression which they experienced as Raza women. While this anger was seldom expressed openly, it was always present and potentially explosive. The advent of a unionization campaign helped to give organized expression to this anger.

EARLY ORGANIZING

Despite most workers in the El Paso region not being organized into unions, some women had been exposed to labor-organizing drives. Women from Mexico had parents who had fled to the United States after their attempts to organize workers in Mexico had failed. They had lost everything in the process. Some women, as children, had witnessed bloody strikes in the textile mills and mines of northern Mexico. Among those women, some had even worked as children in these industries. Others had undergone the dislocation and hardship of migrant life in the United States.

Among Chicanas at Farah, some had fathers, mothers, brothers, and husbands who belonged to unions in El Paso's smelting and packing plants. There was the example of the prolonged and successful strike of garment workers for union recognition at the Top Notch clothing plant in the 1960s. But experience with organized labor was by no means widespread among workers at Farah. The overwhelming majority of the women in the plant during the late sixties and early seventies had little or no idea about the day-to-day activities of a union, and virtually no examples of working women's struggles in unions to guide them. Yet, Farah workers from both sides of the border had grown up in working class families, and many had had tragic personal experiences that dramatized for them the need for unionization. One woman recalled the early death of her father from lung cancer.

> He died when he was young, only forty-four years old. Because where he was working, they didn't have no union and he was doing dirty work, smashing cans and bumpers. When you smash them, smoke comes up and he inhaled it and that's what killed him. He didn't have no protection; they didn't even give him a mask. He put only a handkerchief to cover his face. He died of cancer because of all the things he was inhaling. That's what the doctor told us. He died before I was seventeen. They operated and said he had only half a lung and wasn't going to live long. He lasted three weeks. I'd do anything for him, I was very close to him. He told me it was too late to have another job. I couldn't stand it and would go into the next room to cry so that he wouldn't hear me. He was so husky until the sickness ate him away.

This woman never lost the conviction that her father's life could have been prolonged if he'd had a union's protection on the job. "When I started to know about the union," she concluded grimly, "I joined right away because of my father."

The earliest attempt by workers at Farah to present an organized response to management attacks was a brief petition campaign among markers at the Gateway plant in 1968. A more systematic effort to address workers' grievances began in 1969 when male workers from the cutting and shipping departments contacted organizers from the Amalgamated Clothing Workers of America (ACWA).[4] They acted in spite of Farah's repeated violent tirades against unions. Farah presented films about union corruption on company time and pronounced to his workers, "See what a union does? You don't want anything to do with that!" But Farah overestimated the impact of his blitz on organizing. He was sufficiently confident of union defeat in an upcoming election that he urged cutters to vote, insisting that not to vote was to vote for the union. The cutters turned out in force for the election, and on October 14, 1970, they voted overwhelmingly to affiliate themselves with the union. Not about to accept the unexpected turn of events, Farah immediately appealed the election result with the National Labor Relations Board (NLRB). The cutting-room election was tied up in court until 1972, when the election victory was set aside on grounds that the cutting room was not an appropriate bargaining unit. But by that time, organizing had long since spread to the rest of the plant.

Soon after this first election, a handful of cutters began attempts to sign up workers in other departments. Reactions to the organizing drive varied. Most women had little idea of what the activists hoped to gain from union recognition. Others were fearful—with good cause—of supervisors' retaliation. Furthermore, many workers believed what Willie Farah said about labor unions taking their money and benefits.

Even so, some women were moved by their fellow workers' persistence in the face of personal harassment and threats to their jobs. Several workers signed cards and began to talk to their coworkers about the new organizing drive. Efforts to sign up workers took place clandestinely because of the virulence of management tactics against the organizers. Women hid union cards in their purses, met hurriedly in the bathrooms, and whispered in the halls to persuade the indifferent. The cafeteria was the heart of the organizing efforts. During lunchtime, workers circulated among the tables to sound out each other's sentiments about the union. The first union meetings in people's homes were a completely new experience. "Oh, I did like them," a striker reminisced. "There was a lot of—you know, talking about new things, about the union. And especially, I felt that somebody was talking for us."

Management responded to organizing activities with a series of repressive measures. Supervisors were stationed in the halls to monitor sympathizers and interrogate employees concerning their union loyalties. "They would say, 'What are they saying in there?' and I would respond, 'Who? I don't know what they're saying,'" a striker recalled.

> They'd say, "Don't believe about the union, the union's a bunch of bullshit. They only want to take your money away." That's what they'd say. And I just heard them, and I didn't say anything. But once they knew you were involved with the union, they'd start pressuring you. Some of us just quit, some were fired.

All personal conversations were restricted during work time, and conditions worsened even for those not involved in organizing. "When we began organizing," one woman recalled, "[the company] put even harsher supervisors who tried to humiliate people more. If there was a shortage of work on a line, they made me sweep. I refused, but other workers were afraid of being fired and obeyed. They did it to humiliate us and to assure that no organization would succeed."

Company intimidation frightened many people away. Workers treated union organizers as if they had some kind of disease. Union sympathizers were fired, among them four women. One woman described her firing, saying, "My supervisor sent me to another line because my line had no work."

> After lunch, he told me to go back to my machine because now there was work, and I worked at the machine the rest of the afternoon. About half an hour before quitting time, another foreman asked me what I was doing at my machine since I had been told to work in the other line. I told him that I was only following orders. Without another word he sent me to the office where they asked me to turn in my badge and scissors. I still did not know what was going on but the bell rang and I went home. The following day when I returned to work, the supervisor did not let me punch in and told me I was fired. Farah says I was fired for disobedience. Some people have spread the rumor that I was fired because I was lazy or that I quit to go to work for the union. But none of this is true. I was fired to stop me from organizing and to scare other people.

The firings intimidated workers, but also angered them. As one of the women who was fired observed, "It did give them some courage. They wanted to know why I was fired after all these years, with no earlier work problems." Few workers were willing to openly confront their supervisors, but as their anger grew they discussed the union among themselves more frequently.

Organizing continued at the Gateway plant, though there were no immediate plans to take action. The activists who were fired went down to the union office and vowed to continue the struggle. One woman organized a group of students from a nearby high school to distribute leaflets in front of the Gateway, Paisano, and Third Street plants. They were insulted, their leaflets were torn up and thrown in their faces, and some of them were assaulted. But the woman came every day at 6:00 A.M. and stood her ground until the day of the walkout.

THE WALKOUT

The campaign to unionize the Farah plants intensified in the spring of 1972. In March, twenty-six workers were fired when they attempted a walkout at the Northwest plant in El Paso. But it was a series of events in San Antonio that triggered the large-scale strike in El Paso.

One weekend, members of the union organizing committee in El Paso sponsored a march. Farah workers from San Antonio made the twelve-hour drive between the two cities to join the demonstration. Some of them did not return to San Antonio in time for work on Monday morning. On Tuesday, a supervisor confronted a worker with pictures of him marching under union banners in El Paso and then promptly fired him. Workers who objected to his dismissal were also fired. More than 500 San Antonio Farah workers walked out in protest.

Six days later, when El Paso Farah workers learned of the San Antonio strike, their frustration with working conditions and with Farah's continued suppression of union activity exploded into a spontaneous strike. On May 9, the machinists, shippers, cutters, and some of the seamstresses walked out. The walkout, which continued for almost a month, initially took the company by surprise. Women who had worked docilely at their machines for years, women who had been reduced to tears by a supervisor's reprimand, women who had never openly spoken a word in favor of the union, suddenly began to speak up.

> That day that we walked out, the supervisor saw that I had a little flag on. He went over and he looked at me, sort of startled, and he said, "You?" And I said, "Yes!" And he said, "What have we done to you?" I said, "Oh, I wouldn't know where to begin." He said, "We haven't done anything to you." I said, "But you have done a lot to all of the people around me. I've seen it going on."

The startled management soon rallied with a skillful combination of promises and threats. On the first day of the walkout, as activists walked through the factory urging the workers to join them, supervisors followed them, telling the workers to let the dissidents go out on strike and suffer and lose their jobs. The loudspeaker system broadcasted "La Golondrina," a Mexican song of farewell, in a sardonic gesture to the strikers. The shop floor and the cafeteria were full of people shouting, arguing, or quietly trying to decide what to do. For many women, the decision was a difficult one that took several days to make, while the management did its best to frighten or cajole the women who were still undecided. For all of the strikers, the day on which they decided to walk out remains a vivid and memorable one:

> I remember the first time of the walkout we were all in break, eating, having some coffee. And then suddenly there was a whole bunch in the cutting room—the girls and everything. They went over to my table and said, "Alma, you've got to come out with us!" And I just looked at them. I was so scared I didn't even know what to do. What if I go and lose my thirteen years? So long, having seniority and everything. I just looked at them and said, "Yeah, yeah, I'll go." That's all I said. And I had a whole bunch of people sitting there with me and I said, "Let's go!" And one of them said, "Well, if you go, we'll go."
>
> So the next day I went and put pants on. I always wear dresses. I used to love to wear dresses. So I put some pants on and said, "I don't know what's going to happen. Maybe there's going to be fighting or something." You know, we were scared. We were scared maybe they would beat us and everything.
>
> But I remember that day. When I was passing, the girls started yelling at me, "Alma, you'd better go out! We need you out here!" And I said, "Yeah, yeah, yeah. Wait, wait." "No, you're happy. That's what's the matter with you. You're just a happy one. The way they treat you in there, and you're still in there."
>
> So around nine o'clock I started gathering everybody. "We're going out! Right now! When you see me get off my machine." So you should have seen all those supervisors around me. Somebody pinched a finger on me and told them I was going to go out. You should have seen them all around me. They said, "Alma, you're a good worker. We'll pay you what you want. Alma, the way you sew, the way you work, the way you help us.'" And I would just say, "Yeah, I know. I know." They thought I was going to stay there.
>
> At nine o'clock I got off [the machine]. I went to the restroom and I started telling everybody, "Let's go!" So some of them just didn't go. I took a lot of people out with me.
>
> Then I started walking through the middle of the—where all the people were working—they thought I was very happy [with work at Farah]. And they started, "Alma! Alma!" And everybody started getting off the machines. I couldn't believe it. It was something so beautiful. So exciting.
>
> And then suddenly a supervisor got a hold of me on my shoulder, and he

says, "Alma, we need you! Don't go!" So everybody started. . . . I took a
lot of people that were real good. I took them all out with me.
     When I started walking outside, all the strikers that were out there,
yelling, they saw me, and golly, I felt so proud, 'cause they all went and
hugged me. And they said, "We never thought you were one of us." And I
said, "What do you think? Just because I'm a quiet person?"
     But it was beautiful! I really knew we were going to do something. That
we were really going to fight for our rights.

As the walkout continued and spread beyond the shipping and
cutting rooms, it began to include a wide variety of women. Some
came from families with histories of union involvement, while others
had no previous contact or experience with unions. Some who walked
out had taken an active role in the union organizing campaign leading
up to the strike, while others had never even signed a union card. For
all of them, however, the act of walking out began a process of change
in the way they looked at themselves and their work. "For me," one
striker recalled, "[the day of the walkout] was something out of this
world. I was pleased with myself, but at the same time I was afraid.
That night I couldn't sleep. I couldn't see myself out of Farah. So
many years."

THE STRIKE

The Amalgamated Clothing Workers of America quickly moved
to support the Farah workers; the strike was declared an unfair labor
practice strike. One month later a national boycott of Farah products
was begun, endorsed by the AFL-CIO. In El Paso the strikers began to
picket the Farah plants and local stores that carried Farah products.
But in a town where many regarded Willie Farah as a folk hero, the
strikers found that public reaction to the walkout was often hostile.
One woman remembers:

People were just very cruel. Everybody thought that Farah was a god or
something. I swear, they'd even turn around and spit on you if they could.
There was one lady, I was handing out some papers downtown and she got
her purse and started striking me. When she started hitting me, she said,
"Ah, you people, a bunch of dumb this and that! Farah's a great man!"

Passers-by told the picketers that they were lazy bums who just wanted welfare and food stamps. The strikers were repeatedly reminded that Farah was a major employer in an area where unemployment was high, and that they should be grateful to him for giving them jobs.

Antiunion sentiment was not limited to random comments on the street. It was also expressed in a virtual blackout in the local media. A reporter for the *El Paso Times* who wanted to write a series of feature articles on the strikers was told that the strike was a "private affair" between Farah and his workers. The editor added, "Maybe if we let Willie Farah run his business he'll let us run our newspaper." It wasn't necessary for Farah himself to exercise direct censorship. His importance in the El Paso business community ensured that no newspaper would print material that was damaging to him. A striker describing the extent of his informal influence wryly observed, "Willie Farah conquered El Paso."

There was also considerable racism in the antiunion sentiment. Some members of the Anglo community felt that Mexican-Americans were "aliens" and that Mexican-American strikers were ungrateful troublemakers who should be dealt with severely. One woman angrily remembers:

> When we were on strike there was a program on TV and anybody could call up. You know, one man called the TV station and told them why didn't they send all the Mexicans back to Mexico? How ignorant! Here I was born in the United States and this stupid man has the nerve to say to send them all back to Mexico because we were on strike!

Racial tensions between Anglos and Chicanos, an ever-present feature of life in El Paso, were exacerbated by the strike and the political mobilization of Chicana workers that accompanied it.

However, opinions about the strike did not simply divide along racial or ethnic lines. The strike split the Chicano community. Many workers at Farah crossed picket lines and continued to keep the plant operating. They were known as the "happies" because they wore buttons which featured a smiling face and the slogan, "I'm happy at Farah." Especially at Farah's Third Street plant, where many of the people had worked for Farah since World War II, vehement opposition to the strike was expressed.

There was this woman who was married to one of the supervisors. She even yelled at us that we were going to starve. She said, "Don't worry! We'll give you the cockroaches!"

They used to call us a lot of names. "You should be ashamed after so many years that Willie has been supporting you with work." "Why don't you start working? All you want is to be loafing around. At your age!"

The strike divided families. Several women told of walking out while their sisters remained inside the plant. There was even one family where the husband was on strike and his wife was continuing to work at Farah. "He'd drive his wife up to the door," one striker recalled, "and get out of there as fast as he could. Now this was ridiculous!"

Striking workers were quickly replaced by strikebreakers from El Paso and . . . Juarez. There was no lack of applicants for the jobs: El Paso unemployment figures have soared as high as 14 percent in recent years, while Juarez, like much of Mexico, has a current unemployment rate of 40 percent.

Until shortly before the strike, Willie Farah, who liked to style himself as a superpatriot, had refused to hire Mexicans to work in his plant even if they had green cards. But when the strike began and he needed workers, he abruptly changed his policy, and willingly hired Mexican nationals. Large numbers of green-carders appeared in the plant. Farah's hiring practices were partly successful in pitting workers against each other. Some Chicano strikers blamed Mexican workers for being hired by Farah, rather than blaming Farah and other employers along the border for using job competition to divide workers. However, many of the strikers recognized that the economic situation in Juarez forced people to find work wherever they could. And in spite of the economic squeeze, a small number of Juarez residents joined the strikers.

People on the picket lines faced continuing harassment from company personnel. Farah hired guards to patrol the picket line with unmuzzled police dogs. Several strikers were hit by Farah trucks, and one woman was struck by a car driven by Willie Farah's mother. Farah obtained an injunction limiting pickets to one every fifty feet; 1,008 workers were cited for violations, and many were ordered to report to the police station in the middle of the night and required to post four-hundred-dollar bonds. One woman was jailed six times. (The

Texas law which permitted such injunctions was later declared unconstitutional, and all charges were dropped.)

Support

Although the strikers suffered physical and psychological harassment from opponents of the strike, they also discovered new sources of support. The ACWA sent organizers to El Paso, gave weekly payments of thirty dollars to each striker, administered a Farah Relief Fund, and sponsored classes for the strikers on labor history and union procedures. For many workers, the films shown by the union were their first exposure to the history of labor struggles in the United States. One woman was deeply moved by a film about a strike in Chicago; another striker especially liked the movie "Salt of the Earth," because it showed the role of Chicanas in a strike in New Mexico.

Immediately after the strike began, the union organized a national boycott of Farah pants which became a crucial factor in the success of the strike. By January 1974, forty union representatives were working on boycott campaigns in more than sixty cities.[5] The ACWA issued leaflets, posters, and public relations kits, and worked closely with other unions and church and student groups to implement the boycott. Many Farah workers went on speaking tours to promote the boycott. All these efforts transformed the Farah strike from an isolated local struggle to a national campaign with widespread support.

The Catholic Church was another source of help for the strikers. Father Jesse Muñoz, a priest at Our Lady of the Light Church, made church facilities available for union meetings and participated in several national speaking tours to promote the boycott of Farah products. He also came to the picket line at the Gateway plant to bless the strikers on Ash Wednesday. Bishop Sidney Metzger of El Paso publicly endorsed the boycott in a letter to his fellow bishops. Metzger said, "The fact that today over 3,000 workers are on strike is evidence that both grievances and resentment are real. And by listening to the people over the years one gradually became aware that things at Farah were not actually as they were made to appear."[6]

In El Paso, a town with a large and devout Catholic population, the approval of the church was a source of emotional as well as organizational support for the strikers and a setback for their opponents. Muñoz received threatening letters from unknown sources, and he contends that Farah hired someone to put LSD in his Coca-Cola at a union dinner.

When a group of happies announced that they planned to picket the church, the strikers quickly organized a counteraction. The happies arrived to find the church surrounded by strikers. One striker spotted the black ribbons worn by the protesters and called out, "What happened, did Willie die already?" The happies took stock of the situation and retreated.

Father Muñoz suggests that there were many reasons why the church chose to back the strikers in spite of the continuing controversy. He points out that the church has a commitment to social justice, which he personally had supported by joining the southern civil rights protests of the 1960s. "So when I came here and there was a roaring tiger in my backyard, I wasn't going to ignore it." Muñoz was also concerned that the strikers would be incited to violence by "Communists from Red China, Cuba, and Berkeley," whom he charges came to town to disrupt the strike. By inviting the strikers to use church facilities, he hoped to isolate them from what he viewed as dangerous influences.

Workers at Asarco and the few other union plants in town also expressed their support for the strikers. Even more surprising to the strikers, given the prevailing mood of hostility, was the support given them by some local businesses.

> We got on that truck and we went to ask everybody if they could give us some food. That was when, I tell you, my life started changing. There you know who your good friends are and who cares about people. We went to that fruit stand on Alameda. He gave us, I guess, about twenty bags of potatoes. Then we went to that Payton [meat] packing company, and they gave us wienies. Mostly we went to the stores to ask for baby food. Then we went to the *tortilleria* in Ysleta [east of El Paso] and that man gave us about twenty dozens of tortillas and tamales, and some juice. Then we went back to report to the people, to tell them that we had support.

The strikers were also encouraged by messages of solidarity and financial support from other unions around the country. Particularly important to them was the visit to El Paso of Cesar Chavez. In addition, a variety of Chicano, student, and leftist organizations in El

Paso and around the country supported the strike by publicizing the boycott and the conditions at Farah.

New Responsibilities

But the most profound changes among the Farah strikers began when they took on new responsibilities for organizing strike activities. Some women went to work for the union on a volunteer basis, writing strike relief checks, keeping records, and distributing the goods that arrived from outside El Paso. Almost immediately they began to realize that their capabilities were not as limited as they had been taught to believe. One striker asserted, "If I had not walked out, I would not have been able to realize all those things about myself."

> You know, when we used to register the people from the strike, would you believe that we organized all those cards, all those people on strike? And you know, not realizing, here you can do this anywhere! You know, you think to yourself, "How in the world did I ever think I couldn't do anything?" This is one of the things that's held us back. We didn't think we could do it. Until you actually get there and sit down and do it, and you find out, "I'm not so dumb after all!"

Other strikers went on speaking tours organized by the union or by strike support groups to publicize the boycott and raise funds.

> I had never travelled as much as I did when I was on strike. The only place I had gone was to L.A., one time, but that was about all. But I never thought that I could go to New York, or Seattle, or all these places. To me it was just like a dream, something that was just happening and I was going through, but I couldn't stop to think about it. I just had to go and talk to those people about the strike. The first week it was hard [to get used to talking to groups of people]. Because over here I just used to talk to one or two persons when I was working—they hardly let you talk at all. Sometimes I would try to talk just as though I was talking to the strikers right here. I just didn't think that they were people that I didn't know.

One woman observed that antiunion harassment took similar forms all over the country; when she stopped to talk to workers at a nonunion plant, a supervisor appeared and shooed the workers back inside. When she spoke on the East Coast she noticed that racial and ethnic differences often kept workers isolated from one another. She returned to El Paso with a heightened perception of the difficulties involved in building a strong union.

Financial Troubles

As the months wore on, strikers faced increasing financial hardship. The union strike relief payments of thirty dollars a week were inadequate for many families. In one household both husband and wife were on strike, and there were eight children to feed and clothe. Unable to handle their house payments, the family moved in with the husband's mother. The uncertainties of the strike, the financial troubles, and the change in living arrangements were a strain on the marriage:

> My husband was worried too, because of the financial [situation], and he would start to drinking to take it off his mind. I even told him to go to the hospital, because he was getting awful. And I had an operation too at that time. And he did, he went to the hospital and he got cured. . . .
>
> [Drinking was a big problem among the strikers] because there was nothing for them to do. He had to be there [on the picket line] from 7:30 until 4:30 in the afternoon, because he was the [picket] captain. Mostly the kids wouldn't see him at all, and neither did I, until two in the morning when he got home.

For single women workers living with their parents, the situation was somewhat easier. Their parents supported them, and working brothers and sisters often helped with car payments and other bills. But many single women were themselves working to support widowed parents and younger siblings. For them the strike meant financial desperation.

Women who could find work in other clothing factories did so, continuing to picket at Farah before and after work and on Saturdays. Only the small number of unionized plants in El Paso were willing to hire Farah strikers. At nonunion plants, however, the jobs only lasted as long as the striker's identity was unknown.

> On my application I lied. I said I had worked at Farah and then I had

gotten married and I had left. I had an interview with this man. He was real nice about it. He said, "How come you didn't go back to Farah?" I said, "Oh, my husband says they're having a lot of trouble in there." [laughs] So he said, "I might as well put you as an inspector on the lines."

It was a very good job, better than being an operator. He called me in when I had about two months there, and he says, "I like your work. You're going to get a raise, but don't tell anybody about it." About four months later he called me in again. "Listen," he says, "I'm thinking of giving you a bigger raise." Well, finally what I earned there in six months I didn't earn in those seven or eight years that I had in Farah!

But there were some of the girls in the plant that had brothers and sisters that were happies and they would say, "She's the striker from Farah, and doesn't anybody know about it?" "No, but she's an inspector and she got a better job than I did!"

The third time they called me into the office and he also had a tape recorder there. And then they got my application out and he said, "You know what's going to happen, don't you?" And I said, "Yeah, I guess you're going to fire me. Tell me, why am I getting fired? It couldn't be about my work—you just gave me two raises!" And he [pointed at the tape recorder and snapped at the other man in the office], "Turn it off!"

For strikers who could not find other work and for those who had to meet unexpected expenses, getting food stamps and other forms of aid was crucial. After a lengthy delay some strikers were declared eligible for food stamps. Unemployment benefits, of course, were unavailable to strikers. When one woman began work at another factory and was laid off after a year, she found that she could not collect unemployment benefits because she was a Farah striker.

Because of these problems, it was imperative that strikers obtain contributions and money from other unions across the country. They staffed an emergency committee which dispensed funds to strikers who could not meet medical and other payments. They formed a Farah Distress Fund to supplement the fund-raising efforts of the union-sponsored Farah Relief Fund. They helped to arrange their own speaking tours in addition to speaking on the union tours. Strikers who did not need the groceries distributed by the union passed them on to those who did. But in spite of all these measures, their financial situation continued to decline. One ex-striker comments tersely, "A lot of people lost their homes, cars—you name it, they lost it."

Social Relations

If the strike created new pressures and anxieties, it also cemented new relationships. "The good thing about the strike," recalls one woman, "is that we started knowing a lot of people—what they felt, who they were, what their problems were." Women who had been too busy or too shy even to speak to their fellow workers found themselves involved in discussions and arguments.

> I never used to come and talk to people about their beliefs. I never used to go and tell someone "do this" or "do that" or "this is good for you" or "bad for you." But everyone was so enthusiastic that I started [saying to the nonstrikers], "Come on, girls! It's for your own good!"

Picket duty and strike support activities brought new groups of people together.

> People made a lot of friends. Some of us know each other by nicknames, that's all. Believe it or not, I have a whole bunch of friends at Farah, and they call me up, and they have to tell me their nicknames, because I won't know them by their first name or their last name.

The difficulties of being a striker in an antiunion town also inspired camaraderie. When groups of women were arrested for mass picketing and ordered to report to the police station, they took advantage of the inexperience of the police in dealing with female detainees, and created havoc.

> We got on the scale and they weighed us, and then they got our finger-prints, and they asked us how old we were, and then we used to say, "You really want to know?" And then they said, "What's your phone number?" "Ai, you *really* want to know!" We were just playing around. The jailman was going all kinds of colors, because he was an old man.

In working-class areas, particularly in the sprawling eastern end of town, many workers felt a sense of solidarity with their neighbors.

> Here the whole neighborhood, you know, the majority of us were on strike! The guy on the corner was on strike, the girl across the street, the one on the corner over there, then there was Virgie and all her sisters, and then we had

one lady down the other corner that was working. My neighbors in front—her father's always been fighting for unions. A lot of these things, I think, kind of made you feel good.

The Home

As women became more and more involved in running strike support activities, and as they developed new friendships among the strikers, they began to spend more time outside the home. This was a source of tension in many households.

> I was so involved that I was forgetting everything. My husband started getting very angry at me, and I was giving him a hard time. You know, at that time I didn't realize that I was hurting my kids and my husband. At the time I just felt that this was something I had to do, and if my husband liked it or didn't like it he was going to have to accept it. Lucky that he was able to accept [it], because this went on and on during the strike. Now I stop to think, and I tell myself, good grief, he really did put up with a lot! How would I like it if he was gone every day of the week! So I'm just glad that he was able to stand behind me, and it didn't destroy our marriage, but it did destroy a lot of marriages.

In some cases, differences of opinion about the merits of the walkout were fueled by financial insecurity. In other homes the husbands did not think that attending public meetings was an appropriate way for their wives to spend their time.

> Well, at the beginning they didn't like it. They thought [the women] should be at home, because here they were kind of old-fashioned, the women were always supposed to be home. The only time she'd be working was if she had to work to keep up with the bills, and both wife and husband had to work. Otherwise there was no way that the man himself could support the house. But that's about all they thought about, just for them to work—they didn't think they could go to meetings.

But the women felt strongly enough about their involvement in the strike to put up a spirited defense of their activities.

> My ex-husband told me, "You're not gonna make it, and I'm not gonna help you!" And I said, "If God made it, and his followers made it, like

Peter, he left his boat behind, all his belongings to follow God, yet he didn't die! Right now he's in better shape than we are. He's in heaven, holding that door—isn't that true!"

For many women the changes in their marriages were more profound than a few disagreements over meetings or money. The strike made them more confident of their ability to make decisions, and they began to question their own attitudes toward their husbands.

Maybe it's just the Mexican woman, maybe it's just that the Mexican woman has been brought up always to do what somebody tells you, you know, your father, your mother. And as you grow up, you're used to always being told what to do.

For years I wouldn't do anything without asking my husband's permission. I've been married nineteen years, and I was always, "Hey, can I?" or "Should I?" I see myself now and I think, good grief, having to ask to buy a pair of underwear! Of course, I don't do this anymore. [The time of the strike was] when it started changing. All of it. I was able to begin to stand up for myself, and I began to feel that I should be accepted for the person that I am.

Most marriages survived the ordeals of the strike, and many women feel that their growth as individuals has strengthened their relationships with their husbands. But it was also not uncommon for husbands threatened by the new eloquence, assertiveness, and political awareness of their wives simply to walk out.

The strike also transformed the relationship of women workers to their children. Many brought their children to meetings and to the picket line. "My little boy was only three months, and you should have seen me, I had him always in my arms, going everywhere," remembers one striker. Children who were slightly older took an active part in strike support work, and formed their own opinions about unionization.

See my little boy? I used to take him with me to go picket. We [adults] used to go give people papers, and they would hold their papers, or throw them at us right in the face, or say "Shove it down your you-know-what." He would get them—you know, he's a small boy. People would not pay attention to him. So he would say, "Here, sir!" "OK!" He would put it in his pocket, or read it. He was always out with me, always out picketing. He was about seven or eight. Anybody talks about unions, he'll tell you, "Go out there and join the union." Tell him, "Unions are no good." "They're good. They educate. They educated my mother."

One teenager commented, "Mom used to be a slave. But since the strike she thinks for herself. It's a lot better."

Women also consciously reevaluated their ideas about child rearing and their hopes for their children.

I used to be a very nervous person when my kids were little. I almost had a nervous breakdown. My husband used to drive me batty, you know. The kid couldn't be bawling over there in the other room—I had to get up and run and see what's the matter with the kid! Because my husband was an overly protective person with his children . . . So here's the idiot wife, running like crazy to look after these kids, and it was driving me batty!

These are the things that I was able to begin to stand up for. It was crazy, you couldn't watch the kid constantly. And I've come to where now I don't feel this pressure. I don't feel this anymore. I'll look out for my kids the best I can.

My ideas are a whole lot different than they used to be. I want my kids to be free. I never want them to feel oppressed. I want them to treat everybody as an equal. I don't think they should slight someone because he's black or he's any different than they are. And this is what I want—I want them to be free people. And to be good people.

I want my daughter to be able to do what she's gotta do, and not always comply to whatever her boyfriend or her husband [wants] . . . that she should be the person that she is. And I want my boys to be the person that they are.

You know, it's very funny, when my daughter and my son were little, you know my husband wouldn't let my boy wash dishes? So he grows up never washing a dish! And I tell my husband, "I think it's your fault that he doesn't know how to wash dishes!"

You know, I think it [the strike] has made my kids more outspoken. Maybe some people would call it disrespect. I don't. I think that being outspoken is not harmful if you do it in the right way. Like my son—if someboy, if an adult, gives him a hard time, I expect him to stand up and speak for his rights.

Unidad Para Siempre

Women strikers turned a critical eye on their personal lives and their home; as they became more experienced they developed criticisms of the union campaign as well. Some women felt that the

ACWA was not promoting the strike and boycott actively enough, particularly in El Paso.

The union, hard-pressed to pay each striker thirty dollars a week, stopped encouraging more workers to come out on strike. (The union organizers felt that the strike could not be won unless there was a successful national boycott, and that funds should be channeled into boycott organizing rather than support of additional strikers.) There were squabbles about eligibility for emergency funds and relief payments. More important, many strikers felt that they were not being encouraged to take independent action to raise funds or publicize the strike. They wanted the process of education which had begun with the walkout to continue. One woman remembers that she and her fellow activists "were trying to get those people to reorganize—not only the union, but actually to really try to stand on their own two feet . . . trying to talk things out for yourself without having somebody else talk them out."

Some strikers began to meet independently of the union, in a group which was known simply as the rank-and-file committee. (This group took the name Unidad Para Siempre—Unity Forever—when it was reactivated after the strike.) The members of the group—about forty—shared a strong sense of themselves as workers and a desire to build a strong and democratic union. They put out their own leaflets, participated in marches and rallies, helped to found the Farah Distress Fund, and talked to other strikers about the need for a strong union. "We wanted a union with action, not just words. That's why we were having meetings and going out, really doing more, making our own papers."

Politicization of Women

For the women on strike at Farah there was no artificial separation between personal and political change. Their experiences during the strike altered the way they looked at themselves as women and as workers.

> Of course, we never did anything wrong, really. What we were fighting for was our rights, because we were very oppressed. For one thing, I was a very insecure person way back then. I felt that I was inferior to my supervisors, who were at the time only Anglo. None of this affects me anymore. I have

learned that I am an equal. I have all the rights they have. I may not have the education they have, and I may not earn the money they earn. But I am their equal regardless. And it's done a lot for me, it's changed a lot for me. It made me into a better person.

It used to be if a supervisor got after me for anything I'd sit there and cry. Well, they don't do this to me anymore. They don't frighten me anymore. Two of them can take me into the office—it does not affect me at all. I have my say, and if they like it or not, I'm going to say so. . . . Before I wouldn't say anything. I would just hold it in and cry it out, and stay and stay.

And I believe very much in fighting for your rights, and for women's rights. I don't believe in burning your bra, but I do believe in our having our rights, that even if you're married you can make your marriage work. I know that sometimes we have to put up with a little bit more, but it has changed a lot of things for me.

Maybe the company doesn't feel this way, but it's done a lot for us.

The strike made women more conscious of political and social movements that they had regarded as "outside" and irrelevant to their own lives. These ranged from the support of local union struggles to the struggles of the United Farm Workers (UFW) and Texas Farmworkers to the women's movement.

"During the strike," says one woman, "every place I turned around there'd be a strike. They [other strikers] used to go to the stores where they were selling Farah pants, and they used to picket at the stores, and in return we used to go and help them picket." Farah workers have supported recent strikes at a local cannery and the municipal bus lines. Some of them joined the picket lines when Asarco, a nearby smelting plant, went on strike in the summer of 1977.

Recently, ex-strikers have also been involved in other unionizing drives. One woman who now works in a hospital is contemplating an organizing campaign among health-care workers. Another has helped her father and uncles to begin signing up people at a bread factory. Several other women have joined a Texas Farmworkers support committee, which publicizes the working conditions of the farm workers and tries to raise funds for their unionizing campaigns.

People have also begun to discuss the women's movement in their homes. Although it is still perceived as a movement that is taking place somewhere outside of El Paso, it evokes both sympathy and support:

Well, all of us women, we like it. And we sure would like to join them. Some of the husbands they don't like it at all. They're not happy about it. [My husband] doesn't like it. Sometimes [we argue] and my daughters help me, my daughters back me up. [My sons] like it too.

For all of the women, the strike made them more conscious of themselves as working people with interests distinct from other classes. One woman began to argue with her dentist, who complained to her that her strike was causing him to lose money he had invested in Farah Manufacturing Company. She commented that he could afford to lose money, and added,

> It's like I tell him, "Just because you happen to be one Mexican out of many that made it to the top—and I bet you worked your butt off to get up there. I'll respect you for your ideas as long as you respect me for mine. I happen to be of the working class, and I happen to be one of the minority (i.e. Chicana), that I feel work at the lowest type of job there is, and I feel that we have a right to fight.

For others the strike altered the way they looked at their jobs, and for the first time made them feel that their workplace was the site of an important struggle:

> For myself, I would like to continue working where I am. I think about going to school and getting a secretarial job, and I think it would be a boring thing. I like to be where the action is. For my kids, if they want a college education, I expect to give it to them. I'd rather have them have a better job than me.
>
> But I like being there. I like the challenge. You don't know what the next day's going to bring you. You might get fired! I don't think I could see myself sitting there in back of a desk, answering phones. When you could be fighting somewhere else, in a grievance, fighting with your supervisors, giving them hell.
>
> [Before the strike] it was just a job to go to. Now it is kind of challenging, you know, you can never tell what's going to happen.

Inside the Plant: The Pressure Builds

By the beginning of 1974, the nationwide boycott organized by the ACWA was having a noticeable effect on Farah's business. Sales, which were $156 million in 1972, dropped to $126 million in 1974.[7]

By the end of 1973 four Farah plants outside of El Paso had been closed, and the El Paso plants had been put on a four-day week.

The five El Paso plants, which had been operating with "scab" labor throughout the strike, began to resemble ghost towns. One striker who maintained a close friendship with a strikebreaker recalls:

> She told me all the things that happened in there. That sometimes there wasn't even work and they would send them home. She said sometimes they would just play tic-tac-toe for hours. She said she used to get tired of staying waiting hours in there for material. And they would just sit down and talk, or go into a bathroom and spend thirty minutes in there. I think that their orders weren't coming in [because of] the boycott.

Even among the business community in El Paso, there was concern that the city was acquiring a reputation as a bad place to invest, and there was embarrassment at the outrageous and frequently racist statements that Farah periodically made to the press. When Farah publicly blamed the Catholic Church for his problems with the union, national press coverage was not sympathetic.

The final blow came at the end of January 1974, when an administrative judge of the National Labor Relations Board issued a decision which accused Farah of "flouting the (National Labor Relations) Act and trampling on the rights of its employees as if there were no Act, no Board, and no Ten Commandments." Farah was ordered to offer reinstatement to the strikers (whom the company asserted had voluntarily quit), to reinstate with back pay several workers who had been fired for union activity, and to allow the union access to company bulletin boards and employee lists.

Farah initially indicated that he would appeal the decision, but several weeks later he abruptly changed course. On February 23, apparently after preliminary discussion with union officials, he recognized the ACWA as the bargaining agent for Farah employees. The union simultaneously announced that it would terminate the boycott.

The strikers, exultant and relieved, celebrated that fact that they had outlasted El Paso's major business figure.

> It's like Rome. Remember, at that time, Caesar and all of them, he had a big throne. He said, "I am a god. I make these people do that and and I make these people do this." Yet his throne, his empire, crumbled down.

That's what happened to Farah. It was an empire. And yet, his empire came down. Farah's empire came down.

However, for many strikers the feeling of triumph was marred by confusion about who had decided to end the strike. They resented not being involved in the discussions which preceded Farah's capitulation. Many people first heard the news on the picket line.

> All of a sudden the strike was over. [We heard about it] the day before, because they said, "Nobody's gonna picket tomorrow." After I got out of the check committee I went out picketing. [The picket captain] knew, I'm pretty sure he did, because he's working now as a business agent.
>
> We really didn't know what was going on. "We don't picket tomorrow." "Why don't we picket?" "I don't know. The strike is over, I guess." "Oh, really?" And then the newspaper, the headlines. . . . I didn't like it, because I thought it was something they had already made up their minds to it, you know. We were not involved. I wasn't really pleased about it, but I said, "Well, at least we got the union in."

Most strikers believed that the decision to end the strike had been made in New York.

When the negotiating committee for the first contract was elected, strikers discovered to their dismay that happies were to be represented on the committee. In the few weeks before Farah recognized the union, his supervisors had been ordering people to sign union cards, telling them that if they didn't comply the factory would close. As nominal union members, these people had the right to participate in contract negotiations. The committee was thus badly split.

> You know, we were strikers, and they told us we were going to have a committee for the negotiations as strikers. And I believe that as long as you're on strike, that you have the right to decide what contract you want. They [the union officials] decided that it was only fair that the people that were inside [should] have another committee.
>
> So there was the table, this side were happies, and this side was strikers. We wanted something, they voted against us. We wanted thirty cents, they wanted five cents. That's where I believe we got screwed. If we had the chance, not having that committee there, I believe we would have gotten a better contract.

Other strikers on the negotiating committee felt that they were powerless, that the union officials had decided what they wanted before they held meetings with the workers. "The negotiating committee never really had much to say. . . . [The officials] say they know what is right and what isn't." If a member of the negotiating committee raised a question about a specific contract provision in negotiations, recalls one committee member, the senior union official would say: "Well, let's have a little break now." And he would talk to the people and say, "You shouldn't do that, you know. They know how much they can give you."

The final contract included pay increases of fifty-five cents an hour over three years, a medical insurance plan financed by the company, job security and seniority rights, and a grievance procedure. It also gave union representatives the right to challenge production quotas for individual operations. It was ratified at a meeting of employees on March 7.

Many workers were angry that there was little time taken to explain the contract or hear people's questions and objections.

> They put us all in the cafeteria of one of the factories. And we were in there along with all the people. There was a lot of people, a lot of noise. Some of the clauses that were in there, we didn't even get to understand them very well. He [a union official] would explain it in English, and the ACWA Joint Board Manager would just translate it. But he was going so fast with it that we didn't have a chance to really understand it. But then they said that we had to take that contract regardless because Mr. Farah had said that if that contract was not signed he wasn't about to change his mind and go for another contract. That contract had to be taken or else he would just close down the factory and that was that. . . .
>
> So he read the contract real fast and then he asked, "Does anybody disapprove?" and then a few of the people raised their hands and they were ignored. He said, "OK, this means we go back to work." We didn't vote on it.

Strikers felt that two years of suffering entitled them to a stronger contract. But Farah was in financial trouble as a result of the boycott and a series of management mistakes, and his threat to close the factory was a real one. The strikers, inexperienced at contract negotiations, felt outmaneuvered by a process in which the company set the terms and the union lawyers made most of the decisions.

AFTER THE STRIKE

In spite of their misgivings about the contract, and a pervasive feeling that the situation was no longer under their control, most strikers concluded that the contract was "all right for a first try," and that it was "a beginning." They realized that their fight for better working conditions was by no means over, but at least they now had the protection of a union and a grievance procedure. They were determined that they would no longer be intimidated by supervisors; if they were mistreated they were going to climb off their machines and protest. "I'm going to say something if I have to say it," one striker insisted. "And I'll be nice if they're nice. If they're not very nice I can also be very unnice."

When they returned to work in the spring of 1974, the strikers faced tremendous obstacles. Texas was (and still is) a right-to-work state, so workers were not required to join the union. If enough workers took the benefits without joining the union, the company could move to have the union decertified. This made the task of organizing the unorganized at Farah both very necessary and immensely difficult. It was complicated by the fact that the conclusion of the strike did not dilute Willie Farah's antiunion sentiment. He had recognized the union with great reluctance, and was determined to break it. Finally, there were serious divisions among the workers in the plant. Strikers determined to build a strong union would have to overcome tensions between themselves and the happies, as well as divisions between Chicanas and Mexicanas which had been created during the strike.

When the strikers returned to the factory, they found that the organization of production had changed dramatically during the two years of the strike. In an attempt to keep up with the changing men's clothing market, Farah was diversifying production to include men's leisure suits and jackets. Workers were placed in new production lines without adequate retraining. Women who had been sewing straight seams for ten years were suddenly expected to set sleeves. One woman said, "They just sat me on the machine and said, 'Try to do this.' That was my training."

Workers who previously had been working with a six-piece pattern for pants were now working with a thirty-piece pattern for jackets. Seamstresses accustomed to sewing cotton fabric suddenly had to adjust to sewing brushed denim, plaids, and double-knits—fabrics which were much more difficult to handle. In addition, sewing collars and cuffs of jackets was much more delicate and time-consuming work than most operations involved in the production of pants.

These changes in materials, patterns, and techniques were not taken into account when new production quotas were established. Women whose wages had been based on their ability to produce a certain number of pieces at one operation were expected to produce just as many at a new operation. As a result, quotas were often impossibly high. Unable to meet their new quotas within the pre-scribed time limit, many women suffered wage reductions and even-tually were fired for low production. Some ex-strikers believe that by selectively assigning them to the most difficult new operations and establishing high quotas, the company hoped gradually to weed them out of the plant.

At the same time that Farah was changing production, the com-pany plunged into a serious financial disaster. The recession of 1974–1975 hurt the company, and in addition, Willie Farah made major miscalculations in production and marketing.[8] He had always been able to stockpile his most dependable styles and sell them on a stable market year after year. Lightning changes in styles meant that Farah could no longer predict the market. For example, one year he would corner the market in leisure suits, stockpile thousands of them, and then find that the next year no one was wearing leisure suits. In 1974 Farah decided he wanted to produce his own fabrics, and opened a textile mill in El Paso. The venture was a six-million-dollar flop.

Farah's financial predicament was exacerbated by marketing prob-lems. In the past, Farah had been known for the high quality of its merchandise. But under severe pressure to meet quotas on new operations, workers were simply unable to concern themselves with perfection. "When you're pushing people they can't get their work out right," one ex-striker commented.

> So they were getting it out as fast as they could, without caring how it was coming out. They made all these jackets lopsided and crooked. Who are you going to sell them to once the stores see how they are? They are definitely going to return them. And that is what started happening. They were sending back truckloads of jackets, sportcoats, and pants.

In addition, retailers who disliked Farah's high-handed business practices had gladly removed Farah pants from their shelves during the boycott, and were reluctant to resume dealing with the company again after the strike.

All of these management problems resulted in a 40 percent decline in sales and a $3.5 million loss in the last quarter of 1976. Five thousand of the original nine thousand employees were laid off. Several Farah plants were closed, including plants in San Antonio, Victoria, and Las Cruces, New Mexico.

Union Troubles

These financial setbacks hindered the efforts of union activists to continue organizing. First, there was a visible cutback in services provided for the workers by the company. Bus service to and from the plant was curtailed, coffee and donuts no longer were served during breaks, the already inadequate medical care available to workers was cut back, and Thanksgiving turkeys and Christmas parties were no longer provided. Many workers complained that the plants were dirtier and more dust-covered than they had ever been in the past. Since these cutbacks coincided with the end of the strike, many nonunion members blamed the union, not Farah, for the decline in their working conditions.

A more serious consequence of Farah's financial setback was that it required a drastic reduction in the size of the work force. This need to lay off workers provided Farah with an opportunity to harass and eliminate his most vocal opponents among the union activists. Some were given extremely erratic work schedules. Some days they would be required to work until noon, other days until three o'clock, and frequently they were called to work on Saturdays. They were rarely given much advance notice of their hours. Some ex-strikers were switched to production lines that were scheduled to be phased out. Others were placed on extended layoff and after one year were let go by the company.

Farah's management devised several further strategies that undercut the ability of union activists to organize. One was to isolate union members. At the end of the strike almost all of the strikers were assigned to the large Gateway plant. (By keeping them all in one place the company apparently hoped to prevent strikers from "infecting" other workers in the various plants.) After the strike, one woman recalled,

> We were closer. We didn't let our chain break. They tried to break it. At first they put us all together. And then suddenly they knew that we were so strong, they started separating us. They went to Northeast, and the other ones went to Paisano. So then suddenly you were all separated. Then they put happies with you. It was hard to make them understand.

While in the past an effort had been made to assign women to the plant nearest their homes, after the transfers many workers found themselves working at plants across the city from their residences.

Grievances

It is against this background of changes in production, financial setbacks, the establishment of high quotas, and transfers of workers that many grievances were filed. (During negotiations for the second contract in March 1977, union officials stated that more grievances were filed at Farah than at all other ACWA plants in the United States combined.) When workers had grievances, it was up to the shop stewards to investigate the complaint, collect all the necessary information, discuss it with the immediate supervisor, fill out the forms, and deliver them to the union office. If a grievance could not be resolved on the shop floor, it would be turned over to a business agent.

Most shop stewards were inundated with grievances. Some were responsible for lines of a hundred workers, stretched out over a quarter mile. Unlike the supervisors, they did not have roller skates and bicycles at their disposal to traverse the distances within the plant. They had to do all union-related work during lunch hours and breaks. One ex-striker said:

> I'm a very active person and I *love* to help people. They wouldn't let you talk during work, they wouldn't let you talk about the union or anything. At breaktimes I would go real fast, and I would go in the plant and start talking to the people, start going line by line.

Work for the union did not end with the end of the working day at Farah, and most shop stewards spent several hours each day driving to and from the union office. "Some people don't understand the time you put into it," one shop steward complained,

> the time you have to leave your kids to go fight their cases. We don't get paid for being shop stewards, we don't get gas money, we still pay our union dues, everything. We get nothing out of it, other than our self-satisfaction that we are helping our people.

In addition to being overworked, shop stewards were systematically harassed. One union activist noticed that every time she went to the bathroom a supervisor followed her, and if she took time to smoke a cigarette, the supervisor would hurry her back to work. Another found that whenever she had problems with her sewing machine and signaled the supervisor, he would consistently ignore her, and it would be hours before the machine was repaired.

The ability of shop stewards to effectively solicit and process grievances was further hindered by their isolation from other union activists and from workers in general. "They have a great big cutting room," one shop steward commented,

> and on the corner where all the machines start, that's where I'm at, on the very corner. They kind of keep me isolated from the other people. I had one woman tell me—she saw me in the bathroom. She said, "Are you the shop steward here?" I said, "Yeah." And she said, "You know, I'd never seen you before here." I said, "Yes, I've been here, but I've never been on the other side." She said, "Well, they keep telling me there was one [shop steward], but I never saw you."

In at least one case a steward was fired for carrying out her duties. In this instance, an ex-striker who had filed a grievance was being harassed by the supervisor. The entire production line had stopped work to watch the argument. The shop steward stepped off her machine and walked down the line to investigate. The supervisor started yelling at her to return to her machine. Outraged that she had climbed down from her machine in the first place, and then refused to go back, he phoned the plant manager, who fired her for disobedience. She had witnesses and was rehired after her case went to arbitration.

A final factor that made the shop stewards less effective than they might have been was the continuing apathy of nonunionized workers. The ex-strikers clearly understood that they had to organize to defend their interests, and were continually frustrated by the complacence and lack of support from workers who refused to act on their own behalf.

There were never enough women willing to serve as shop stewards. When shop stewards were laid off, or transferred from one plant to another, there were rarely other workers willing to take their places.

The effectiveness of the grievance procedure depended largely on the resources of the union staff. The business agents, hired by the union, were chosen from among the ex-strikers. Inexperienced and inadequately trained, they were overwhelmed by the volume of grievances. In addition, some ex-strikers charge that the union carefully selected the most passive and malleable strikers to work full-time for the union.

Another union staff member who played a decisive role in implementing the grievance procedure was the union engineer. Because of the changes in production from pants to leisure suits and the introduction of new operations, many of the grievances dealt with allegedly unfair quotas assigned to those operations. Quotas for new operations were initially set by company engineers. If they were to be challenged, a grievance had to be filed within thirty days; then a union engineer would be sent to the plant to determine whether or not the quota set by the company for that operation had been reasonable.

There was only one union engineer for the five Farah plants, and he was responsible for all the other ACWA plants in El Paso as well. Not only was the union engineer overworked and unable to investigate every dispute, but all too often, ex-strikers complained, the union engineer would back up the quotas set by the company.

One union activist, switched to a new production line and given an impossibly high quota, received a pink slip for low production. She called in the union engineer to observe the operation. She could not even produce half of the quota, and another person he observed was not able to make the quota. Nonetheless, he agreed with the company that the quota was a reasonable one. The repeated occurrence of similar cases led many strikers to conclude that the union engineer could not be counted on as an advocate for the workers.

Many ex-strikers felt victimized by a combination of the company's determination to manipulate and undermine the union and the union's reluctance to actively challenge the company. The union seemed willing to take to arbitration only those cases in which a favorable decision was certain. Only a small percentage of all the grievances filed were taken to arbitration.

Decline of Unidad Para Siempre

Militant union members were left in a particularly vulnerable position. The rank-and-file group, Unidad Para Siempre, pushed for reforms that had not been included in the contract. These reforms included elimination of the quota system, compensation and training for shop stewards, and greater rank-and-file participation in settling grievances between workers and the company. In this way, they hoped to build a stronger and more responsive union. The continued growth of Unidad was hampered by the fact that a large number of its members—the most vocal and militant union activists—were among the first to be laid off by Farah during his cutbacks in production. Unidad members feel that the union did not actively prosecute their cases because, like the company, it felt threatened by their presence. By 1977, few members of Unidad still worked in Farah plants.

Unidad's ability to form a strong organization was further inhibited by fundamental divisions among the workers. There were differences among the ex-strikers and nonstrikers about how much and when to criticize the union. Among the workers at Farah, some still actively opposed the union. They blamed the union for Farah's financial predicament; they blamed the union for the termination of services they had previously enjoyed. They did their best to harass union activists in the plant. "Oh, I had so many things done to me," one shop steward remarked.

> They [workers hostile to the union] used to get into my car, put gum on my chair. One time I was setting the cuff. People would come by and knock them all down. They would take all my union papers and leaflets. They'd take them off or throw them on the floor. One time somebody cut all the threads off my machine. Can you imagine?

Other workers were simply indifferent to the union. As far as they

were concerned they could take advantage of union benefits without paying dues or suffering the harassment inflicted upon union activists. Some Mexicans feared that they might lose their green cards if they became union activists.

Union members viewed the union in a variety of ways. Some uncritically supported it. In their view the major obstacle to the growth of a strong union was the apathy of the workers who refused to share the responsibility of working to improve conditions. Another group of union activists expressed frustration with passive, nonunion workers in the plant, but attached equal importance to the weaknesses of the union machinery. Still another group, many of whom belonged to Unidad, emphasized the extent to which the union had collaborated with the company and saw democratizing the union as the major requirement. Finally, a small group of ex-strikers became disillusioned with the union, and simply signed out.

The Second Contract

The continuing layoffs, loss of rank-and-file activists, tensions among workers in the plant, and inadequate support from the international union all combined to weaken the position of the workers during contract negotiations in early 1977.

Negotiations took place with both sides assuming that Farah was in serious financial difficulties. Workers on the negotiating committee spent several days listening to detailed descriptions of Farah's woes, and finally were told, "You can ask for the moon, but if we give it to you we'll fold tomorrow and you'll all be out on the street."

This bleak picture was accepted by union lawyers, who urged the negotiating committee to accept Farah's terms. The union officials clearly were worried about Farah's financial status, and felt that no further challenges to the company's authority should be mounted. Instead of giving an organized voice to workers' grievances, they tried to devise a strategy that would help the company back to financial health. As one union official put it, "Once Farah was a union plant, it was in the union's interest to sell pants." If selling pants more cheaply meant accepting a serious setback in working conditions, the union officials were willing to pay that price to keep Farah from going under.

The 1977 contract granted the workers a scanty thirty-cent pay raise over a three-year period. It eliminated dental benefits and retained the hated quota system. Most damaging of all, it permitted Farah to lay off experienced workers and call them back to work on a different production line—at the minimum wage. Some members of the negotiating committee reluctantly voted to accept the contract, certain that once it was taken to the workers for ratification it would be rejected.

Many workers now believe that the company exaggerated its problems so that the union would settle for a weak contract. Although it is still uncertain whether Farah Manufacturing Company will recover from its economic crisis, it is already clear that under the terms of the 1977 contract, the workers are paying for Farah's problems.

The contract was hastily presented in a short meeting held in the cafeteria at the Gateway plant. The meeting was called at the end of the working day, and most workers did not know until the last minute that the meeting was to take place. The contract was read in legalistic Spanish which few workers could understand, and questions from the floor were discouraged. When a vote was called the ACWA Joint Board Manager requested that those in favor of the contract stand up. Since the room was packed, most people were already standing up. There is a great deal of controversy about what happened at this point. Many who attended the meeting say that a clear majority of workers raised their hands in opposition to the contract. No formal count was made, however, and the union official declared that the contract had passed.

Before workers could raise their objections to the terms of the contract and the way in which the vote was conducted, the bell signaling the end of work rang. Workers swarmed out of the Gateway cafeteria, many angrily pulling their union buttons off their shirts and throwing them onto the ground. Lacking experience as well as the presence of a strong rank-and-file organization, the remaining union activists were unable to challenge the proceedings. This created even greater divisions among the workers, as many felt that they had been sold out by union militants.

Since March 1977, Farah has closed another of its El Paso plants. The number of workers at Farah, particularly union members, continues to decline.

CONCLUSION

Events at Farah since the strike show the continuing difficulty of union organizing in the Southwest. The right-to-work law, the consolidated opposition of powerful employers, the timidity of union officials, and the many incipient tensions in the border area which employers can use to divide the work force—all of these are formidable obstacles in the way of a strong workers' organization.

The story of the ACWA at Farah also illustrates some of the problems specific to organizing workers in the garment industry. In contrast to relatively monopolized, capital-intensive industries such as auto and steel, the garment industry is highly competitive, volatile, and labor intensive. In this context of constant business fluctuations, it is possible for a large and established company like Farah to suffer a dramatic decline within a period of several years.

The development of runaway shops during the last decade has made this instability even more pronounced. Increasing workers' organization and the relatively high cost of American labor have prompted labor-intensive industries such as garments and electronics to move south across the border, or to Southeast Asia, where labor is cheaper and less organized than in the United States. In border cities such as El Paso, industries have been able to take advantage of the proximity of an abundant supply of documented and undocumented workers from Mexico.

In an attempt to prevent industries from leaving the country, many unions such as the ACWA have adopted the strategy of bailing out the company in times of financial hardship. As recent events at Farah suggest, this may often be done at the expense of the workers. Although this is not a problem whose ultimate solution lies solely within the borders of the United States, current union strategy has not even provided a partial answer. Instead, it has failed to prevent runaway shops and simultaneously has helped to undermine the development of a strong union movement.

It is clear from the Farah experience that a successful unionization effort does not end when the union wins a contract. Organizing and training of workers in everything from a grievance procedure to labor history must continue on a long-term basis. In addition, workers must develop a strong rank-and-file movement—one that can overcome divisions among the workers, build a democratic local union, and encourage women workers to develop leadership skills and an analysis of their working situation.

While the Farah strike did not produce a strong, mature rank-and-file movement, it did help to create the conditions under which one can develop. The workers who made the strike were irreversibly changed by it. All of them say that they would organize and strike again; most of them recognize the need for strong support from an international union like the ACWA, as long as it does not undermine the independent organization of rank-and-file workers. "We're sticking in there and we're not going to get out and we're not giving up!" one ex-striker insisted.

> I believe in fighting for our rights, and for women's rights. When I walked out of that company way back then, it was like I had taken a weight off my back. And I began to realize, "Why did I put up with it all these years? Why didn't I try for something else?" Now I want to stay here and help people to help themselves.

The Chicanas who comprise the majority of strikers learned that they could speak and act on their own behalf as women and workers, lessons they will not forget.

NOTES

(Unnumbered note p. 227)

1. El Paso, Texas, is located on the western tip of Texas, near the point where the boundaries of Texas, New Mexico, and Mexico intersect. In July 1975, the population was estimated by the U.S. Bureau of Census at 414,700 people, of whom 57 percent were "Spanish American." El Paso is directly across the U.S.-Mexico border from Ciudad Juarez, which has an estimated population of 600,000.

2. General Executive Board Report, "Farah Boycott: Union Label," Amalgamated Clothing Workers of America, 1974 Convention, 1.

3. Allen Pusey, "Clothes Made the Man," *Texas Monthly* (June 1977), 135.

4. In June 1976, ACWA merged with the Textile Workers Union of America, and became the Amalgamated Clothing and Textile Workers Union. Since the events in this article occurred before the merger, the union will be referred to as ACWA.

5. "Farah Boycott," ACWA Report.

6. Bishop Sidney Metzger to Bishop of Rochester, Oct. 31, 1972, reprinted in *Viva La Huelga: Farah Strike Bulletin No. 15* (Amalgamated Clothing Workers of America, AFL-CIO).

7. *Moody's Industrial Manual* (New York: Moody's Investors Service, Inc, 1975), 1099.

8. Critics of the union have blamed the strike and boycott for the company's business troubles. The boycott never actually destroyed Farah's profit margin, however. In fact, some analysts argue that the short-term effect of the strike was beneficial because it forced the company to stop overproduction. They note that "during the only full year of the boycott (1973), the company jumped from $8 million in losses to a modest $42,000 profit" (Pusey, "Clothes Made the Man," 135). The losses predate the union and can be traced to management errors on Farah's part.

CHAPTER 9

A Stitch in Our Time: New York's Hispanic Garment Workers in the 1980s

Elizabeth Weiner and Hardy Green

TODAY'S HISPANIC worker in a New York clothing shop is likely to be a woman who recently immigrated here from a Central or South American country. Chances are that she came here along with other members of her family or met up with a relative who had come before. Upon arrival, she immediately started looking for work and found her first job when a friend or family member told her about an opening not far from home in a women's clothing factory. During her first week, she learned how to operate an industrial sewing machine through tortuous experimentation with the pieces she was given to sew. At the end of the week she found her pay to be pitifully small, perhaps less than $10 a day. But with practice, her speed increased and her earnings increased as well.

Many women, especially undocumented workers (or "illegal aliens"), stick with their first jobs for a long while, reasoning that the boss at a new place might ask questions about immigration status or that such jobs might be located in unfamiliar neighborhoods. Sometimes a worker will find a better job when her factory temporarily runs out of work and closes, maybe a job in a union shop that has steadier work, higher wages, and even paid vacations or a few benefits. But there are more bad jobs than good jobs nowadays in New York apparel shops.

With 150,000 production jobs by official count, apparel is still the largest industry in the New York metropolitan area, but it could not compete against manufacturers operating in the low-wage countries of the Third World without a supply of immigrant women workers.[1] Most United States production is carried out by contractors who pressure their workers to accept lower and lower pay, in much the same way that jobbers force the contractors to underbid each other. This setup has created a two-tiered industry: a legitimate sector and an "underground" sector. Surveying the legitimate jobs, the Department of Labor notes that apparel work pays just under $5 an hour on the average.[2] But no accurate wage statistics exist for off-the-books jobs. And no one really knows how many women work in crowded, unregulated factories for wages far below accepted minimums, although one New York state senator's investigation counted over 3,000 such factories, employing over 50,000 workers.[3]

Whether they work underground or on legitimate jobs, the majority of sewing machine operators usually sew pieces of a garment only—a sleeve, a collar—and they are paid a set rate for each piece sewn. There is little room for advancement, and the work is stressful and unhealthy. To cope with the difficulties that the jobs entail, both at work and at home, they depend upon a network of friends, family, and others from their homelands. But family responsibilities also add to the burden of working women, and those who are mothers must find babysitters or consider sewing at home.

Less universal as means of coping with life and work, but resources upon which some workers depend, are the church, state and city agencies, and labor unions. But these institutions can be mixed blessings for those who rely on them.

GOOD JOBS AND BAD: TWO WOMEN'S EXPERIENCES

Olga Velasco came to the United States from Ecuador in 1970 with other members of her family. She got her first job in a lower Manhattan dress shop through the recommendation of a friend who also lived in the Ecuadorian community on the city's Upper West Side. Though she earned only around $100 a week, Olga worked at the crowded, cluttered, dirty shop as a sewing machine operator until it closed a year and a half later. Then another friend recommended her to the boss at Prudence Manufacturing, also in Manhattan. At Prudence, Olga learned to operate a jump-stitch machine, which basted the seams of the men's vests she turned out by the dozens. Since this was a relatively skilled job, she was paid a time rate rather than a piece rate, the more common arrangement under which there is often a relentless pressure to produce. She made around $185 a week.

With its almost one hundred employees, union representation, and the greater stability of the men's (as opposed to the women's and children's) apparel industry, Prudence was a good place to land a job, and Olga stayed there for eight years. She got involved with the union, serving as a shop steward, and last year she left sewing behind and accepted an offer to join the union staff as an organizer.

Isabel Magriz came to New York fifteen years ago from Puerto Rico. Since that time she has worked in a number of clothing shops. For the last six years she has worked at F & M Co., a small shop near her home in a South Bronx housing project. She is paid less than the legal minimum wage, working off-the-books so that the government will not stop sending her welfare payments.

She also supplements her income by working at home, sewing women's dresses in her bedroom until the early morning hours. On a good week she might make $130 total from sewing in the factory and from the 15 to 40 cents per piece she earns at home. With the $87.50 she gets from welfare, the money must stretch to support her daughter and herself and leave a little extra to send occasionally to her mother in Puerto Rico.

"The boss takes 6 percent out of my pay for giving me the privilege of working off-the-books," she said. "I just want the kids to stay in school and not turn to crime to get what they need. But now I have to work constantly, and always get left behind."

THE BUTT END OF PRODUCTION

Apparel production in the United States today is a different industry than it was twenty years ago. Although New York is still the center of the women's apparel industry, as it has been since the advent of ready-to-wear clothing manufacture in the latter half of the nineteenth century,[4] its condition today is fragile. Official counts show the industry with less than half of the jobs counted in 1949, and the state Labor Department has predicted further job loss for the future.[5] Long-established marketing structures keep the city's industry going. Chic showrooms with displays of designers' collections are clustered on Seventh Avenue between 31st and 42nd streets. Buyers from around the nation descend upon the city twice a year to select next season's look.

But the "butt end" of production, its remnants here, increasingly resemble a Third World ghetto. The internationalization of production, now affecting the nation's auto and steel industries, has long been at work in apparel, shifting the labor-intensive, low-technology jobs to low-wage areas. And the more companies packed their production off to such parts of the world, the more the industrial segment that remained came to resemble the factories abroad.

During the 1950s, New York lost jobs to low-wage domestic areas in Pennsylvania, where the wives of unemployed miners welcomed whatever jobs they could find, to Massachusetts, and to the South, where over 40 percent of United States apparel workers now reside.[6] With further breakdown of work into low-skill operations, and with improvements in cargo transport during the next decades, manufacturers turned to the populations of Southeast Asia, where workers make as little as 25 cents an hour.[7] As a result, imported clothes, which sell at wholesale prices 20 percent below domestic products, now constitute over 20 percent of the nation's clothing market.[8]

Mainland production, however, still offers some advantages: chiefly, skilled workers and a greater ability to adjust to shifts in fashion. Thus half of the production workers in New York are engaged in making the most fashion-oriented women's clothing.[9]

Such workers' shops are small. Eight out of ten New York women's wear shops have fewer than fifty employees, while over half of the nation's apparel makers employing fewer than twenty workers are located in the metropolitan region.[10] They are kept small by fashion, which dictates short production runs, since only small orders of a similar style can be sold. (Longer production runs mean a more standardized product, which in turn allows a greater division of labor and larger scale production, as in Levi's and Farah's sunbelt factories.[11]) Fashion has also inhibited the automation of the industry: The low volume of production and a high rate of business failure due to abrupt changes of style make investment in laser-beam cloth-cutting equipment or advanced sewing machines a risky venture. In the mid-1970s, in the industry as a whole, capital invested per worker was around $9,000, or less than a quarter of the ratio for all manufacturing.[12]

Finally, the built-in relationships of the industry create further downward pressure on the wages of New York apparel workers. There are relatively few "inside" shops in which all production and sales functions take place. More typically, jobbers are the entrepreneurs producing samples from designers' patterns, buying the materials, and cutting the pieces. The work of assembling the garments is sent to "outside" contract shops. Seventy percent of the production workers in the city's dress industry work in such contract shops.[13]

Contracting provides the industry with a great deal of flexibility, relieving any firm of the need to maintain factories large enough to fill maximum orders. But since it costs only a few thousand dollars to open a contract shop, there are always more contractors vying for work than there is work to be done. This situation presents jobbers with an excellent opportunity to push down labor costs, forcing the contractors to bid each other down, with the ultimate victor forcing his workers to take lower and lower wages.

Average industry wages are so low that they compare unfavorably to welfare.[14] This means that apparel industry jobs are often filled by those for whom the comparison is irrelevant: undocumented aliens who do not apply for welfare out of fear of detection. At a maximum of $6,176.40 a year for a family of four, the welfare grant is itself an inadequate income. Consequently, even among women who receive welfare payments, many seek work in underground shops offering an unrecorded income, which, however meager, can supplement their benefits.

INSIDE NILDA'S FACTORY

In a shop in the middle of the garment district on an upper floor of a large dingy building, Nilda Rodriguez got her first sewing job. With no prior experience, Nilda was forced to rely on the generosity and patience of her coworkers to learn how to operate an industrial sewing machine. Her Ecuadorian boss and his wife also helped out. "Within the first few days, they knew I couldn't sew," recalled Nilda. "But the boss's wife said, 'Fine, I'll teach you.' In nonunion shops, they'll teach you—it's all piecework, so they're not losing out. It's your problem."

While 80 percent of the industry functions on piece rates[15]—or payment per garment rather than by the hour—there seems to be no agreement among workers about its merits. Some operators argue that piecework allows them to work without the constant vigilance of their employers, so that they feel as if they work for themselves.[16] Others say the nonstop pressure to keep up pace with faster workers, or just to make enough money, is oppressive. Employers seem to have no such disagreement: Piecework keeps the factory humming and the garments flying. Nilda sided with the workers who dislike the system. "Piecework is terrible," she said. "It pits you against the other workers, puts you in competition. If the styles change, they just throw it at you and you have to figure it out yourself. It takes at least a day to do one garment the first time."

The piecework system, with its attendant burdens for the worker, is not uncommon in other manufacturing jobs. More particular to the garment industry is the absence of a seniority system. In a highly seasonal industry, plagued with constant layoffs, veteran workers and newcomers alike share the skimpy or ample work load in union shops. The International Ladies' Garment Workers Union (ILGWU) has codified the arrangement in its collective agreements.[17] Some critics suggest that by keeping all workers insecure, this policy inhibits the militancy that often arises from a more stable group of workers. But the work-sharing clause also eliminates the contractors' prerogative to keep favorites supplied with work.

The garment factory has little room for personal advancement. While the most skilled women work for manufacturers or jobbers as sample makers—fashioning original samples of a design for display and often working closely with designers—over half of apparel workers are sewing machine operators. Once responsible for the assembly of an entire garment, operators increasingly do "section work," repeating the same insert of a sleeve or closing the same seam on blouse after blouse. Other workers—called floor workers, trimmers, and general workers—turn out belts and collars on special machines, snip extra threads and look for irregularities, and hang up newly-pressed goods, slipping on the cellophane for shipping.

Within the narrow range of upward mobility in the factory is the opportunity to learn how to operate the newest machines. Nilda recalled that she insisted on learning the merrow machine, which binds seams with an automatic overstitch and allows operators to work rapidly. Other useful skills include knowing how to operate special buttonhole machines, which sew on buttons and perform various specialized functions. There is no tradition of automatic advancement in a sewing factory, however, no built-in increments or union-guaranteed training opportunities. Therefore, many women stay at one task all their working lives, afraid to insist on training, or unwilling in the short run to absorb the loss of time and pay that training would entail.

Rarely are women able to penetrate the domain of men's work. Men are the cutters, cutting hundreds of layers of fabric at once into pattern pieces. The aristocrats of apparel workers, cutters are relatively highly paid and often work on the premises of the jobber, where the crucial cutting process can be strictly supervised. Men are also pressers, pressing seams and finished garments to prepare them for shipping. Some men do cross over as operators and floor workers, but women are not considered strong enough for the hot, heavy irons or the now-motorized cutting tools.[18]

When Nilda demanded training on new machines, it was no accident of character. She is a New York-born Puerto Rican, and that circumstance distinguished her from her coworkers. Because she could maneuver equally well in English and Spanish, she was often viewed with suspicion by her employers. "They were afraid of my knowing the minimum wage laws, regulations and of demanding these rights," she said. But as far as her coworkers were concerned, Nilda said she fit right in. She described a warm and supportive atmosphere where women shared ideas, doubts, and family problems, and stood by each other with a sense of unity.

Nilda said the shop talk among the workers from all over Latin America was often stimulating.

> We tend to think that workers don't have anything to talk about. But they talked about everything and anything. Not just bullshit, but about their country's politics, religion, student strikes, the situation in Nicaragua. We would exchange information about each other's countries, and everyone would bring in their favorite native food for the others to taste. It was interesting to hear their views and to give them yours. You learn a lot.

As a novice, Nilda also found other workers generous about teaching her.

> Whenever I got stuck, someone would stop for a second and show me the

best way to do it. Of course, you have to show you're a good worker, that you work as hard as they do. They'll complain when people don't work hard and the work piles up on them—that's only fair. They're only slightly competitive. It's the boss who's trying to make it competitive. But there's always a little gossip.

More than for gossip, Nilda's coworkers relied on the advice and sympathy of the others.

All the women had problems with their husbands and children and no one to help. It helped them to come into the shop and talk about it. We'd talk about how we viewed men, or children, women's lib, everything. Many women said they would rather be at work than at home. If someone started crying, they would always get sympathy.

In the event of an accident, Nilda said, "The whole place stops. A woman got her finger caught in a buttonhole machine, and everyone stopped working while they got her some help. If that happens, though, it shows you're a real pro, you go around showing everyone your scar." The women also banded together to keep the bathroom facilities clean. "We always had to fight about toilet paper," Nilda laughed.

Health hazards in a typical New York City garment shop go far beyond an unsanitary bathroom. Compared with factories in which high-hazard jobs expose workers to harmful chemicals and heavy machinery, a sewing factory, at first glance, appears benign. But under the frequently dusty, chaotic surface are a number of serious health and safety problems. According to the New York Committee for Occupational Safety and Health, garment workers suffer from high levels of stress (aggravated particularly by piecework, low job security, and lack of child care), skin rashes and allergies caused by chemical cleaners and dyes, joint pain from repetitive manual tasks, eye strain from striped and printed fabrics and poor lighting, and circulatory problems as a result of constant sitting or standing.[19]

Most commonly, workers find their own ways of coping with discomfort. A woman will bring a cushion from home to sit on, wrap a cloth around the knee press to insulate her leg from the heat, and share tips with coworkers about how to assuage various aches and pains. There have been some instances of collective action when conditions reached crisis proportions. In one case, at least thirteen women staggered off the job, coughing and fainting, into their local union office. They had been suffering for over two weeks from the effects of high levels of carbon monoxide gas from a leaky boiler.[20]

The ILGWU openly acknowledged the serious cumulative effects of garment production on the health of its workers when it set up for the first time a Health and Safety Department in 1980. With a three-year grant from the Occupational Safety and Health Administration (OSHA), it proposed to research the health hazards of chemical fabric treatments, inadequate workplace design, noise, job stress, and other problems. In conjunction, some New York City locals began to survey conditions of factory buildings in an attempt to identify the worst of the old, decaying industrial housing throughout the city. Only the most cosmetic changes or the most essential reforms have been pressed for, however. Most shops operate on marginal cash flow, and their proprietors plead poverty when faced with demands for major repairs, while shop landlords are often elusive.

Only in recent times have occupational health and safety become items on the agenda of American workers. Child labor, on the other hand, is assumed to have been dealt with effectively decades ago. Few people, however, have been inside a contemporary sweatshop. While the children are not employees, they have not disappeared from the shops. After school hours, school-age children are on the premises waiting for their mothers; preschool and older children may be found playing in corners and even sorting buttons and doing occasional errands.[21] "Some women sit their kids next to them at the machine," said Nilda.

The presence of children in the sweatshops does not represent a return to the outmoded practice of child exploitation. Rather, it indicates the burden placed upon garment workers and their children in the absence of day-care facilities. Olga Velasco said, "The workers in my shop complain about it all the time." When they can find a satisfactory arrangement, she said, "women often have to take their kids a long distance to the baby sitter before they go to work. Then, a good bit of their earnings goes to pay the sitter."

Olga Diaz, manager of the Shirt and Leisurewear Joint Board of the Amalgamated Clothing and Textile Workers Union (ACTWU), said, "We should have day-care centers in every area."

> In centers, kids learn how to get along with each other. Instead, what happens is that workers have to depend on sitters. There's a woman in my

building in the Bronx who lives on welfare plus what she earns for taking care of four kids. The kids don't get out of doors, and they aren't learning anything. They're actually being hurt. When their mothers come home from work, they are too tired to do anything for them.

AT HOME IN THE CITY

The lack of day care is perhaps one of the most stressful aspects of a garment worker's life, both inside and outside the workplace. The pressure of the dual roles of wage earner and homemaker, compounded for some women by such additional insecurities as earning low wages, being undocumented, being on welfare, and perhaps being physically ill, leads a number of women to accept homework as a "solution." Able to keep an eye on the children, fix meals, and work off-the-books while staying safely at home, women workers turn their homes into sewing factories.

Isabel Magriz is one of the growing number of garment workers who do their labor at home, though the practice has been against the law since the 1940s. Such workers receive no benefits, no extra compensation for overtime, nor are any payments made on their behalf into the Social Security fund. Further savings accrue to employers because homeworkers absorb overhead costs, including thread, electricity, and machine repairs. Nonetheless, Isabel prefers homework. "My apartment is more comfortable than the factory," she said. "When my kidney ailment causes pain, I can take breaks and lie down for a while."

Elsa Perez, a Dominican woman who works in her Brooklyn apartment so that she can care for her two chronically ill children, added, "It would be better to go to the factory, to get all the work done at once, but I have so much to do here. So I work in *los ratitos*, the little bits of time in between."

It is in the very nature of the "underground" dilemma that few broad social institutions touch the lives of such garment workers. In the polyglot of cultures and nationalities that is New York City, immigrants tend to live in close-knit neighborhoods, among people from their own native country, and often from the same province or town. There they find an entire network of *paisanos*, or compatriots, to lead them to jobs, stores, travel agencies, and mutual aid societies.

Often those who came before are well established in their new communities as small business people and can serve the constant stream of new immigrants. Since the initial investment for a contract shop is small, and since a willing labor force is assured, local sewing factories run by the immigrants' compatriots are common. Sometimes the native bond is reassuring to the workers: Old customs are respected, and tips on the new society are shared. In other cases, however, the closeness creates an obligation, monetary or moral, that keeps workers indebted and trapped.[22]

Among the many Central and South American immigrants, there is a strong dependency on the Catholic Church. Throughout the boroughs of New York City, local parishes have swelled in size and need as Dominicans, Salvadorans, Ecuadorians, Mexicans, and others have arrived here looking for work. Unable or unwilling to relate to the vast government social service bureaucracy, because of lack of language skills or legal status, most Hispanic immigrants turn to the church for guidance and concrete aid.

The church has responded to the need. For example, in the Williamsburg section of Brooklyn, the Transfiguration Church provides its entirely Spanish-speaking parishioners with immigration counseling services, employment and training programs, food, and shelter. The hard-working clergy, moreover, have respected the confidence entrusted in them: During the 1980 census, the officials of the Brooklyn Catholic diocese refused to cooperate with the government to count the undocumented population unless guarantees for amnesty and safety were granted. The latter were never made; and the results of the 1980 census were challenged in court for underrepresenting the New York City Hispanic population.[23]

Some community organizations are also beginning to open their eyes to the problems of local garment workers. In the Washington Heights area of northern Manhattan, a grass-roots health project formed a "Committee on Sweatshops" after their state senator found over 100 underground shops in the district. The committee sponsored a series of workshops, open to workers and officials alike, on the health, legal, and political issues raised by such workplaces, as well as on the possibilities for unionization.

The city government, from its distant perch, occasionally devotes its resources to examining the problems of the garment industry. At least once in each administration, a report is issued on industry problems. But the city's interest is narrow. Well aware that the apparel industry is one of the few remaining employers in the manufacturing sector, city officials concern themselves with the problems of infrastructure—keeping the city attractive to jobbers by holding onto loft buildings with strict zoning regulations, improving the midtown traffic flow, and keeping theft in the district to a minimum. The world of the garment worker touches city policy only insofar as local politicians and government bureaucrats relate to the leadership of the well-regarded ILGWU.

THE UNIONS

If you ask a New York garment worker, especially an unrepresented worker, whether it is better to have a union or not, most will say it is better to have a union. "When you work in a shop with a union you get vacation with pay and you expect to make a little more money," said Marie Noree, a Haitian press operator at a union shop in Manhattan. "Without a union you don't have anything."

"We have such low wages and no health benefits," said Carmen Collado, one of twenty-three workers employed in a coat manufacturing shop in the Williamsburg section of Brooklyn. "We decided to get a union because everything is so expensive now . . . you can't afford to go to the hospital." With a union, the workers get vacation pay and holidays, modest health benefits, a little more in wages, and very modest pensions. Employers get labor peace, and the contractors among them get a more steady flow of work since the unions channel work to them.

It does not seem to be a bad tradeoff for a worker stuck in so blighted an industry. But if you talk to workers who are members of either of the two predominant labor organizations in the industry, the ILGWU or the ACTWU, they will soon tell you that it is not enough. Wilma Najarro, an ACTWU member, said,

> I worked for five years in one shop making women's blouses. It was a good job with wages of five dollars an hour, and I got along well with the boss. Then one day the floor lady fired me. She was jealous of the boss's admiration for my work, I guess. The union business agent came and didn't do anything to help me. He sided with the floor lady and didn't even get me the vacation pay they owed me.

The unions do not function as strong advocates of workers' rights, and union members frequently complain that in disputes "the union always takes the management's side."[24] Such union policies are a result not of indifference or corruption, but of the unions' historic position as partners in the industry.

Larger and more stable than any of the employers with whom they deal, the unions long ago took on the responsibility for imposing order upon a chaotic industry. As early as 1913, the ILGWU undertook time-and-motion studies of its members in order to set a uniform piece rate, and to help unionized firms increase productivity.[25] In the same year, the union first sought a solution to the "organized anarchy and irresponsibility" of the contracting system in the coat and suit industry, proposing that all contractors be registered and that jobbers and manufacturers be forbidden to take on new contractors so long as their current contractors were not working full time. In the words of ILGWU official Gus Tyler, "The union realized that its central problem was not the determination of a wage level, not the setting of a proper work week, not fringe benefits, not grievance procedure—but the contracting system."[26]

Both unions also have a long history of going the extra mile to get along with employers. Following the mass strike of 50,000 cloak makers in 1910, the ILGWU and employers agreed to a settlement proposed by attorney Louis Brandeis known as the Protocol of Peace. Under this agreement, the union won collective bargaining and the "preferential union shop" (which meant that union members got first crack at jobs), but surrendered the right to strike, allowing that all disputes would be settled through outside binding arbitration. Similar agreements were reached later in the men's clothing industry, as Amalgamated president Sidney Hillman became one of labor's foremost apostles of arbitration over more confrontational methods of settling problems.[27]

The ILGWU has been quite open about its practice of holding the line on wages. Echoing the union's rationale for the policy, one observer has pointed out that "the rate of movement to other areas might have been even faster if the ILGWU had not sought in recent years to protect the job opportunities of its members in the older cities by modifying its wage demands."[28] This policy dates back to the 1950s. The bypassing of wage increases in that decade brought about a sharp relative decline in the wages of dressmakers; whereas their earnings in the late 1940s had been higher than those of auto and steel workers, in the 1950s they earned less than half of the wages of such workers. The ILGWU's policy was also demonstrated in the union's opposition to minimum wage laws in the 1960s.[29] Given such a tradition, it is not surprising that in current times, when the nation's industry is in trouble, the unions act to smooth over problems on the shop floor and to moderate wage demands in negotiations.

The unions' record on political and social issues which directly affect their members is also mixed. As many as 30,000 of the ILGWU's 109,000 New York area members are undocumented aliens.[30] After years of sharing the anti-immigrant position of the AFL-CIO, ILGWU locals in New York and in Los Angeles began actively organizing the undocumented in the mid-1970s. The union as a whole was forced to consider the issue of immigration, and for a time to act as advocate of undocumented workers' rights, calling for unconditional amnesty for all workers who were residents of the country, and opposing sanctions against employers who hired them. Now it appears that the union has abandoned this advanced position under pressure from the AFL-CIO.

At the same time the organization is engaged in a highly visible union label campaign, attacking "cheap foreign labor" rather than the international system of oppression, and encouraging consumers to view the ILGWU label as "a little American flag in your clothes." One of the most stridently anti-Communist native unions, the ILGWU has consistently supported United States military adventures in the Third World and has played a key role in the work of the CIA-funded American Institute for Free Labor Development. The effect of such a course has been organizationally suicidal, as many of the beneficiaries of the policy are also the sources of cheap apparel imports—kept cheap by the repressive antilabor policies of United States-backed regimes.

The ACTWU's policies, although also contradictory, are less extreme. More apt to be critical of United States foreign policy (it was among the first AFL-CIO unions to oppose the Vietnam war) and of such right-wing governments as those in Chile and South Korea, it has been less outspoken on the issue of immigration. At its national convention in the summer of 1981, delegates approved a resolution calling for both an amnesty program for undocumented residents and legal penalties against employers who hire the undocumented.[31]

Possibly because of the paucity of female union leaders, neither union has emphasized "women's issues" in organizing or legislative campaigns. Although the ILGWU's membership is about 90 percent female, its leadership remains mostly male—there are only two women on its twenty-six member executive board. With a 66 percent female membership, and five women on its executive board of forty-four, ACTWU's representation is only marginally more representative.[32] Sexist hiring and promotion practices, pay discrimination, and sexual harassment are issues that have received considerable attention in recent clerical organizing attempts, but such concerns are given short shrift by the apparel unions.

The unions have placed slightly more emphasis on the women's issue of need for child-care programs. Although it has no centers in New York, ACTWU has established seven child-care centers in Baltimore and Chicago and has pressed for government-funded centers operating twenty-four hours a day. The ILGWU's efforts here have been less successful, with only one model program in Philadelphia.

But the unions' greatest failure is their inability to come up with a remedy for the abuses of the underground sector. "They are losing ground all the time," Yale Garber of the Apparel Manufacturers Association said of the ILGWU's organizing efforts in New York.[33] A long way from having the sort of base among Latino or Chinese immigrants that was gained among turn-of-the-century Jewish immigrants, the unions are prone to look for legal solutions rather than to put the required effort into organizing. To date, the only significant legal achievement has been successful lobbying for a New York State law that increases penalties for violations of the industrial homework statutes, that allows any interested party to obtain an injunction to shut down a law-breaking employer's operation, and that mandates a state study of violations of minimum wage, child labor, and overtime pay laws, to be conducted with a garment industry advisory committee.[34]

The ILGWU is also lobbying on behalf of a New York State bill (much like existing legislation in California) which would require all garment manufacturers to be registered with the state and bonded. Such a statute would place upon the state the burden of identifying the often hard-to-find contractors and limit the companies' ability to pack up and run away from wage-and-hour inspectors and union-organizing drives.[35]

Meanwhile, competition for the unorganized shops has sprung up. At least fifteen unions, including five AFL-CIO affiliates, have begun organizing the garment industry, along with the ILGWU and the ACTWU. Many of these groups have links to organized crime; their sole purposes are to block organizing efforts of legitimate unions and to rip off members' dues and welfare money. Through the terms of sweetheart contracts—which stipulate low wage rates, few holidays, and few welfare or pension provisions, and which are rarely enforced—manufacturers are able to reduce costs 20 to 30 percent below the costs of legitimate, union-affiliated competitors.[36] It is not unusual for union organizers and even workers to discover that a shop they are trying to organize already has a union contract, or to have a "gangster union" intervene at a boss's request and foul up an election by filing unfair labor practice charges, delaying the vote until pro-union momentum is broken. Said ACTWU organizer Nick Unger,

> Nothing is clean and every victory requires more union staffing than these small shops seem to be worth. With a very diverse work force and the fractured life of a city without community, you might need to send ten people out on evening house calls in the process of organizing a shop of fifteen people. . . . But these immigrants, documented or undocumented, often *do* want to be organized. They are willing to hold meetings in their homes, and to stay out late to go to such meetings in spite of the city's dangers. Many are very anxious to improve their lives.

CONCLUSION

One of the oldest forms of women's work, garment making, survives as one of the world's most labor-intensive and exploitative jobs. In the United States it has long been and continues to be work done by recent immigrants, since the pay is low and the tasks are tedious, and since employers look on it as the kind of work any woman can do. Every woman knows something about sewing, the reasoning goes, and can build upon training she has had since girlhood and the experience of work performed for family members.

Boundaries between family and home and the workplace are blurred in many ways for garment workers. Many workers supplement their shop earnings by taking work home; other employees work only at home, never inside a shop. When there is no baby sitter, workers bring children with them into the factory. And if the boss is looking to hire someone, one of the workers can usually suggest a relative or a friend who is looking for work.

Bosses and unions, though, are pretty clearly outside of the circle of family and community. The scramble for meager profits in the garment industry leaves little space for paternalistic relations between employer and employee in a sewing factory, even though the boss may be of the same nationality as a worker or live in the same neighborhood. The unions have taken on the role of distant managers of a chaotic system of production, and with officers and staff drawn primarily from ethnic groups represented in earlier waves of immigration, they involve themselves only sporadically in the noneconomic lives of their members.

The workers in one of the most traditional fields of women's work are thus left to rely upon women's traditional sources of support— family, religion, and a sisterhood of coworkers. In this regard, for the thousands of workers in this unglamorous part of the economy, the story continues much as it began.

NOTES

1. Herbert P. Rickman and Lance I. Michaels, *Interim Report of the Task Force on the Apparel Industry* (New York: Office of the Mayor, 1978), 2.

2. United States Department of Labor, *Wage Survey: Women's and Misses' Dresses*, (Aug. 1977), 14–15; United States Department of Labor, *Industry Wage Survey: Men's and Boy's Suits and Coats* (Apr. 1979), 1, 36.

3. New York State Senator Franz Leichter, "The Return of the Sweatshop," pt. 2, unpublished manuscript, Feb. 1981, 3.

4. Roy Helfgott, "Women's and Children's Apparel," in Max Hall, ed., *Made In New York: Case Studies in Metropolitan Manufacturing* (Cambridge, Mass.: Harvard University Press, 1959), 21.

5. Rickman and Michaels, *Interim Report*, 2.

6. Helfgott, "Women's and Children's Apparel," 86–87.

7. "Apparel's Last Stand," *Business Week* (May, 1979), 60, notes that workers make 50 cents an hour in Taiwan and 25 cents in Sri Lanka, the fastest growing source of apparel imports to the United States.

8. Ibid., 60.

9. Charles Brecher, *Upgrading Blue Collar and Service Workers* (Baltimore: The Johns Hopkins University Press, 1972), 17.

10. U.S. Dept. of Labor, *Industry Wage Survey*, table 2, 2; George Roniger and Gail Morris, *Metropolitan New York: An Economic Perspective* (First National City Bank, 1974), 20.

11. Helfgott, "Women's and Children's Apparel," 33.

12. North American Congress on Latin America, "Capital's Flight: The Apparel Industry Moves South," *NACLA's Latin American and Empire Report*, 11 (Mar. 1977), 5. Harold Wool's *The Labor Supply for Lower Level Occupations* (New

York: Praeger, 1976), 279, cites a much lower figure: $3,000, which he says is one-ninth the corresponding ratio for all manufacturing in 1973.

13. U.S. Dept. of Labor, 2, *Industry Wage Survey*, text table 3.

14. One study concluded that in 1979 citizen or legal resident working women with children could make 95 cents an hour more on welfare (counting taxes that would not have to be paid) than working in an apparel shop. See Amerigo Badillo-Veiga, Josh DeWind, and Julia Preston, "Undocumented Immigrant Workers in New York City," *NACLA Report of the Americas*, 13 (Nov.-Dec., 1979), 38.

15. NACLA, "Capital's Flight," 8.

16. Interview with garment worker, member of Local 23–25, ILGWU, 1979.

17. Collective agreement between the New York Skirt and Sportswear Association, Inc., The International Ladies Garment Workers Union, Local 23–25 and Local 10, 1979–82, Article 27.

18. Interview with Jerry Himmel, Business Agent, Local 23–25, ILGWU, 1980.

19. The New York Committee for Occupational Safety and Health, unpublished survey, New York City, 1979.

20. Incident took place in spring 1980, Local 23–25, ILGWU, New York City.

21. Personal visit to Mary Fran Dress Shop, 830 Westchester Avenue, Bronx, New York; interview with ILGWU organizer, Louis Bertot.

22. Roger Waldinger, "Labor Migration and Labor Market Structure: A Case Study of Undocumented Workers in the New York Garment Industry," unpublished manuscript, Harvard University, Department of Sociology, 1979, 23–25.

23. *New York Times*, Dec. 6, 1979.

24. For further examples of this sentiment see Carol Smith, "Immigrant Women, Work and the Use of Government Benefits: A Case Study in New York's Garment Industry," unpublished manuscript, Adelphi School of Social Welfare, March 1980, 91; Badillo-Veiga et al., "Undocumented Immigrant Workers," 26.

25. NACLA, "Capital's Flight," 19.

26. Gus Tyler, "Pattern of Garments," unpublished and undated article, ILGWU education department, 7–8.

27. An account of the forging of the Protocol and of the rank-and-file reassertion of the strike weapon may be found in James R. Green, *The World of the Worker: Labor in the Twentieth Century* (New York: Hill and Wang, 1980), 73–77. On Hillman and and the ACWA see Matthew Josephson, *Sidney Hillman: Statesman of American Labor* (Garden City, N.Y.: Doubleday, 1952), 59–85.

28. Helfgott, "Women's and Children's Apparel," 88.

29. Michael Myerson, "The ILGWU: A Union That Fights for Lower Wages," *Ramparts* (1971), 51–53. Helfgott, "Women's and Children's Apparel," 88.

30. Figures on current ILGWU membership in *Women's Wear Daily*, Nov. 20, 1981; percentage of undocumented among ILGWU membership in Rinker

Buck, "The New Sweatshops: A Penny For Your Collar," *New York Magazine* (Jan. 1979), 44.

31. Amalgamated Clothing and Textile Workers Union, "Resolution of Civil Liberties," unpublished document, ACTWU public relations department, 1981.

32. *New York Times*, Nov. 29, 1981, 56; ACTWU, *Report of the General Executive Board* (June 1981), 9.

33. Quoted in *Women's Wear Daily*, Nov. 20, 1981.

34. *ILGWU Justice*, Aug. 1981, 1–2.

35. *Women's Wear Daily*, Mar. 5, 1981, 11.

36. *Women's Wear Daily*, Nov. 16 and 17, 1981.

INDEX

Abramovitz, Bessie, 124–125, 130, 185; marriage to Sidney Hillman, 123–133
ACTWU. *See* Amalgamated Clothing and Textile Workers Union
ACWA. *See* Amalgamated Clothing Workers of America
Adams, Abigail, 10
Addams, Jane, 124
Adler Brothers, 107
Advance (ACWA), 209–211, 221–223
AFL. *See* American Federation of Labor
AFL-CIO: anti-immigrant position, 291; Industrial Union Department, xx; present-day organizing, 292
AFSC. *See* American Friends Service Committee
Alpern, Libby, (UGWA), 101–102
Amalgamated Clothing and Textile Workers Union, 286; present-day policies, 291–293
Amalgamated Clothing Workers of America: in Baltimore strike, 201–204; 207–223; in Chicago strike, 131–133; early years, 88–90; in Farah strike, 191, 228, 243, 248, 250, 262–264, 270–276; male domination of, xiv, xv, xviii–xx, 136, 206; Out-of-Town Organization Committee, 215; Women's Department, 209, 216–218; women participants in, xiv, 185–186, 195–196, 203–207, 213–223, 260
Amalgamated Clothing Workers of America Biennial Convention: Second, 207; Third, 214; Tenth, 222; Twelfth, 220
American Federation of Labor, 88–90, 119, 175, 201, 207, 219
American Friends Service Committee, xix–xx

American Institute for Free Labor Development, 291
"Americanizing" immigrants, xiii, 12–13, 125
American Labor Party, 223
"A Mistaken Charity," 11
Ansorge Brothers, 195–196, 223
Anthony, Susan B., 15, 60, 104
Apparel industry: before mechanization, 23–25, 27–30; decentralization of, 39, 51–52; health hazards in, 285–286; movement west and south of, xvi, 3, 131, 190, 220, 223, 229, 279; during 19th century, 39–44, 84–85, 97–98; post–World War I, 189–190; post–World War II, xvi, 281; present-day conditions of, xvi–xviii, xx–xxi, 191–192; 223–224, 285–287; sex segregation of duties in, xi–xii, 96, 116–118, 188–189, 204; sewing machine introduced into, xii, 26, 41–50, 71; and Third World, xvi, xvii, 190, 192, 275, 279, 281; in World War II, 211
Ashbridge, Elizabeth, 3–4
Asian Law Caucus, xix
Asian workers, xvi, xix, 185, 187. *See also* Chinese immigrant workers
Association of Waist and Dress Manufacturers (New York), 169, 171

Baker, W. E., sewing machine inventor, 35
Balch, Emily Greene (Wellesley College), xiv
Baltimore apparel industry, 84, 198
Baltimore Clothiers' Board of Trade, 197
Barnum, Gertrude, (WTUL), 124, 146, 155
Bellamy, George, (Hiram House), 158

|